THE **MARZANO ACADEMIES** MODEL

TEACHING IN A COMPETENCY-BASED ELEMENTARY SCHOOL

Robert J.
MARZANO

Seth D.
ABBOTT

555 North Morton Street
Bloomington, IN 47404
888.849.0851
FAX: 866.801.1447
email: info@MarzanoResources.com
MarzanoResources.com

Printed in the United States of America

Library of Congress Control Number: 2021052078
ISBN: 978-1-943360-39-0 (paperback)

Production Team
President and Publisher: Douglas M. Rife
Associate Publisher: Sarah Payne-Mills
Managing Production Editor: Kendra Slayton
Editorial Director: Todd Brakke
Art Director: Rian Anderson
Copy Chief: Jessi Finn
Senior Production Editor: Laurel Hecker
Content Development Specialist: Amy Rubenstein
Acquisitions Editor: Sarah Jubar
Proofreader: Jessi Finn
Text and Cover Designer: Abigail Bowen
Editorial Assistants: Charlotte Jones, Sarah Ludwig, and Elijah Oates

ACKNOWLEDGMENTS

I would not be the teacher I am today had it not been for the support and encouragement of countless students, teachers, coaches, and administrators. I am honored to have the opportunity to help shape the lives of all the students who pass through my classroom—their smiles, love, jokes, successes, struggles, and tears have taught me way more than I could ever teach them. I have been surrounded by amazing teachers and coaches like Carla Bigum and Carrie Strand, who provided mentorship and support when I needed it most. I have been fortunate enough to have principals like Justin Davis and Brian Kosena, who allowed me the freedom to be innovative and established a stable foundation from which to grow. I have been lucky enough to work in a district with leaders like Pamela Swanson, Oliver Grenham, and Jeni Gotto, who are bold enough to be pioneers of personalized competency-based education. Additionally, it has been an absolute honor to work with Bob Marzano, who encouraged my drive to develop his competency-based principles into practical application within my classroom and gave me a forum to share my practices with the world.

Finally, I am blessed with wonderful parents and an amazing family who have always believed in me, every step of the way. To my children: Ben, Emily, Kate, and Luke, you inspire me to be the best version of myself. To my wife: Julie, I am eternally grateful for your unwavering support. You have stood by my side through all the challenges of life as a teacher: back-to-school nights, committee meetings, parent conferences, and countless other commitments, the inflexible hours and stressful days, and all the late nights grading papers and lesson planning. Thank you.

—Seth D. Abbott

TABLE OF CONTENTS

CHAPTER 4

CHAPTER 5

ABOUT THE AUTHORS

Robert J. Marzano, PhD, is cofounder and chief academic officer of Marzano Resources in Denver, Colorado. During his fifty years in the field of education, he has worked with educators as a speaker and trainer and has authored more than fifty books and two hundred articles on topics such as instruction, assessment, writing and implementing standards, cognition, effective leadership, and school intervention. His books include *The New Art and Science of Teaching*, *Leaders of Learning*, *Making Classroom Assessments Reliable and Valid*, *The Classroom Strategies Series*, *Managing the Inner World of Teaching*, *A Handbook for High Reliability Schools*, *A Handbook for Personalized Competency-Based Education*, and *The Highly Engaged Classroom*. His practical translations of the most current research and theory into classroom strategies are known internationally and are widely practiced by both teachers and administrators.

Dr. Marzano received a bachelor's degree from Iona College in New York, a master's degree from Seattle University, and a doctorate from the University of Washington.

To learn more about Dr. Marzano, visit www.marzanoresources.com.

Seth D. Abbott is a teacher at John E. Flynn, a Marzano Academy, in Westminster, Colorado. He has taught in Westminster Public Schools (WPS)—a pioneer in personalized competency-based education (PCBE)—for thirteen years, where his innovative style quickly brought him to the forefront of the PCBE movement. Within WPS, Seth has been a leader in the development of competency-based tools, practices, and procedures, and has represented the district on an international scale. He has advised, consulted, and conducted trainings for districts and organizations around the world in advocacy of PCBE.

In February of 2019, Seth became the first teacher to achieve Level 3 in the Marzano Resources High Reliability Teacher™ program. He has written for numerous blogs and has been featured on podcasts as an expert in the field of competency-based teaching. He is a regular presenter at the WPS Summit, a national competency-based education conference held annually in Colorado.

Seth received a bachelor's degree from Metropolitan State University of Denver.

Introduction

This book is about effective instruction. Of course, there are many books on this topic, and there will continue to be more every year. Unlike most of those books, this one focuses on instruction in competency-based classrooms (also known as standards-based classrooms, proficiency-based classrooms, and the like). Specifically, it focuses on a model of competency-based instruction that we refer to as the *Marzano Academies model* or simply the *academy model.*

The History and Foundations of the Marzano Academies Model

The Marzano Academies model, as described in this book, is the product of decades of interrelated efforts to translate research and theory into practice starting with efforts in the 1980s to integrate direct instruction in thinking skills into the K–12 curriculum (for instance, Marzano et al., 1988). Such efforts have proceeded up to the present, with works that cover a wide variety of topics, including instruction, leadership, curriculum, assessment, vocabulary, standards, grading, high reliability organizations, professional learning communities, personalized competency-based education (PCBE), student motivation, social-emotional learning, teacher and leader evaluation, and taxonomies of knowledge and skill, to name a few. In short, the model presented here is the integration of numerous research and theory efforts over multiple decades, all of which were developed such that every piece is designed to fit with every other piece. This type of systematic planning is in contrast to the efforts in many schools to put together separate and sometimes disparate programs designed independently by different experts and organizations. While such efforts are well intended and have a certain intuitive appeal, they often fail because the selected initiatives might clash and cancel each other out, even though all are effective in their own right. Throughout this book, we systemically reference and describe the previous works on which the Marzano Academies model is based so that readers might consult those original sources, if they so choose.

Marzano Academies brings all these pieces together into a comprehensive model that produces consistent, high-quality education. This model is a departure from traditional structures of schooling in a number of ways. First, it is a competency-based system. *Competency-based education* (CBE) refers to the practice of promoting students to the next level only when they have demonstrated mastery of the academic content at the previous level. Time is not a factor—a student can progress at an accelerated rate in one subject and take more time in another. For example, a student might be working on fourth-grade English language arts (ELA) content and sixth-grade mathematics content. Students are organized into classes and groups by their ability rather than by age, allowing teachers to provide more targeted, effective instruction. CBE ensures that students actually learn before advancing, so they master the content the school considers important at each level and are prepared for the next one.

Second, to determine the content that students will learn at each level, the Marzano Academies model defines its academic program in a highly precise manner. For each topic that students must master, a *proficiency scale* delineates the progression of learning, from basic knowledge and skills, to the target level that students are expected to reach, to opportunities for advanced applications. A manageable set of proficiency scales for each content area at each level ensures consistency—students master the same content and skills no matter which teachers they learn from. Proficiency scales show exactly what students need to know and how they will get there. Furthermore, teachers assess students, score work, and report grades based on proficiency scales. Feedback to students lets them know where on the scale their current level of knowledge falls, making it easy for them to see what they need to do to improve. When grades are reported, it is not as an omnibus percentage or letter grade, but rather as a set of individual scores for each topic that the student is currently working on.

To support students in learning the academic content defined by proficiency scales, the Marzano Academies model also employs a robust, schoolwide vocabulary program. Vocabulary is foundational to learning in general, and direct vocabulary instruction is the best way to ensure that all students know the words they need to know to be successful in school and in life (see Marzano, 2020, for a discussion of the research). At the elementary level, the focus is on acquisition of basic and advanced high-frequency terms—that is, words that appear often in general language use. Thus, students have a base vocabulary that prepares them to learn domain-specific academic vocabulary (for example, technical terms related to science) in secondary school.

A third way that the Marzano Academies model differs from a typical traditional school is its recognition that effective education goes beyond academic content. The model includes directly teaching cognitive and metacognitive skills, such as analytical thinking, problem solving, impulse control, and collaboration. These skills are as essential to preparedness for life and career as academic content, so age-appropriate learning progressions for each skill are defined through proficiency scales. Students learn information and processes related to each one, and teachers give feedback on students' mastery thereof.

The Marzano Academies model also includes social-emotional components. The community of the school sets the environment for learning, and the quality of that community impacts the quality of students' education. Thus, this model emphasizes relationships and a sense of belonging among students, teachers, leaders, and other stakeholders. In addition to regular social-emotional learning on topics like mindfulness and empathy, students in a Marzano Academy participate in inspiring programs like those presented by Rachel's Challenge, an anti-bullying organization that focuses on kindness and compassion (www.rachelschallenge.org).

The final unique component we will mention here is the Marzano Academies approach to instruction. An *instructional model* defines in detail the practices associated with excellent teaching. The Marzano Academies instructional model includes forty-nine elements of effective instruction for CBE, ranging from content-delivery elements like recording and representing content to elements related to the classroom context, such as showing value and respect for all learners. With support from school leaders, teachers are expected to set goals and develop their abilities relative to the elements of the instructional model. Instruction in the Marzano Academies model also includes the systematic use of strategies known to improve students' retention of information, such as cumulative review.

The Marzano Academies instructional model is the primary focus of this book. The next section provides an overview.

The Marzano Academies Instructional Model

One of the defining features of a competency-based classroom is that students move at different paces through the content. One student might progress through content quite quickly. Another student might progress through the content quite slowly. While there are certainly other characteristics of CBE instruction, this is the core. Clearly, this feature of CBE has significant implications for the nature of classroom instruction. The instructional model that teachers use in a competency-based system must therefore be designed with CBE in mind. In this book, we provide a CBE-specific framework and strategies based on research and experience (Marzano, 2007, 2017). The instructional model we present has a number of specific elements embedded in an overarching framework, as depicted in figure I.1.

Overarching Domains	Feedback	Content	Context	Self-Regulation
Design Areas	I. Proficiency Scales	III. Proficiency Scale Instruction	V. Grouping and Regrouping	VIII. Belonging and Esteem
	II. Assessment	IV. General Instruction	VI. Engagement	IX. Efficacy and Agency
			VII. Comfort, Safety, and Order	X. Metacognitive and Life Skills

FIGURE I.1: Marzano Academies framework for CBE instruction.

At the highest level, the instructional model consists of four overarching areas, which we refer to as *domains*: feedback, content, context, and self-regulation. Each domain contains two or three *design areas*. As their name implies, design areas are important to the process of effective preparation and planning. The domain of feedback refers to information provided to students regarding their current status and growth. It involves proficiency scales (design area I) and assessment (design area II). Proficiency scales are at the heart of the academy model and provide a unique perspective on curriculum, instruction, and assessment within a CBE system.

The domain of content deals with core instructional strategies—the tools teachers use to help students initially learn and then further develop their understanding of the content within the curriculum. There are two design areas in this domain. Proficiency scale instruction (design area III) focuses on instructional strategies for content within the various levels of specific proficiency scales. General instruction (design area IV) focuses on strategies that help students continually develop and revise their knowledge.

The domain of context involves creating a classroom environment that maximizes support for student learning. It includes grouping and regrouping (design area V), engagement (design area VI), and comfort, safety, and order (design area VII). These design areas develop the foundation for effective teaching and learning.

Finally, the domain of self-regulation includes strategies designed to help students become independent learners and take responsibility for their own learning. It involves three design areas:

belonging and esteem (design area VIII), efficacy and agency (design area IX), and metacognitive and life skills (design area X). This domain is uniquely important to a competency-based system that empowers students.

It is important to note that each of the ten design areas includes a number of elements. Each element of the instructional model represents a tacit responsibility for teachers—something they must do in the classroom to provide effective CBE instruction. For example, consider design area II, assessment. It involves four elements.

IIa. Using obtrusive assessments

IIb. Using student-centered assessments

IIc. Using unobtrusive assessments

IId. Generating current summative scores

Each of these elements is an important practice on its own, but when a teacher successfully enacts all of them, he or she effectively addresses assessment as a whole. There are a total of forty-nine elements embedded in the ten design areas. The design areas and their associated elements are shown in figure I.2.

Finally, teachers can address each element through a variety of specific instructional strategies. For example, element IIb, student-centered assessment, involves instructional strategies such as personal tracking matrices and student-generated assessments. In all, there are over three hundred specific instructional strategies in the model.

In summary, the academy model of instruction contains four domains. Those four domains have ten embedded design areas. The ten design areas involve forty-nine elements, and the forty-nine elements involve some three hundred specific instructional strategies. These layers are depicted in figure I.3 (page 6).

As teachers use the instructional activities associated with each of the elements in the academy model, they should be cognizant of how well those strategies are working. In two widely read books, John Hattie (2009, 2012) popularized the notion that the standard for judging the effectiveness of instructional strategies should be "visible evidence." The titles of his books communicate this central theme: *Visible Learning* (2009) and *Visible Learning for Teachers* (2012). Within the Marzano Academies model, we have applied the concept of visible evidence to what teachers should do and how students should react relative to the instructional strategies within each element. Specifically, for each of the forty-nine elements in the instructional model, there are concrete visible behaviors that teachers should display. If the teacher executes these behaviors effectively, there are specific visible behaviors that students should exhibit. To analyze their effectiveness regarding the strategies in the forty-nine elements, teachers should examine whether they have produced three types of visible evidence.

1. Evidence of effective instruction and guidance on their part
2. Evidence of desired student actions and behaviors relative to the strategies
3. Evidence of students' understanding and awareness relative to the strategies

So that teachers may reflect on their instructional practice, we provide examples of these three types of evidence for each element in the model. It is important to note that we include examples of visible evidence beyond those specifically mentioned in our discussion of each element. For detailed discussions of the strategies that are not directly discussed in this text, readers should consult one or more of the following sources.

Feedback	Content	Context	Self-Regulation
I. Proficiency Scales Ia. Providing Proficiency Scales Ib. Tracking Student Progress Ic. Celebrating Success **II. Assessment** IIa. Using Obtrusive Assessments IIb. Using Student-Centered Assessments IIc. Using Unobtrusive Assessments IId. Generating Current Summative Scores	**III. Proficiency Scale Instruction** IIIa. Chunking Content IIIb. Processing Content IIIc. Recording and Representing Content IIId. Using Structured Practice IIIe. Examining Similarities and Differences IIIf. Engaging Students in Cognitively Complex Tasks IIIg. Generating and Defending Claims **IV. General Instruction** IVa. Reviewing Content IVb. Revising Knowledge IVc. Examining and Correcting Errors IVd. Highlighting Critical Information IVe. Previewing Content IVf. Stimulating Elaborative Inferences IVg. Extending Learning Through Homework	**V. Grouping and Regrouping** Va. Supporting Group Interactions Vb. Supporting Group Transitions Vc. Providing Group Support **VI. Engagement** VIa. Noticing and Reacting When Students Are Not Engaged VIb. Increasing Response Rates VIc. Using Physical Movement VId. Maintaining a Lively Pace VIe. Demonstrating Intensity and Enthusiasm VIf. Presenting Unusual Information VIg. Using Friendly Controversy VIh. Using Academic Games **VII. Comfort, Safety, and Order** VIIa. Organizing the Physical Layout of the Classroom VIIb. Demonstrating Withitness VIIc. Acknowledging Adherence to Rules and Procedures VIId. Acknowledging Lack of Adherence to Rules and Procedures VIIe. Establishing and Adapting Rules and Procedures VIIf. Displaying Objectivity and Control	**VIII. Belonging and Esteem** VIIIa. Using Verbal and Nonverbal Behaviors That Indicate Affection VIIIb. Demonstrating Value and Respect for Reluctant Learners VIIIc. Understanding Students' Backgrounds and Interests VIIId. Providing Opportunities for Students to Talk About Themselves **IX. Efficacy and Agency** IXa. Inspiring Students IXb. Enhancing Student Agency IXc. Asking In-Depth Questions of Reluctant Learners IXd. Probing Incorrect Answers With Reluctant Learners **X. Metacognitive and Life Skills** Xa. Reflecting on Learning Xb. Using Long-Term Projects Xc. Focusing on Specific Metacognitive and Life Skills

Source: © 2020 by Marzano Academies, Inc. Used with permission.

FIGURE I.2: Marzano Academies instructional model.

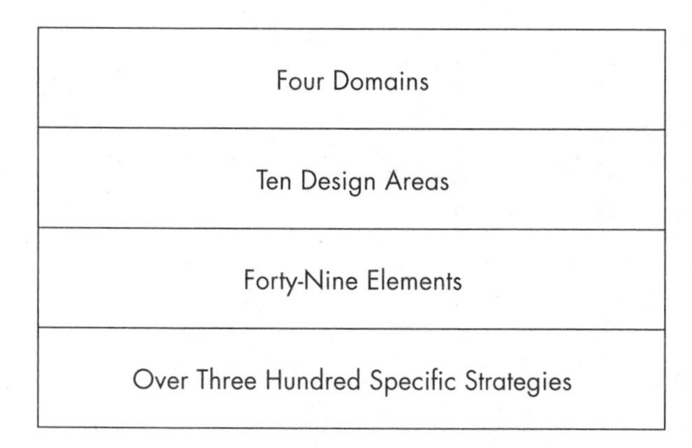

Source: Adapted from Marzano, Rains, & Warrick, 2021.

FIGURE I.3: Complete academy model of instruction.

- *The New Art and Science of Teaching* (Marzano, 2017)
- *The Handbook for the New Art and Science of Teaching* (Marzano, 2019a)
- *The Marzano Compendium of Instructional Strategies* (Marzano Resources, n.d.)

While the Marzano Academies model includes a number of instructional strategies that will be new to teachers who do not have experience in a CBE system, it also involves many traditional instructional strategies. However, these traditional strategies are typically employed in new ways within a competency-based classroom.

How This Book Is Organized

Chapter 1 of this book addresses feedback, the first domain of the academy instruction model, and the two design areas within that domain. Chapter 2 addresses the domain of content and its two related design areas. Chapter 3 focuses on the domain of context and its three related design areas. Chapter 4 addresses the domain of self-regulation and its three design areas. For each design area, we detail the associated elements that teachers must address in their classrooms. In addition, for each design area, there is a section devoted to understanding and planning. These sections elaborate on the individual elements by addressing specific issues teachers should consider when planning units and lessons. By delving into the nature and function of each design area, teachers will develop a deep understanding of how the various parts of the model operate as an integrated whole. Chapter 5 focuses on the different ways of thinking teachers must engage in to fully implement the academy model. We refer to this as *the CBE mindset.*

While this book is certainly useful to teachers in schools that are Marzano Academies or schools that are in the process of becoming academies, it is also intended for teachers in schools that are not pursuing that process but do wish to use some of the components of the academy model within their current system. Schools that wish to go through the formal process of becoming an academy should contact MarzanoAcademies.org.

CHAPTER 1

Feedback

The first domain of the Marzano Academies instructional model is feedback. Within the model, feedback means that, at any point in time, students clearly understand their current level of performance regarding the specific topics they are studying, how much they have grown in their understanding of those topics, and what they must do to improve their current status. To accomplish this, content must be articulated in a specific way, and students must be assessed in specific ways. Feedback involves two design areas.

I. Proficiency scales

II. Assessment

Proficiency scales are foundational to the vast majority of instructional activities in the academy model. Assessments within the academy model are always based on proficiency scales and provide teachers with a wide array of options for determining students' status and growth. The integration of the activities in these two design areas represents a highly focused feedback system for students, teachers, and parents and guardians.

Design Area I: Proficiency Scales

The overall purpose of this design area is creating proficiency scales and communicating these scales to students. As stated in the introduction (page 1), a proficiency scale defines a learning progression from basic content to target content to advanced applications. Within the Marzano Academies model, each proficiency scale focuses on a specific topic referred to as a *measurement topic*. The proficiency scale associated with a given measurement topic articulates the progression of knowledge and skill expected of students for that particular measurement topic. Measurement topics and proficiency scales are inextricably linked. Throughout this book, when the term *measurement topic* is used, the reader should assume that it has an accompanying proficiency scale. When the term *proficiency scale* is used, the reader should assume that the scale refers to a specific measurement topic (indicated by the title of the proficiency scale).

The Marzano Academies model employs a very specific type of proficiency scale, the format for which has been developed over decades and widely used since 1996 (Marzano, 2000, 2006, 2010; Marzano & Kendall, 1996). To illustrate, consider the proficiency scale for the third-grade mathematics topic of rounding depicted in figure 1.1 (page 8).

4.0	The student will: • Use mental computation and estimation strategies to assess the reasonableness of an answer at different stages of solving a problem (for example, when given that a boy has 374 more baseball cards than a friend who has 221 baseball cards, and when given that he then buys another 186 cards, use rounding to estimate that the number of baseball cards the boy started with should be close to 600 and the number of cards he ended up with should be close to 800).
3.5	In addition to score 3.0 performance, partial success at score 4.0 content
3.0	The student will: Round a given number to the nearest 10 or 100 (for example, round the numbers 23, 50, 95, 447, 283, 509, and 962 to the nearest 10 and the nearest 100).
2.5	No major errors or omissions regarding score 2.0 content, and partial success at score 3.0 content
2.0	The student will recognize or recall specific vocabulary (for example, *digit, estimate, hundreds, number line, ones, place, place value, round, round down, round up, tens, thousands*) and perform basic processes such as: • Identify multiples of 10 and 100. • Identify relationships between place values. For example, explain that ten 1s are equal to one 10 and that ten 10s are equal to one 100. • Explain that rounding a number to a given place estimates or approximates the value of the number to the nearest multiple of that place. For example, rounding a number to the nearest 10 approximates the value of that number to the nearest multiple of 10. • Explain that rounding a number to a given place will leave a value of 0 in each place that is smaller than (to the right of) the targeted place. For example, rounding a number to the nearest 100 will leave a value of 0 in the tens and ones places. • Use a number line to find the nearest multiple of a specified place for a given number. For example, when given the number 146 represented on a number line, identify 100 as the closest multiple of 100. • Explain that a number will be rounded up to a given place if the digit in the place immediately to the right is greater than or equal to 5, and will be rounded down if the digit is less than or equal to 4. • Identify situations in which rounding might be useful. For example, explain that rounding two addends and quickly calculating their sum can be useful for assessing whether or not the calculated sum of the unrounded addends is accurate.
1.5	Partial success at score 2.0 content, and major errors or omissions regarding score 3.0 content
1.0	With help, partial success at score 2.0 content and score 3.0 content
0.5	With help, partial success at score 2.0 content but not at score 3.0 content
0.0	Even with help, no success

Source: Adapted from Marzano, Norford, & Ruyle, 2019.

FIGURE 1.1: Proficiency scale for the third-grade measurement topic of rounding.

The fulcrum of an academy proficiency scale is the content at the score 3.0 level. Score 3.0 is the desired level of knowledge and skill that students are expected to attain to demonstrate proficiency relative to the measurement topic. In the case of figure 1.1, that content involves rounding to the nearest 10 or 100. The score 3.0 level of a well-designed proficiency scale should also provide specific examples of student behaviors that would indicate proficiency. In this case, such behaviors include students rounding the numbers 23, 50, 95, 447, 283, 509, and 962 to the nearest 10 and to the nearest 100.

The score 2.0 level of the scale contains important vocabulary and basic skills that will be taught directly. Such content is important foundational knowledge necessary for students to attain 3.0 status. The scale in figure 1.1 identifies basic skills like identifying multiples of 10 and 100.

The score 4.0 content represents knowledge or skill that exceeds the expectations at the 3.0 level. If students can demonstrate the expectations at the 4.0 level, they have reached a status beyond what is considered proficiency for a given measurement topic. At the score 4.0 level, proficiency scales commonly include a specific task that would indicate 4.0 status, as exemplified in figure 1.1. However, it is also a common convention in schools to articulate the 4.0 level as a general statement such as, "Students will make inferences and applications that go beyond what was explicitly taught in class."

In addition to the three levels of explicit content for a given measurement topic, academy proficiency scales also contain score values of 1.0 and 0.0, but these do not involve new content. Rather, a score value of 1.0 indicates that, with help, a student has partial success with score 2.0 and 3.0 content. The score value of 0.0 indicates that even with help, a student does not demonstrate partial success with any of the content.

Finally, academy proficiency scales also have half-point scores. The half-point values indicate partial movement to the next level of the scale. For example, a score of 2.5 indicates that a student has partial competence with the score 3.0 content. In effect, the three levels of explicit content (scores 2.0, 3.0, and 4.0) in a proficiency scale can be translated into nine different score values that range from 0.0 to 4.0, based on evidence provided by classroom assessments.

In the academy model, it is the school's responsibility to design the proficiency scales that all teachers in the school will use. This creates a uniform interpretation of standards that is consistent from teacher to teacher. The very structure of proficiency scales provides students with a detailed and unequivocal articulation of what they are expected to learn, and it provides teachers with a detailed and unequivocal articulation of what they are expected to teach. Many schools have already developed or are in the process of developing their schoolwide proficiency scales. Teachers in a school that does not have proficiency scales can create their own using the standards from their state or district. A number of books provide specific guidance to this end (see Hoegh, 2020; Marzano, 2018; Marzano et al., 2019).

Proficiency scales are foundational to the types of feedback a teacher uses within the Marzano Academies model. There are three elements embedded in this design area.

- Ia. Providing proficiency scales
- Ib. Tracking student progress
- Ic. Celebrating success

The following sections detail each one.

Ia. Providing Proficiency Scales

For this element, the teacher's responsibility is to present and communicate the proficiency scales that represent the content students are expected to master. Proficiency scales are as much (if not more) for students as they are for teachers. When well-written proficiency scales are in place, teachers know exactly what to teach and the sequence in which they should address the content. It is important to note, though, that even when a school provides all teachers with the proficiency scales they are expected to use, it is the job of teachers to communicate and interpret each scale to students.

Furthermore, even when scales are school-level creations, setting a consistent curriculum, academy teachers have significant latitude in augmenting scales to meet the unique needs of their students.

Teachers should give students the proficiency scales at the beginning of each unit of study. Teachers first introduce and explain the proficiency scale to them, but then help students unpack each new scale. This is because each bulleted item at the score 2.0, 3.0, and 4.0 levels represents a specific learning goal. Students should recognize this about proficiency scales and view the bullet points in the scales as the roadmap to their learning within a particular unit. Educators refer to the bulleted points on a proficiency scale in a variety of ways, including *learning goals*, *learning targets*, *target content*, *targets*, *elements*, or simply *bullet points*. In this book, we primarily use the term *learning targets*.

One of the concrete actions teachers can take to facilitate the use of proficiency scales is to have students keep data notebooks. Throughout this book, we mention data notebooks a number of times. A data notebook is simply a repository where students keep information and evidence about how well they are doing on specific measurement topics. This repository can be a three-ring binder, a large folder that holds multiple pieces of paper, an electronic notebook where items have been scanned and converted to digital records, or a combination of these options. At the beginning of each unit, students add the scale for that unit to their data notebooks as a reference and to facilitate tracking their progress on the learning targets (see element Ib, page 13).

During each unit, the teacher can post a class copy of each new proficiency scale on a corresponding focus board. As its name implies, a focus board is simply a whiteboard or space on the wall where teachers post content that is important to a particular lesson or unit. Figure 1.2 depicts a proficiency scale for mathematics that has been provided to students in a unit titled Fun With Fractions. Note that the proficiency scale includes a code used by the school district for this measurement topic (in this case, MA.05.NF.07.04). Because teachers at this school consistently use these codes, students become familiar with them as shorthand abbreviations. The codes also appear in reports and charts that display the status of individual students and groups.

When starting this unit, the teacher would go over this scale with students, pointing out the individual learning targets it includes. The teacher would engage students in a whole-class discussion focused on the scale and invite questions from students. Some of these questions might be posted alongside the scale to refer back to when their answers become clear.

Some elementary teachers like to provide space in a scale for students to record examples or notes from the lesson that helped them understand particular content in the scale. To illustrate, consider the proficiency scale in figure 1.3 (page 12) on the topic of celestial motion. This scale is formatted with a separate row for each of the three score 3.0 learning targets, which are closely interrelated and thus part of the same measurement topic. (Such decisions about including multiple score 3.0 elements in a single scale would be made at the school or district level when educators are writing the scales that all teachers will use.) The score 2.0 content that supports each score 3.0 target is listed below it. The last column in this scale provides space for students to record examples of the content they had generated in a specific lesson or in their notes. These entries help students understand the specific targets in the scale. For example, next to one learning target, a particular student might record the comment, "This is what Mr. Abbott was talking about when he was using the globe and the wastepaper basket to represent the Earth and the Sun." Such entries are strictly for students as aids that remind them about the content in a scale and help them make connections between lessons and learning targets.

After introducing students to specific proficiency scales, teachers should encourage students to reference the scales and learning goals by name using the code in the scale. Again, when students are familiar with the district codes that accompany specific measurement topics, they are able to interpret charts and reports from the district that summarize group performance on these measurement topics.

Measurement Topic: MA.05.NF.07.04—Multiplying and Dividing Fractions	
Target Description: • Solve real-world problems involving division of unit fractions by non-zero whole numbers and division of whole numbers by non-zero unit fractions. Use visual fraction models and equations. • Solve real-world problems involving multiplication of fractions and mixed numbers. Use visual fraction models or equations.	
Proficiency Scale	
Score 4.0	Take it further: perform an in-depth application of a fractional division or multiplication problem-solving process. For example, plan an all-school party by multiplying (or dividing) desired recipes to account for the number of guests.
Score 3.5	In addition to score 3.0 performance, partial success at score 4.0 content
Score 3.0	The learner will: • Use visual models or equations to solve real-world division problems where fractions are divided by whole numbers, and where whole numbers are divided by unit fractions. • Use visual models and equations to solve real-world problems where fractions and mixed numbers are multiplied.
Score 2.5	The learner has no major errors or omissions regarding score 2.0 content, and partial success at 3.0
Score 2.0	The learner will recognize or recall specific vocabulary (for example, *denominator, divide, fraction, mixed number, multiplication, numerator, product, scaling, unit fraction*, and *whole number*) and perform basic processes such as: • Interpret a fraction as division. • Interpret the product of a fraction and whole number as a part of a set. • Find the area of a rectangle with fractional side lengths. • Interpret multiplication as scaling (resizing). • Compare the size of a product to the size of one factor.
Score 1.5	Partial success at score 2.0 content, and major errors or omissions regarding score 3.0 content
Score 1.0	With help, a partial understanding of some of the simpler details and process and some of the more complex ideas and processes
Score 0.5	With help, a partial understanding of some of the simpler details and processes
Score 0.0	Even with help, no understanding or skill demonstrated

FIGURE 1.2: Proficiency scale for Fun With Fractions unit, grade 5.

Name: ____________________

SC.05.ESS1.02.05—Celestial Motion		Example From Lesson or Notes
4.0	Go beyond what was taught in class. For example, investigate how humans have used the patterns created by Earth's movement around the sun in technology.	
3.0	Describe how the Earth's movement in relation to the sun creates patterns of day and night.	
2.0	☐ Explain how the spherical shape of the Earth is illuminated unevenly by the sun. ☐ Describe the pattern of how the sun rises, moves across the sky, and sets during the day. ☐ Explain that Earth rotates on its axis completely every twenty-four hours.	
3.0	Describe how the Earth's movement in relation to the sun creates patterns that affect the appearance of shadows.	
2.0	☐ Relate length of shadow to time of day and position of the sun in the sky. ☐ Track the shadow cast by the sun on an object throughout the day. ☐ Relate the sun's position in the sky to time of day.	
3.0	Describe how the Earth's movement in relation to the sun creates patterns that affect the appearance of constellations in the night sky.	
2.0	☐ Explain why the position of the Earth in its orbit affects which constellations are visible at night. ☐ Identify constellations in the night sky. ☐ Explain that the sun is stationary and that the Earth orbits around it every 365 days (revolution).	

Source: © 2021 by Westminster Public Schools. Used with permission.

FIGURE 1.3: Proficiency scale for celestial motion, grade 5.

Teachers can periodically encourage students to set within-one-week (WOW) goals as students refer to the scales. For example, a student might say, "My goal for today is to show evidence for a 3.0 score on proficiency scale R1.01." Such activities keep scales in the forefront of students' thinking.

Teachers should keep in mind that proficiency scales are not just artifacts to be posted on the board and ignored. Rather, scales should be a living, breathing part of daily life within a competency-based classroom. Ensuring that students are continually developing their understanding of specific elements in scales and becoming increasingly more aware of their status on those scales should be regular parts of teachers' interaction with students.

As mentioned in the introduction, teachers should use visible evidence to judge how well strategies for each element are working. Figure 1.4 lists visible evidence for element Ia.

Visible evidence for effective instruction and guidance includes teachers doing the following.
• Explaining to students the meaning of the content in proficiency scales that they are about to use • Developing routines that encourage students to pay attention to the proficiency scales (for example, reviewing the scale at the beginning and end of class) • Creating student-friendly versions of proficiency scales • Having students archive proficiency scales in their data notebooks • Developing personal tracking matrices for students • Having students set personal goals relative to their growth on specific proficiency scales
Visible evidence for desired student actions and behaviors includes students doing the following.
• Making reference to proficiency scales as they talk with their peers • Making reference to proficiency scales as they interact with the teacher • Setting goals for themselves regarding proficiency scales
Visible evidence for students' understanding and awareness includes students doing the following.
• Explaining the proficiency scale in their own words • Explaining which learning goal from a specific proficiency scale is being addressed in the current lesson • Describing how the current instructional activity relates to a specific proficiency scale • Explaining the progression of content in a specific proficiency scale

Source: © 2021 by Robert J. Marzano.

FIGURE 1.4: Visible evidence for element Ia.

Ib. Tracking Student Progress

The teacher responsibility inherent in this element is to help students track their progress as they learn the content within specific proficiency scales. Operationally, the teacher should facilitate students' progress tracking on each scale in such a way that, at any point in time, students will know their current level of performance and how much they have increased their competence in the content of the scale. As a byproduct of such knowledge, students should also be aware of what they must do to achieve the next level of performance on the scale.

Operationally, students should track progress on individual proficiency scales within their data notebooks using a *personal tracking matrix*. To illustrate, consider figure 1.5 (page 14), which depicts the personal tracking matrix for the fifth-grade proficiency scale for the measurement topic of multiplying and dividing fractions (figure 1.2, page 11). This tracking matrix would be employed in the Fun With Fractions unit described in the discussion of element Ia. The teacher in this case designs lessons or learning activities around the specific learning targets, beginning with score 2.0 content from the proficiency scale and progressing accordingly. As students complete assignments and receive feedback, they use the personal tracking matrix to rate their level of understanding or skill.

Note that each individual learning target from the proficiency scale has its own row in the personal tracking matrix, and that students are asked to rate themselves on their understanding or skill

Level	Indicator	My Rating			My Evidence
		I'm still confused about this topic.	I've learned some but not all of the topic.	I've got this now.	
4.0	Perform an in-depth application of a fractional division or multiplication problem-solving process.				
3.0	Use visual models or equations to solve real-world division problems where fractions are divided by whole numbers, and where whole numbers are divided by unit fractions.				
3.0	Use visual models and equations to solve real-world problems where fractions and mixed numbers are multiplied.				
2.0	Interpret a fraction as division.				
2.0	Interpret the product of a fraction and whole number as a part of a set.				
2.0	Find the area of a rectangle with fractional side lengths.				
2.0	Interpret multiplication as scaling (resizing).				
2.0	Compare the size of a product to the size of one factor.				
2.0	Recognize the critical vocabulary listed in the scale.				

FIGURE 1.5: Personal tracking matrix for Fun With Fractions.

relative to the content in each row. Students use the following scale to rate their current level of understanding for each element.

- I've got this now.
- I've learned some but not all of this content.
- I'm still confused about this topic.

There is also a column in the personal tracking matrix where students record the evidence to support their personal judgment of their competence. In this column, students list or describe the activities they engaged in that support their self-evaluation scores. For example, a specific student who rated herself "I've got this now" for "recognize the critical vocabulary listed in the scale" might record as her evidence the fact that she correctly answered 100 percent of the items on the virtual vocabulary quiz for this scale. Over the course of a unit (and even after a unit has been completed), students continue to update their status on the various components of the proficiency scale.

Personal tracking matrices are dynamic data-gathering and recording devices. In addition to making students aware of their own status and growth, personal tracking matrices establish a clear line of communication between students and the teacher. To illustrate, consider a specific student who initially rates himself as "still confused" on all of the score 2.0 content. As he works to attain proficiency on these targets and receives feedback and scores from activities and assignments, he changes his rating on each score 2.0 learning target to "I've got this now," with the exception of the row for "interpret multiplication as scaling (resizing)." For that particular target, he rates himself as "I've learned some but not all of this topic." The student determines that he would like to get some additional help with this particular learning target. He requests a meeting with the teacher, who meets with him to provide further instruction. Through a probing discussion with this student, it becomes apparent to the teacher that the student is having some trouble understanding certain key vocabulary terms from the proficiency scale. In this case, the teacher determines that the student has developed an incorrect understanding of the word *scaling*. The teacher spends a few minutes reteaching some key information about the relationship between multiplication and scaling, showing the student some examples, and directing him to specific instructional videos and online practice for support. The teacher also pairs the student with an "expert" peer from the class who has already demonstrated proficiency at the 4.0 level. After all these activities, the student updates his self-rating and both the student and the teacher are confident that he has mastered all the 2.0 targets.

In this example, the student has independently identified a specific piece of content he would like to improve on. He advocates for himself by reaching out to the teacher and asking for support, and receives specialized instruction and additional resources. He uses the resources available to him to deepen his understanding until he deems through reflection and self-assessment that he is proficient.

Even primary students are capable of tracking their progress on specific measurement topics. To aid primary students in this endeavor, teachers should utilize visual representations of each learning goal that students can check off as they progress through each scale. For example, consider the proficiency scale for first-grade literacy in figure 1.6 (page 16).

Initially, the teacher would go over this scale with students, describing and perhaps exemplifying each element. Next, the teacher would provide students with a personal tracking matrix for the scale that includes picture clues as to the expectations at each level. This is depicted in figure 1.7 (page 17), where an illustration of the intended knowledge and skill represents each element of the proficiency scale. As in the previous example of a personal tracking matrix, primary students would keep track of their performance on each element of the matrix using the "My Rating" scale.

Measurement Topic: LI.01.R1.02—Key Details	
Target Description: • Identify the main topic and retell key details of a text (nonfiction). • Retell stories, including key details, and demonstrate understanding of their central message or lesson (fiction).	
Proficiency Scale	
Score 4.0	Take it further: make a central message connection between two books. For example, find another book that has a similar central message or lesson and talk about their similarities and differences.
Score 3.5	In addition to score 3.0 performance, partial success at score 4.0 content
Score 3.0	The learner will: • Find the main topic of a text and retell key details. • Retell a story by including important details, and discuss its central message or lesson.
Score 2.5	The learner has no major errors or omissions regarding score 2.0 content, and partial success at 3.0
Score 2.0	The learner will recognize or recall specific vocabulary (for example, *central idea, detail, lesson, message, story, text,* and *topic*) and perform basic processes such as: • Recognize or recall the central message or lesson of a story (fiction). • Retell key details of a text (nonfiction). • Retell a story and include details (fiction).
Score 1.5	Partial success at score 2.0 content, and major errors or omissions regarding score 3.0 content
Score 1.0	With help, a partial understanding of some of the simpler details and process and some of the more complex ideas and processes
Score 0.5	With help, a partial understanding of some of the simpler details and processes
Score 0.0	Even with help, no understanding or skill demonstrated

Source: © 2021 by Westminster Public Schools. Used with permission.

FIGURE 1.6: Proficiency scale for first-grade literacy.

Personal tracking matrices are not the only way students can track their progress. To illustrate, consider figure 1.8 (page 18), which shows a form students use to keep track of their progress across a number of proficiency scales within various subject areas. This matrix lists various levels of achievement in the columns titled "My Progress." This district's numbering convention for grade levels uses PK for prekindergarten, 00 for kindergarten, 01 for first grade, and 02 for second grade. Each row represents a different subject area. For each subject area and grade level, the total number of measurement topics is listed, with a blank for students to fill in how many they have mastered.

To illustrate how the matrix might be used, consider the last row for the subject area of physical education. As indicated by the number five noted at the kindergarten level, students must

Level	Indicator	My Rating			My Evidence
		I'm still confused about this topic.	I've learned some but not all of the topic.	I've got this now.	
4.0	Retell a story by including important details, and discuss its central message or lesson.				
3.0	Recognize or recall the central message or lesson of a story.				
3.0	Retell a story and include details.				
2.0	Recognize key vocabulary words.				

FIGURE 1.7: Personal tracking matrix with visual representations of learning targets.

demonstrate competence on five physical education proficiency scales to complete the kindergarten-level expectations. When a student demonstrates proficiency on these five scales, he or she would fill in the blank to show 5/5. Students can thus use this one competency tracker to keep track of their status and progress on multiple subject areas spanning PK through grade 2. Students would keep this recording device in their data notebooks.

In addition to the activities described previously, many other methods of tracking progress can be used. Teachers can easily acquire information from students that helps them track their progress through the use of informal assessment techniques such as the following.

- Digital surveys (such as Google Forms) that pose questions about their perceptions of their current status on specific learning targets
- Quick checks for understanding regarding specific learning targets, perhaps using polling apps or paper alternatives (such as Plickers)
- Self-rating exercises regarding specific learning targets, such as fist to five (in which students use their fingers to rate their levels of understanding)

Figure 1.9 (page 19) lists visible evidence for element Ib.

Primary Level Competency Tracker

Student Name: ______________________ Grade: __________

Content Area	My Progress			
Mathematics	PK	00	01	02
	___/5	___/9	___/10	___/10
Literacy	PK	00	01	02
	___/10	___/34	___/34	___/34
Science	PK	00	01	02
	___/7	___/11	___/11	___/12
Social Studies	PK	00	01	02
	___/7	___/11	___/11	___/12
Technology	PR			
	___/6			
Visual Arts	00	01	02	
	___/4	___/4	___/5	
Performing Arts	00	01	02	
	___/5	___/7	___/10	
Physical Education	00	01	02	
	___/5	___/8	___/6	

Step 1. Circle the performance level you should be starting this year based on your traditional grade level.

Step 2. Mark your progress for each content area then star (*) your goal level for the year.

Source: © 2021 by Westminster Public Schools. Used with permission.

FIGURE 1.8: Primary competency tracker.

Visible evidence for effective instruction and guidance includes teachers doing the following.
• Requiring students to track their progress on the proficiency scales • Providing students with personal tracking matrices • Making adaptations for primary students in the proficiency scales and their related personal tracking matrices • Tracking the progress of the entire class by showing what percentage of students scored at a proficient (3.0) level or above for a particular assessment • Asking students to set goals relative to the proficiency scales and track their own progress • Helping students archive evidence of learning in their data notebooks
Visible evidence for desired student actions and behaviors includes students doing the following.
• Periodically updating their status on a proficiency scale by tracking their progress • Providing evidence for their self-evaluation scores in their personal tracking matrices • Setting goals relative to increasing their status within specific proficiency scales
Visible evidence for students' understanding and awareness includes students doing the following.
• Describing how they have progressed on a particular proficiency scale • Defending the evidence they recorded in their personal tracking matrices • Describing in their own words what they need to do to get to the next level of performance on a proficiency scale

Source: © 2021 by Robert J. Marzano.

FIGURE 1.9: Visible evidence for element Ib.

Ic. Celebrating Success

To enact this element, the teacher must recognize and celebrate students' success at mastering the knowledge and skill inherent in proficiency scales. To this end, it is important for teachers to celebrate two types of success: status and growth. Of course, these celebrations are made possible by the existence of proficiency scales. *Status* refers to current scores on a specific scale. When students reach the level of 3.0 or higher, it is certainly a reason for celebration. *Growth* refers to the change in a student's score on a specific scale. Whether a student has progressed from score 1.0 to 2.0 or from score 3.0 to 4.0, it is still an occasion to celebrate growth of one full level. Such celebrations can range from informal and unplanned to formal and planned.

Teachers can celebrate individual students and the class as a whole as they move through the various levels of a specific proficiency scale or the curriculum in general. For example, during a post-lesson reflection, a teacher might ask, "Did anyone make a change to their tracking matrix today?" Students could then share their answers with the whole class or in small groups. When doing so, it is useful for them to use the sentence stem, "I used to think ______ but now I think ______."

For the purpose of celebration, notes, comments, stickers, stamps, and so on can be affixed to assignments, with teachers commenting specifically about students' progress toward their individual learning goals. Of course, this requires teachers to be cognizant of students' personal goals. A student who has been working hard to understand a mathematics concept can relish a score of 2.5 even though he has not yet shown complete proficiency. Teachers should jump at the chance to pat a student on the back, literally or figuratively, whenever they see hard work pay off. Classes can also celebrate success routinely at the end of a unit, or whenever students attain proficiency on a scale. Perhaps once a week when the teacher examines student data and enters overall scores into a gradebook, he or she can play celebratory music or have students ring a bell, chime, or gong to signify attainment of proficiency or a specific amount of growth.

Consider a student who is working toward proficiency (that is, score 3.0) on her fifth-grade multiplication and division of fractions scale. At the student's request, the teacher gives her several additional assignments and lets her redo two exit tickets in order to demonstrate competence at the level 2.0 learning goals. Following the teacher's guidance, the student watches several teacher-created videos and comes in during lunch and recess to work on her assignments, receiving support from the teacher when needed. The day after she turns in her final assignment redo, the teacher gives her a "kudos," and the whole class gives a cheer for her success. The teacher then follows up later in the afternoon by giving the student's mother a quick phone call detailing her hard work.

Just as individual students' accomplishments can be celebrated, so too can the accomplishments of the class as a whole. Classroom status and growth can be acknowledged on a daily, weekly, or monthly basis. Any area for which the teacher collects and tracks data, whether academic or behavioral, is an opportunity to set goals and celebrate if and when those goals are reached. Classroom goals often deal with students' behavior as opposed to students' academic accomplishments. For example, a class that achieves its goal to attain a certain score on a behavioral proficiency scale such as cafeteria behavior can be celebrated. Behavioral skills and other life skills are explicitly addressed in element Xc (page 143) of the instructional model. For the discussion here, it suffices to note that nonacademic skills and content can also be articulated as measurement topics with their own versions of proficiency scales.

For whole-class success on behavioral goals, students might receive tangible rewards such as choosing a theme day (chip day, hat day, fuzzy slippers day, and so on). Celebrations can happen organically as well, and do not need to include some type of reward. Perhaps a class has been working on learning their multiplication facts, with a goal of increasing the number of facts completed during a timed test by five over the course of one week. When the results of that test are revealed, a class that has been working hard toward meeting that goal can celebrate using cheers, high fives, and smiles.

Finally, a whole school can celebrate success together during regularly scheduled assemblies. Schools might choose to hold level-up ceremonies, where students who have completed an entire level of content (such as fourth-grade mathematics) formally begin a new level (such as fifth-grade mathematics). At the ceremony, school leaders recognize and celebrate these significant transitions in front of the whole school. The principal can recognize students with their parents in attendance, and invite them to a principal's luncheon, where they further celebrate their success. During these celebratory assemblies, the school can also acknowledge additional achievements, such as the school receiving an award or recognition from an outside group; teachers completing certifications, master's degrees, or doctoral programs; a staff member having a child; classes meeting data goals; students reaching long-term goals; students completing personal projects (see element Xb, page 140); or the whole student body displaying consistent positive behavior. Much like a family would celebrate the accomplishments of a son, daughter, mom, or dad, a school should celebrate and recognize even the smallest of achievements for all of its members.

Figure 1.10 lists visible evidence for element Ic.

Visible evidence for effective instruction and guidance includes teachers doing the following.
• Celebrating each student's status at different points in time (status celebration) • Celebrating each student's growth over time (growth celebration) • Providing verbal feedback to students regarding their effort and growth by specifically explaining what they did well on a task • Engaging in whole-class celebrations for status and growth
Visible evidence for desired student actions and behaviors includes students doing the following.
• Demonstrating pride regarding their status accomplishments in class • Demonstrating pride regarding their growth accomplishments in class • Striving for higher scores on proficiency scales • Actively participating in status and growth celebrations
Visible evidence for students' understanding and awareness includes students doing the following.
• Explaining what they enjoy about growth and status celebrations • Saying they are proud of their status and growth accomplishments • Telling their families about their accomplishments

Source: © *2021 by Robert J. Marzano.*

FIGURE 1.10: Visible evidence for element Ic.

Understanding and Planning for Design Area I

In the Marzano Academies model, proficiency scales are the foundation for decisions about curriculum, instruction, and assessments—particularly as those decisions pertain to competency-based education. The basic premise underlying the creation of proficiency scales is that the curriculum should be completely transparent to all educators in the system as well as students, parents, and guardians.

To a great extent, proficiency scales can ensure that the intended curriculum, the taught curriculum, and the assessed curriculum are all the same. As first described in *What Works in Schools* (Marzano, 2003b), this has historically not been the case. Unfortunately, the lack of coordination among these three curricula still exists (see Marzano, 2018; Marzano et al., 2019).

As its name implies, the intended curriculum is the content that the state, province, district, or school deems necessary for students to learn at a given grade level. These expectations are typically stated as standards at each grade level. Given the fact that virtually every state or province has standards for the major subject areas, one might conclude that all curricula are perfectly aligned in most schools: the intended curriculum is the content in the state standards, teachers teach the content in the state standards (the taught curriculum), and the tests are based on the state standards (the assessed curriculum). Figure 1.11 depicts this ideal relationship between the three curricula.

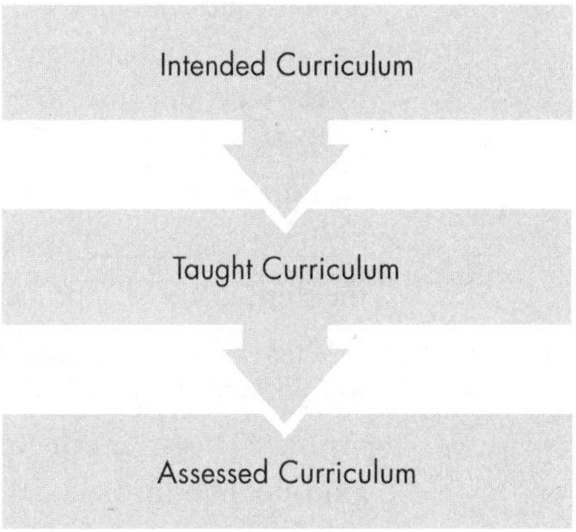

Intended Curriculum

↓

Taught Curriculum

↓

Assessed Curriculum

Source: © *2021 by Robert J. Marzano.*

FIGURE 1.11: Ideal relationship between the three curricula.

Figure 1.11 shows that the intended curriculum completely dictates the taught curriculum, which in turn completely dictates the assessed curriculum. Unfortunately, this line of causality typically falls apart at the outset within K–12 education. This is because standards commonly have so much content that there are many ways to interpret them in terms of the three curricula. Robert J. Marzano, Jennifer S. Norford, and Mike Ruyle (2019) made this point using the following standard: "Understands the properties of operations with rational numbers (e.g., distributive property, commutative and associative properties of addition and multiplication, inverse properties, identity properties) (Grades 6–8, McREL Compendium 3)" (p. 11). If one unpacks this standard, it becomes clear that it contains at least five elements.

1. Understands the distributive property with rational numbers
2. Understands the commutative property of addition with rational numbers
3. Understands the commutative property of multiplication with rational numbers
4. Understands the inverse property of rational numbers
5. Understands the identity properties of rational numbers

While this standard is for mathematics, the same problem holds true for other subject areas. Unpacking standards to identify the specific elements or dimensions is a technical issue and should be undertaken thoughtfully with an awareness of the type of content addressed by a specific standard. Marzano and his colleagues (2019) provided detailed guidance to this end. They offered figure 1.12 as evidence that the phenomenon of standards with multiple embedded elements is ubiquitous across all grade levels and subject areas.

In effect, standards do very little to ensure that the three curricula are aligned for classroom teachers. While all teachers in a school might be working on the same mathematics standard listed previously, there are at least five different things on which they might be focusing.

1. Helping students understand the distributive property with rational numbers
2. Helping students understand the commutative property of addition with rational numbers
3. Helping students understand the commutative property of multiplication with rational numbers
4. Helping students understand the inverse property of rational numbers
5. Helping students understand the identity properties of rational numbers

Consequently, while one teacher's taught curriculum might emphasize elements 1 and 2 from this list, another teacher might focus on elements 4 and 5, and so on. Finally, if the assessment designed by the state, province, district, or school equally addresses all five of the embedded elements, those students whose taught curriculum focused on one or two of the elements would be at a disadvantage simply because they did not have an opportunity to learn some of the content.

A well-constructed proficiency scale addresses this problem at the outset. To illustrate, consider the third-grade ELA proficiency scale in figure 1.13 (page 24).

When a teacher presents this proficiency scale to the third-grade students for whom it is designed, there is no ambiguity regarding the intended curriculum. The teacher will surely provide direct instruction regarding the vocabulary and basic facts in the 2.0 content and will provide practice and guidance in using past and future tense in a short paragraph as described in the 3.0 content. Thus, the taught curriculum becomes unequivocal. Finally, the 2.0 and 3.0 content will be the basis of all assessments relative to this measurement topic, rendering the assessed curriculum concrete and

Subject	Standard and Topics
Reading	6–8, Compendium 3 Uses a variety of strategies to extend reading vocabulary 1. Uses analogies, idioms, similes, metaphors to infer the meaning of literal and figurative phrases 2. Uses definition, restatement, example, comparison and contrast to verify word meanings 3. Identifies shades of meaning 4. Knows denotative and connotative meanings 5. Knows vocabulary related to different content areas and current events 6. Uses rhyming dictionaries, classification books, etymological dictionaries
Writing	K–2, Compendium 3 Uses strategies to draft and revise written work 1. Rereads 2. Rearranges words, sentences, and paragraphs to improve sequence or clarify meaning 3. Varies sentence type 4. Adds descriptive words and details 5. Deletes extraneous information 6. Incorporates suggestions from peers and teachers 7. Sharpens the focus
Social Studies	Grades 3–4, K–4 History, Compendium 3 Knows the ways that families long ago expressed and transmitted their beliefs and values through oral tradition, literature, songs, art, religion, community celebrations, mementos, food, and language (e.g., celebration of national holidays, religious observances, and ethnic and national traditions; visual arts and crafts; hymns, proverbs, and songs) 1. Knows that families long ago expressed and transmitted their beliefs and values through oral tradition 2. Knows that families long ago expressed and transmitted their beliefs and values through literature 3. Knows that families long ago expressed and transmitted their beliefs and values through songs 4. Knows that families long ago expressed and transmitted their beliefs and values through art, including visual arts and crafts 5. Knows that families long ago expressed and transmitted their beliefs and values through religion and religious observances 6. Knows that families long ago expressed and transmitted their beliefs and values through community celebration 7. Knows that families long ago expressed and transmitted their beliefs and values through mementos 8. Knows that families long ago expressed and transmitted their beliefs and values through food 9. Knows that families long ago expressed and transmitted their beliefs and values through language 10. Knows that families long ago expressed and transmitted their beliefs and values through celebration of national holidays 11. Knows that families long ago expressed and transmitted their beliefs and values through ethnic and national traditions 12. Knows that families long ago expressed and transmitted their beliefs and values through hymns 13. Knows that families long ago expressed and transmitted their beliefs and values through proverbs 14. Knows that families long ago expressed and transmitted their beliefs and values through songs
Physical Education	Grades 3–6, Compendium 3 Understands detrimental effects of physical activity (e.g., muscle soreness, overuse injuries, over-training, temporary tiredness, and discovering inability) 1. Understands that physical activity can have detrimental effects 2. Understands the one detrimental effect of physical activity can be muscle soreness 3. Understands the one detrimental effect of physical activity can be overuse injuries 4. Understands the one detrimental effect of physical activity can be over-training 5. Understands the one detrimental effect of physical activity can be temporary tiredness 6. Understands the one detrimental effect of physical activity can be discovering inability
The Arts	Grades 5–8, Compendium 3 Understands how lighting and costuming can contribute to the meaning of a dance 1. Understands how lighting can contribute to the meaning of a dance 2. Understands how costuming can contribute to the meaning of a dance 3. Understands the various ways dance can communicate meaning

Source: Marzano et al., 2019, pp. 13–14.
Source for standards: Mid-Continent Research for Education and Learning (McREL), 2014.

FIGURE 1.12: Multiple topics in content standards.

Score	Description
4.0	In addition to score 3.0 performance, the student demonstrates in-depth inferences and applications that go beyond what was taught.
3.5	In addition to score 3.0 performance, partial success at score 4.0 content
3.0	The student will: RIST—Use simple tenses of irregular and regular verbs correctly (for example, write a short paragraph about last summer's activities and plans for the upcoming summer using past and future tense verbs).
2.5	No major errors or omissions regarding score 2.0 content, and partial success at score 3.0 content
2.0	RIST—The student will recognize or recall specific vocabulary (for example, *future tense, past tense, present tense*) and perform basic processes such as: • Correctly use various tenses of the *to be* verb (such as *am, are, is*). • State that regular past tense verbs are formed by adding *-ed* to verb tenses and that *-y* at the end of a verb needs to be changed to *-i* before adding *-ed* to form the past tense. • Explain when *-s* needs to be added to the end of present tense verbs. • List common irregular past tense verbs (such as *ran, did, bought*). • State that future tense verbs are formed by adding *will* in front of a verb.
1.5	Partial success at score 2.0 content, and major errors or omissions regarding score 3.0 content
1.0	With help, partial success at score 2.0 content and score 3.0 content
0.5	With help, partial success at score 2.0 content but not at score 3.0 content
0.0	Even with help, no success

Source: © 2016 by Marzano Resources. Adapted with permission.

FIGURE 1.13: Sample ELA proficiency scale, grade 3.

focused. In short, the existence of a proficiency scale provides complete transparency relative to the intended, taught, and assessed curricula.

Much of the planning for design area I should be taken care of by the school or district in which a teacher works. That is, ideally, the measurement topics and associated proficiency scales for which a teacher is responsible are designed at the district or school level. If this is not the case, then a teacher's first planning activity relative to design area I is to identify the measurement topics he or she will address during the year and then design the proficiency scales for them. As mentioned previously, *The New Art and Science of Classroom Assessment* (Marzano et al., 2019) provides guidance to this end. If teachers do not have to create their own measurement topics and accompanying proficiency scales, then their planning will be focused on the order in which they will address the measurement topics. Additionally, teachers will make decisions about embedding each measurement topic in its own unit of instruction or include multiple measurement topics within units.

Design Area II: Assessment

When addressing this design area, the teacher constructs and administers assessments that accurately measure students' status on proficiency scales. Furthermore, the teacher helps students understand the relationships between their scores on various assessments and their overall status on proficiency scales. For a detailed and more technical discussion of the assessment process in an elementary academy, readers should consult the books *Making Classroom Assessments Reliable and Valid* (Marzano, 2018) and *The New Art and Science of Classroom Assessment* (Marzano et al., 2019).

In a traditional classroom, the primary function of assessments is to measure and document students' current status on specific content. In the academy model this is still an important function of classroom assessments, but equally important is the use of classroom assessments as a form of feedback between students and teachers. In other words, classroom assessments provide the teacher with information about students' learning needs, and they provide students with information about how to improve. Assessments can take a variety of forms, including obtrusive, student centered, and unobtrusive. Teachers in the academy model also use data from classroom assessments in ways that are not common to traditional classrooms. There are four elements in this design area.

IIa. Using obtrusive assessments

IIb. Using student-centered assessments

IIc. Using unobtrusive assessments

IId. Generating current summative scores

The following sections detail each one.

IIa. Using Obtrusive Assessments

The teacher responsibility inherent in this element is to design concrete assessments regarding the content in specific proficiency scales and administer them at specific times. Such assessments are referred to as *obtrusive* because they require pauses in the flow of instruction. More pointedly, with obtrusive assessments, instruction stops and assessment occurs. This is not negative. Obtrusive assessments signal to students that this is a time for them to demonstrate their knowledge and skill relative to the content in specific proficiency scales. Common formats for obtrusive assessments include pencil-and-paper tests, essays, and discussions.

It is important to recognize that obtrusive assessments are designed differently in a competency-based system than in a traditional one. Each question on an obtrusive assessment focuses on specific content at a specific level of a specific proficiency scale. For example, a sixth-grade mathematics assessment for ratios and unit rates would be broken down into questions for the content at the 2.0, 3.0, and 4.0 levels of the proficiency scale for this measurement topic, thereby allowing the teacher to assess the full range of values on the scale. The questions could be marked to indicate their score value on the proficiency scale. We have found that drafting a test blueprint before actually writing specific test items is foundational to creating a focused assessment. Figure 1.14 (page 26) depicts such a test blueprint.

The example in figure 1.14 indicates that the test planned by this teacher will include fourteen items, each of which focuses on specific learning targets from the proficiency scale. Some learning targets will have multiple items devoted to them. For example, there will be five questions about the score 2.0 learning target related to converting measurement units, and there will be two items about the 3.0 learning target concerning rates and ratios. In all, the blueprint specifies that seven items will address score 2.0 content and seven items will address score 3.0 content. Targets that have multiple items dedicated to them are those the teacher has emphasized during instruction.

With this framework in place, the teacher would then construct the actual items for each learning target. For example, the 3.0 learning target on solving unit rate problems, including those involving unit pricing and constant speed, is slated as the focus of three items. For one, the teacher writes the following short constructed-response item.

> When you talk about how fast a car is going, you typically refer to its speed in miles per hour. For example, you say, "The car was going 60 miles per hour." Normally, you don't say, "The car traveled 120 miles in 3 hours." Explain and demonstrate how you would convert a rate of 120 miles in 3 hours into a unit rate based on minutes.

The teacher would then design the thirteen other items according to the blueprint, using various formats like multiple choice, matching, fill in the blank, and others, based on which formats the teacher believes will most directly and accurately assess the content in the learning targets. It is important to note that developing a test blueprint like that in figure 1.14 allows teachers to design multiple versions of a test for the same learning targets.

MA.06.RP.03.04—Ratios and Unit Rates

Score	Learning Target	Number of Questions
3.0	Find a percent of a quantity as a rate per 100 (for example, 30 percent of a quantity means 30/100 times the quantity); solve problems involving finding the whole, given a part and the percent.	1
3.0	Solve unit rate problems including those involving unit pricing and constant speed.	3
3.0	Understand the concept of a unit rate a/b associated with a ratio a/b with b ≠ 0, and use rate language in the context of a ratio relationship.	2
3.0	Make tables of equivalent ratios relating quantities with whole-number measurements, find missing values in the tables, and plot the pairs of values on the coordinate plane. Use tables to compare ratios.	1
2.0	Use ratio reasoning to convert measurement units; manipulate and transform units appropriately when multiplying or dividing quantities.	5
2.0	Recognize multiple equivalent representations of ratios.	1
2.0	Understand the concept of a ratio and use ratio language to describe a ratio relationship between two quantities.	1

Source: *© 2021 by Westminster Public Schools. Used with permission.*

FIGURE 1.14: Test blueprint designed around levels of a proficiency scale.

To score this test, the teacher would first examine the items designed to assess the score 2.0 content. If students' responses demonstrated that they know this content with no major errors or omissions, they would be judged competent at the 2.0 content in the proficiency scale. The teacher would then move to the items that address the 3.0 content. If students answered these correctly, they would be scored at the 3.0 level.

This is a stark departure from the traditional way of scoring tests where the teacher assigns points to items and then simply adds up the points. In a competency-based system, teachers consider all the items for each scale level as a set and use students' patterns of responses to make decisions about their performance. Marzano and colleagues (2019) described a number of techniques for this type of scoring. To illustrate a points-based approach, consider figure 1.15.

Figure 1.15 depicts the results of a test where the items are organized into three sections: one for the score 2.0 items, one for the score 3.0 items, and one for the score 4.0 items. There are six items at the score 2.0 level, each worth five points, for a total of thirty available points for the score 2.0 items. The last column in figure 1.15 indicates that this particular student has earned twenty-five of these points or 83 percent. The teacher must determine whether this is adequate evidence to indicate that the student has demonstrated competence at the 2.0 level on this particular test. To do so, the teacher sets a cut score for each level. Assuming the teacher set a cut score of 80 percent for this section, the student appears to have adequately demonstrated competence with the score 2.0 content.

With this decision made, the teacher moves on to the two items at the score 3.0 level. There, the student earned thirteen of twenty possible points, or 65 percent, indicating that he appears to currently know a little more than half of the content at that level. The teacher would likely assign a proficiency scale score of 2.5 for this test, indicating no major errors with the basic content and partial success with the target content. This approach to scoring works with essays, performance tasks, demonstrations, and other forms of obtrusive assessment (see Marzano, 2018; Marzano et al., 2019).

One question commonly asked about this approach is, What happens when students exhibit aberrant response patterns? Aberrant patterns occur when a student's collection of responses to items at different levels do not make sense. For example, how would a teacher score a student's test where she answered all the score 3.0 items correctly but missed most of the score 2.0 items? Although logically this pattern should not occur,

Section	Item number	Possible points per item	Points obtained	Section percentage
Score 2.0	1	5	5	25/30 = 83 percent
	2	5	5	
	3	5	0	
	4	5	5	
	5	5	5	
	6	5	5	
	Total	30	25	
Score 3.0	1	10	5	13/20 = 65 percent
	2	10	8	
	Total	20	13	
Score 4.0	1	20	0	10/40 = 25 percent
	2	20	10	
	Total	40	10	

Source: Adapted from Marzano et al., 2019.

FIGURE 1.15: Points-based scoring.

in real-life classrooms, aberrant patterns such as this do sometimes manifest. In fact, this phenomenon is so well known in state and national assessment protocols that testing companies spend a great deal of time and resources identifying aberrant response patterns and revising items to correct for such patterns.

An aberrant response pattern may be the result of a number of factors, including the following.

- The questions were poorly written.
- The questions did not accurately reflect the level of the proficiency scale.
- The student was rushed or tired or failed to put forth the appropriate effort.
- The student did not understand the question as written.
- The teacher's evaluation of a student response was incorrect.

A teacher can address an aberrant response pattern in a number of ways.

- Ignore the aberrant responses.
- Reclassify aberrant questions to a higher or lower proficiency level based on the response pattern of the entire class.
- Engage in a probing discussion with the student in order to determine the cause of the aberrant pattern and make adjustments accordingly.

Probing discussions are an excellent way to clarify an aberrant response pattern, but they are also one of the most reliable and straightforward types of obtrusive assessment in their own right. Simply sitting down and speaking with a student about a specific topic can give the clearest picture of their knowledge and skill relative to a specific measurement topic. In a classroom setting, technology can be especially helpful in conducting probing discussions with students. Google Hangouts, Flipgrid, Google Docs, chats, and even emails can be great venues to discuss the content in a proficiency scale. Additionally, probing discussions can happen anytime and anywhere—the hallway, playground, and cafeteria are great places where students can let their guards down and speak freely with their teachers about the content of a particular proficiency scale.

Consider a fourth-grade student working through a civil rights unit in her literacy class. Her teacher has been working with the class on an ELA proficiency scale focused on including details and examples when explaining what a text is about. After reading an article on the protest tactics of Cesar Chavez and Martin Luther King Jr., her teacher posts a prompt to a discussion website like Google Hangouts or Flipgrid. The student logs on to the site and records herself talking about how both Chavez and King used nonviolent protest tactics like boycotts to advance their cause. However, she does not give any specific examples from the text when stating her case. Her teacher then follows up with her during their next available meeting time (which could be during independent work time, recess, or a trip down the hallway) to further check for understanding. When she meets with her teacher, the student provides details from the text about King's bus boycott in Montgomery, Alabama. Her teacher then makes a record of their conversation in an online gradebook and marks the student as a score 3.0 on the related proficiency scale.

Figure 1.16 lists visible evidence for element IIa.

Visible evidence for effective instruction and guidance includes teachers doing the following.
• Designing, administering, and scoring selected-response and short-answer assessments that relate to specific proficiency scales • Designing, administering, and scoring essay assessments that relate to specific proficiency scales • Designing, executing, and scoring demonstration assessments that relate to a specific proficiency scale • Designing, executing, and scoring probing discussions that relate to specific proficiency scales • Entering scores into the gradebook as evidence of student performance on specific proficiency scales
Visible evidence for desired student actions and behaviors includes students doing the following.
• Using the feedback from obtrusive assessments to make judgments about what they know and don't know • Talking to the teacher about the meaning of their test scores on obtrusive assessments and how they relate to specific proficiency scales
Visible evidence for students' understanding and awareness includes students doing the following.
• Explaining what the score they received on an obtrusive assessment means relative to a specific progression of knowledge • Explaining what their scores on obtrusive assessments mean in terms of their status on specific proficiency scales

Source: © 2021 by Robert J. Marzano.

FIGURE 1.16: Visible evidence for element IIa.

IIb. Using Student-Centered Assessments

To enact this element, the teacher provides students with opportunities to generate and submit evidence as to their current status on a specific proficiency scale. While traditional conceptions of assessment assume that the teacher is in control of all assessment opportunities, the Marzano Academies model encourages students to produce their own evidence of learning. Our discussion of this element will include both student-generated assessments and student self-assessments.

In the psychometric literature, assessment is defined as gathering information about an individual's knowledge and skill at a particular moment in time. In contrast, K–12 educators commonly think of the traditional pencil-and-paper test as the primary or only acceptable form of assessment (for further discussion, see Marzano, 2018). The more expansive technical definition of assessment means that when students present evidence of their knowledge and skill, such evidence qualifies as an assessment if the teacher can assign a score to it. Proficiency scales allow teachers to score this evidence. Stated differently, the existence of proficiency scales makes it possible to use multiple types of evidence provided by students as assessments.

To illustrate, assume a teacher is using the proficiency scale for second-grade mathematics in figure 1.17 (page 30). Imagine that a student decides to create a video demonstrating that she understands the content at the score 2.0 level. She shows that she understands the vocabulary, performs the basic processes such as adding and subtracting numbers on a number line, and explains some basic facts about interpreting picture and bar graphs. The teacher views the video and, based on the evidence, can assign the student a score of 2.0. This constitutes an assessment.

Interpreting Picture and Bar Graphs (2 Mathematics)

4.0	In addition to score 3.0 performance, the student demonstrates in-depth inferences and applications that go beyond what was taught.
3.5	In addition to score 3.0 performance, partial success at score 4.0 content
3.0	The student will: IPBG—Solve problems using information presented in picture and bar graphs (for example, when given that the African savanna exhibit at the zoo has a number of wildebeests, ostriches, gazelles, and lions for a total of twenty-nine animals, and when given a bar graph displaying the number of wildebeests, ostriches, and lions in which the bar displaying the number of gazelles is missing, determine the number of gazelles in the exhibit; determine the number of four-legged animals in the exhibit; and determine how many more or fewer lions the exhibit has than ostriches).
2.5	No major errors or omissions regarding score 2.0 content, and partial success at score 3.0 content
2.0	IPBG—The student will recognize or recall specific vocabulary (for example, *unit*) and perform basic processes such as: • Identify the components of picture and bar graphs (graph title, axes, axis labels, count scale, category labels, key). • Interpret data from vertical and horizontal picture and bar graphs. For example, when given a bar graph, explain what the graph is showing, identify the categories of the graph, and determine how many objects belong to each category. • Add and subtract numbers on a number line. • Explain that the combined number of objects in two or more categories of a picture or bar graph can be calculated by adding the number of objects indicated by the specified categories or by counting the total number of units displayed by each category. • Explain that the difference in the number of objects between two categories of a picture or bar graph can be calculated by subtracting the number of objects indicated by the smaller category from the number of objects indicated by the larger category or by counting the difference in the number of units displayed by the categories.
1.5	Partial success at score 2.0 content, and major errors or omissions regarding score 3.0 content
1.0	With help, partial success at score 2.0 content and score 3.0 content
0.5	With help, partial success at score 2.0 content but not at score 3.0 content
0.0	Even with help, no success

Source: © 2016 by Marzano Resources. Adapted with permission.

FIGURE 1.17: Sample mathematics proficiency scale, grade 2.

Student-centered assessments manifest in two ways: student-generated assessments and student self-assessment. Student-generated assessments involve students designing a task to demonstrate that they understand the content at a particular level of a proficiency scale. Students have a wide variety of options as to how they will demonstrate their competence. They can choose to create artifacts, give demonstrations, or simply have a discussion with the teacher. For example, a fifth-grade student working to show proficiency in mathematics relative to calculating volume might create an irregular

3-D structure out of graph paper and then describe how to compute the volume of the various parts. Other students working on other learning targets might submit and answer questions from an article they have read, create a topographical map of a region they are studying, compose a written summary of a story they are reading, create a knowledge map detailing character traits, and so on.

To render the student-generated assessment process as accurate as possible, students should ensure that their assessments address all aspects of the content in a given proficiency scale. For example, a particular student might choose to create her own assessment to show proficiency in her fourth-grade mathematics unit titled "Lines, Rays, and Angles . . . Oh My!" She would write test questions for each learning goal at the score 2.0 and 3.0 levels and arrange them accordingly. The student would then solve her own problems and provide an answer key for each question along with an explanation as to why her answers are correct.

Student self-assessment is different from student-generated assessments. Student self-assessment occurs when a student asserts that he or she is at a particular level on a particular proficiency scale. This commonly occurs in the context of the personal tracking matrices discussed in element Ib (page 13). Recall that personal tracking matrices employ a scale like the following for each learning target in the scale (see figure 1.5, page 14).

- I've got this now.
- I've learned some but not all of this content.
- I'm still confused about this topic.

Students rate themselves on each learning target (that is, each row in the personal tracking matrix). When they rate themselves as "I've got this now" for all of the learning targets in the matrix, they are, in effect, providing a self-evaluation indicating that they have mastered everything in the measurement topic. When students use a personal tracking matrix for self-evaluation, it is important that they fill in the final column, which requires them to record the evidence they are using to support their self-evaluations. Teachers should examine students' self-evaluation scores and the evidence they provide. If they believe students' evidence supports their self-assessment scores, then teachers can enter the students' self-assessment scores in the gradebook.

Finally, it is important to note that student-centered assessments can also be used for nonacademic skills and processes such as adherence to specific processes for specific tasks. In such cases, the requirement that proficiency scales follow the exact format described previously with the whole-point and half-point scores can be relaxed. Indeed, when student assessment is used with nonacademic skills and processes, the term *rubric* is often used instead of the term *proficiency scale*. To illustrate, assume that a teacher wishes to develop a rubric for hallway behavior. The teacher starts by prompting a discussion by posing questions like "What does good hallway behavior look and sound like?" The discussion leads to students describing behaviors for specific score values in the rubric. In primary classrooms, teachers can use pictures or illustrations instead of text descriptions. For example, a rubric developed in a first-grade classroom for appropriate lining-up behavior could include pictures of students at various stages of proficiency.

Once posted, behavioral rubrics should be considered fluid, living documents that can be changed or added to as time goes on. Ideally, student exemplars for each score are posted alongside the rubric to give the students a concrete idea of what each level actually looks like. To illustrate, consider the example of a rubric for a class code of collaboration in figure 1.18 (page 32). A code of collaboration is a written agreement between students and teachers regarding how they will interact in

Code of Collaboration Rubric	4 I am a role model for others.	3 I can do this myself, without reminders.	2 I have some success with reminders.	1 My teacher is helping me on this goal.
Be helpful to others.	I encourage my classmates to help other people. I discuss with others the importance of being helpful.	I help my teammates when they are struggling. I lend a hand when someone needs it—without being asked. I ask for help from my peers.	I know why it is important to be helpful. Sometimes I have to be reminded to help out when others need me.	I am learning about being helpful. I am trying to be helpful to others.
Be positive.	I am a cheerleader for the class, and always give praise to others for a job well done. I always give a cheer when meeting with partners. I am a school leader for positivity.	I have good things to say about other people. I point out the good parts, rather than focus on the difficult parts. I am a team player.	Sometimes I need reminders to be positive. I sometimes focus on what's difficult, or parts I don't like. I understand the importance of being positive.	I am working with others to try and focus on the things that are good. I can practice being positive with the teacher's help.

FIGURE 1.18: Rubric for code of collaboration.

a collaborative manner (see element VIIe, page 110). Traits related to successful collaboration are listed on the left, with corresponding scores and example behaviors listed beneath each score.

After completing a task that involves collaboration, students would use the rubric to reflect on their performance and make adjustments accordingly. An effective way to use rubrics is to separate a space (whiteboard, hallway, classroom, and so on) into four sections labeled with scores 1–4, and have students place their work or stand in the score they feel pertains to their work or behavior. While this can occur anonymously with names removed or hidden from work, in a classroom with a strong culture built around growth mindset (Dweck, 2006), students typically have no reservations about reflecting on their performance in front of the class.

Figure 1.19 lists visible evidence for element IIb.

IIc. Using Unobtrusive Assessments

The teacher's responsibility relative to this element is to gather information about students' current status on specific proficiency scales in ways that do not interrupt instruction. This type of assessment gets its name, *unobtrusive*, from the fact that it does not interrupt the natural flow of classroom activity. Teachers can employ unobtrusive assessments in any situation that allows them to directly observe students demonstrating their knowledge or skill on a specific learning target or to observe artifacts that reflect students' knowledge or skill of a learning target.

Unobtrusive assessments often occur without students even being aware that they have been assessed. This is possible when skills from a proficiency scale are readily observable. For example, if

Visible evidence for effective instruction and guidance includes teachers doing the following.
• Utilizing assessment activities that translate information from students' personal tracking matrices into scores on specific proficiency scales • Structuring activities that allow students to design their own forms of student-generated assessments and scoring those assessments using specific proficiency scales • Entering scores into the gradebook as evidence of student performance on specific proficiency scales • Using behavioral rubrics for student self-assessment
Visible evidence for desired student actions and behaviors includes students doing the following.
• Using the feedback from student-centered assessments to make judgments about what they know and don't know • Identifying a variety of ways they can show what they know • Talking to the teacher about the meaning of their test scores on student-centered assessments and how they relate to specific proficiency scales
Visible evidence for students' understanding and awareness includes students doing the following.
• Explaining what the score they received on student-centered assessments means relative to a specific progression of knowledge • Explaining what their scores on student-centered assessments mean in terms of their status on specific proficiency scales • Explaining why they think student-centered assessments are accurate indicators of what they know and can do

Source: © 2021 by Robert J. Marzano.

FIGURE 1.19: Visible evidence for element IIb.

the teacher is trying to assess specific aspects of students' writing ability such as editing compositions for transitions between paragraphs, the teacher might happen to observe a particular student engaged in this process while working independently on a composition. If needed, the teacher can ask the student questions to obtain a more concrete indication of the student's status. It is acceptable for students to be aware of the fact that the teacher is observing their behavior.

Again, it is the existence of a proficiency scale that makes unobtrusive assessments possible. Consider again the second-grade mathematics proficiency scale in figure 1.17 (page 30), which deals with interpreting picture and bar graphs. It has several score 2.0 learning targets, including one that requires students to add and subtract numbers on a number line. If a teacher happens to observe a particular student completing an activity that demonstrates this skill, the teacher simply checks off that learning target on the proficiency scale in the gradebook.

Another common way to use unobtrusive assessment is for the teacher to examine evidence in a student's data notebook. For example, a teacher might be perusing a particular student's data notebook and notice some homework assignments that indicate the student can identify the key components of picture and bar graphs. Again, the teacher would simply record a checkmark for the student next to this learning target.

Figure 1.20 (page 34) lists visible evidence for element IIc.

Visible evidence for effective instruction and guidance includes teachers doing the following.
• Utilizing observations of students to assign scores on specific proficiency scales • Examining student artifacts to assign scores on specific proficiency scales • Entering observational scores into the gradebook as evidence of student performance on specific proficiency scales
Visible evidence for desired student actions and behaviors includes students doing the following.
• Using the feedback from unobtrusive assessments to make judgments about what they know and don't know • Talking to the teacher about the meaning of their test scores on unobtrusive assessments and how they relate to specific proficiency scales
Visible evidence for students' understanding and awareness includes students doing the following.
• Explaining what the score they received on unobtrusive assessments means relative to a specific progression of knowledge • Explaining what their scores on unobtrusive assessments mean in terms of their status on specific proficiency scales • Describing why they believe unobtrusive assessments are valid ways for them to show what they know

Source: © *2021 by Robert J. Marzano.*

FIGURE 1.20: Visible evidence for element IIc.

IId. Generating Current Summative Scores

The teacher responsibility inherent in this element is to use each student's recorded evidence on each topic to generate a current summative score. The term *current summative score* is a critical part of the Marzano Academies model. We explain it briefly here, but detailed discussions of current summative scores appear in the books *Making Classroom Assessments Reliable and Valid* (Marzano, 2018) and *The New Art and Science of Classroom Assessment* (Marzano et al., 2019).

In many traditional classrooms, formative assessments are considered practice for a summative test. Stated differently, some teachers adopt the position that students' scores on the summative assessment are the only scores that count. This practice ignores a great deal of useful data about individual students' learning and renders the summative score a very imprecise measure of what an individual student knows about a specific topic at a particular moment in time. In the academy model, elementary teachers use a very different approach. Rather than relying on a single test to determine a student's summative score on a particular proficiency scale, they use multiple assessments for each student and then consider the pattern of these scores. This practice results in more accurate scores because it considers more evidence and reduces the impact of the error associated with any one assessment (see Understanding and Planning for Design Area II, page 38). Here, we discuss several actions teachers should take when generating summative scores.

Building on element IIb, using student-centered assessments (page 29), the process of generating summative scores should involve students. Ideally, teachers should have discussions with students about their scores before entering summative scores into the gradebook. In turn, students should be prepared to have these in-depth conversations with their teachers. It is important to note that these discussions do not have to happen with every single score on every single proficiency scale, but discussions should occur on a regular-enough basis that students become adept at proposing their own summative scores and providing detailed evidence to defend their stance. Teachers might set up a formal schedule of interviews and allow students to schedule a time slot for discussion.

Teachers can also have students fill out a summative score explanation form. This can take place at the end of a unit, once the teacher has entered all evidence for a specific scale into a gradebook. The form should allow students opportunities to detail their progression through the scale using evidence and provide space for explanations that demonstrate their overall understanding. Students can submit their explanations in many ways, such as an online form (figure 1.21), paper and pencil (figure 1.22, page 36), or recorded video discussion. Teachers should guide students through each type of submission and allow students to choose which type of submission they would like to use. Ultimately, a back-and-forth dialogue between the teacher and a student might occur, with both the teacher and student submitting comments and the student submitting additional evidence, until they agree on a final score.

In addition to discussing scores and evidence with students, teachers can use formulas to consider students' formative scores and calculate a current summative score. One of the unique features of the Marzano Academies approach is the use of mathematical models to aid in determining any student's summative score on any measurement topic. Formulas for these calculations are presented in the book *Making Classroom Assessments Reliable and Valid* (Marzano, 2018) and can be applied to any spreadsheet program, such as Excel. These formulas are also embedded in Empower Learning's learning management system (LMS), which all official Marzano Academies employ.

Summative Score Submission—SC.05.ESS2.02

Answer the following questions about your summative score.

(2.0) Describe the amounts and percentages of water and freshwater on Earth.

1	2	3	4
○	○	○	○

What is your evidence for the above 2.0 learning goal? If no evidence, submit an explanation of your understanding.

Your answer

Source: © 2021 by Westminster Public Schools. Used with permission.

FIGURE 1.21: Digital form for summative scores.

Summative Score Explanation

SC.05.ESS2.02—Water

Level	Indicator	My Score	My Evidence	Explanation
4.0	Use a different way to visually represent the ratio of freshwater to saltwater and show distribution on Earth.			
3.0	Describe and graph the amounts and percentages of water and freshwater in various reservoirs to provide evidence about the distribution of water on Earth.			
2.0	Identify the various sources of freshwater on Earth.			
2.0	Describe the amounts and percentages of water and freshwater on Earth.			

Source: © 2021 by Westminster Public Schools. Used with permission.

FIGURE 1.22: Pencil-and-paper summative score survey.

Within the Empower LMS, scores that teachers collect for students on a specific measurement topic are referred to as *evidence scores*. Once the teacher has compiled sufficient evidence for a particular proficiency scale for a particular student, a calculator embedded in the LMS is automatically activated, helping teachers interpret the pattern of evidence scores and assigning a current summative score to that student at that time. This is depicted in figure 1.23.

The scores in figure 1.23 represent about a five-week period of time. The first score the teacher entered for this student was a 2.0 and the last score was 3.5. Altogether, the teacher entered eight scores for this student. Remember that these scores do not all come from traditional pencil-and-paper tests; rather, evidence scores can be derived from any of the types of obtrusive, student-centered, or unobtrusive assessments described in elements IIa, IIb, and IIc. For example, the first score of 2.0 might have come from a traditional test that the teacher administered to the entire class as a pretest. The second evidence score of 2.0 for this student might have come from a probing discussion that the teacher had with this particular student. The third evidence score of 1.0 might have been recorded when the teacher observed the student and determined that he needed help to accurately demonstrate that he understood the content, and so on. The most recent score of 3.5 would likely come from another teacher-designed pencil-and-paper test, perhaps administered to all students as a posttest.

Sometimes students' scores depict a clear trend of improvement which makes it fairly easy to compute a summative score. In figure 1.23, this is not the case. While there was a general upward trend in learning taking the overall view of the score, some evidence scores were significantly higher or lower than adjacent scores. This is where the calculator built into the LMS provides the most help to teachers. The computations are updated after the teacher enters each evidence score, providing an up-to-date view of the student's pattern of scores.

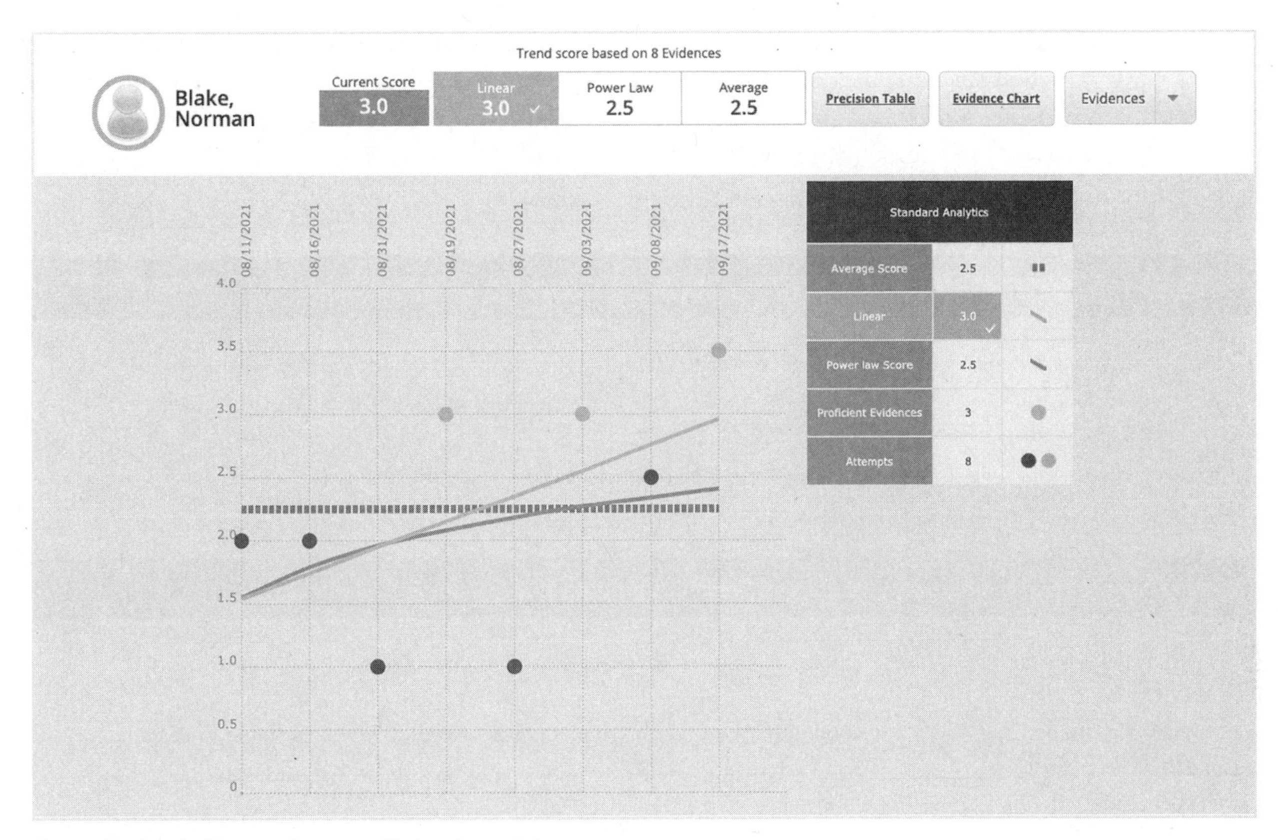

Source: © 2021 by Empower Learning. Used with permission.

FIGURE 1.23: Empower Learning LMS.

The Empower LMS uses three mathematical models to compute the most probable summative score. One model is the average. This model gives equal weight to each evidence score, in effect assuming that little if any learning has occurred over time. The average is depicted by the horizontal dotted line in figure 1.23. A second mathematical pattern is the linear trend. The linear trend is computed under the assumption that students learn at a constant rate. It is the line that moves from lower left to the upper right in a straight line. This means that students learn as much from week 1 to week 2 as they do from week 2 to week 3 and so on. The third mathematical pattern, the power-law trend, is depicted by the curved line that flattens out over time. It is computed under the assumption that students learn quickly in the beginning, but when they get to the more complex content at the higher levels of a proficiency scale, their rate of learning slows down or flattens.

One of the more useful aspects of the LMS is that, in addition to computing these three analyses, it also identifies the mathematical model that has the least amount of error. In figure 1.23, this is indicated by the highlighted rectangle labeled *Linear* with the checkmark in it. This indicates that, in this case, the linear trend is the best model of the three. Thus, the mathematically recommended summative score of "best fit" is 3.0. The teacher uses this information to enter a summative score in the top left of the figure in the box labeled *Current Score*. In this case, the teacher has opted to use the summative score of 3.0 recommended by the mathematical analysis, but it is important to note that teachers can override the calculator if they have reason to believe a different score better reflects the student's current level of knowledge or skill.

Educators who wish to use this type of detailed mathematical analysis but employ an LMS that does not do so can create their own Excel version using formulas in *Making Classroom Assessments Reliable and Valid* (Marzano, 2018), or they can visit www.cbe.empowerlearning.net/marzano-calculator to access a free version of the calculator.

Figure 1.24 lists visible evidence for element IId.

Visible evidence for effective instruction and guidance includes teachers doing the following.

- Systematically entering multiple evidence scores for students on specific proficiency scales
- Periodically translating the set of formative scores into current summative scores for students on specific proficiency scales
- Using discussions with students as information with which to assign a current summative score
- Using mathematical models to assign a current summative score

Visible evidence for desired student actions and behaviors includes students doing the following.

- Using the feedback provided by current summative scores to make judgments about what they know and don't know
- Talking to the teacher about the meaning of their current summative scores and how they relate to specific proficiency scales
- Interacting with the teacher about the summative score they deserve

Visible evidence for students' understanding and awareness includes students doing the following.

- Explaining what the current summative scores they received mean relative to a specific proficiency scale
- Explaining why the summative score they propose is the most accurate representation of their current status

Source: © 2021 by Robert J. Marzano.

FIGURE 1.24: Visible evidence for element IId.

Understanding and Planning for Design Area II

Design area II focuses on the assessed curriculum. The existence of proficiency scales within the Marzano Academies model should help eradicate ambiguity or equivocation in test design since every assessment should relate directly to a specific proficiency scale. As described in the preceding discussion, proficiency scales can make the assessed curriculum identical to the intended curriculum and the taught curriculum. The elements in design area II are also grounded in the psychometric fact that any student's score on a single assessment is typically not a very reliable indicator of the student's knowledge of the content on the test. Recognizing this principle has transformative implications in the world of K–12 educational assessment (for a detailed discussion, see Marzano, 2018).

All tests are designed under the assumption that the score a student receives (called the *observed score*) contains some error. Sometimes the error results in a higher score, as when a student guesses the right answer or the teacher accidentally gives credit for a wrong answer. Sometimes error artificially reduces the observed score, as when a student knows the correct answer but marks the wrong one or the teacher inadvertently fails to give credit for a correct answer. Knowing a test's reliability, teachers and test designers can compute the range of probable scores for any student if the error did not exist. This is referred to as finding the range of scores in which a student's true score might fall.

Table 1.1 depicts the amount of error one can expect in an individual student's score on a single test. The reliability coefficient for a test can range from 0.00 to 1.00; the higher the value, the more precise its scores are assumed to be. To demonstrate the variation in precision of an individual student's score, the rows of this table report the precision of the observed score of 70 across five levels of reliability. The top row of the table reports the best-case scenario. In this case, when the test has a reliability of 0.85, the range of scores that would account for error working for or against the student is between 59 and 81. If the reliability of the test is 0.45 instead of 0.85, the probable true score ranges from 48 to 92.

TABLE 1.1: Error Associated With a Single Score—95 Percent Confidence Interval for Observed Score of 70

Reported Reliability Coefficient for the Test	Observed Score	Lowest Probable Score	Highest Probable Score	Range
0.85	70	59	81	22
0.75	70	55	85	30
0.65	70	53	87	34
0.55	70	50	90	40
0.45	70	48	92	44

Note: The standard deviation of this test was 15, and the upper and lower limits have been rounded.

Source: Adapted from Marzano et al., 2019.

One implication of the unreliability of a single score on a single assessment is that teachers should collect scores for students from multiple assessments related to the measurement topics they are addressing. This does not mean that teachers should design and administer more traditional tests, but it does mean that they should assess students more. In keeping, the Marzano Academies model for classroom assessment provides teachers with many assessment options not available in the traditional classroom. As described in the preceding sections, these options span obtrusive, student-centered, and unobtrusive assessments. Figure 1.25 summarizes the assessment options that were directly or indirectly addressed in elements IIa, IIb, IIc, and IId.

Note that traditional tests are only one type of assessment listed—there are many other types. Some can be quite informal, like probing discussions. Student-centered assessments are a legitimate way of collecting assessment data, equal in value to any of the other types on the list. Again, proficiency scales enable this range of classroom assessment options because the content within the curriculum is so clearly defined.

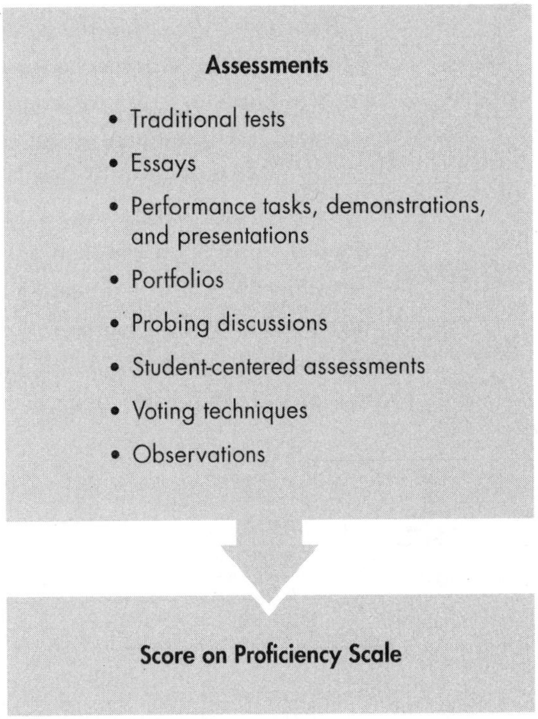

Assessments

- Traditional tests
- Essays
- Performance tasks, demonstrations, and presentations
- Portfolios
- Probing discussions
- Student-centered assessments
- Voting techniques
- Observations

Score on Proficiency Scale

Source: Adapted from Marzano, 2018.

FIGURE 1.25: Conceptual model for classroom assessment.

Another implication of the Marzano Academies model of assessment is that not all students will have the same number of assessments for any given topic. Given that teachers will take advantage of serendipitous opportunities to assess students using unobtrusive assessments and one-to-one obtrusive assessments such as probing discussions, some students will accrue more assessment scores for a particular proficiency scale than other students. When students submit student-generated assessments or self-assessments, those scores also contribute to their evidence for a particular scale. In general, within the Marzano Academies assessment model, teachers are encouraged to seek more evidence for those students from whom they have less confidence in their current summative scores.

Finally, the Marzano Academies model of assessment strongly suggests that any student's final summative score for a proficiency scale during a grading period should be a negotiated decision. Students provide evidence for summative scores they believe are accurate representations of their competence on specific topics at specific times, and teachers judge the validity of such evidence.

Planning for design area II typically focuses on element IIa, using obtrusive assessments, simply because these assessments are independent events that interrupt the flow of instruction. Student-centered and unobtrusive assessments will occur in a more ad hoc or spontaneous manner. Teachers should plan for the type of obtrusive assessments they will use relative to a specific measurement topic. This is particularly true when those obtrusive assessments will be traditional tests, essays, and presentations. Commonly, teachers will design a traditional test to start a unit and a traditional test to end a unit—a pretest and a posttest that are very similar in nature. This can be a great benefit to a teacher's execution of element IId, assigning summative scores, since it establishes consistent and comparable first and last scores for all students, making it easier to interpret the mathematical calculations described in element IId.

Summary

This chapter deals with the domain of feedback in the academy model. This domain includes two design areas. Design area I addresses proficiency scales. The overall purpose of this design area is to create proficiency scales and communicate them to students. Proficiency scales are the basis of the intended curriculum, the taught curriculum, and the assessed curriculum. There are three elements within this design area. Design area II addresses assessments. Here, teachers design and administer assessments that measure students' status on proficiency scales and help students understand the relationship between their scores on assessments and their overall status on a proficiency scale. There is a wide variety of types of assessments teachers can use to this end. There are four elements involved in this design area. Visible evidence for teachers and students was described for each element in each design area to aid teachers in determining how effective their actions are relative to the intended outcomes for each element.

CHAPTER 2

Content

The domain of content addresses instructional strategies for the taught curriculum within the Marzano Academies model. The taught curriculum will mostly certainly involve traditional academic content as defined by proficiency scales, but it will also include nontraditional content such as metacognitive skills and life skills (see element Xc, page 143). Fundamentally, anything that teachers have identified as important for students to learn should be afforded the scrutiny of the design areas in this domain. Such scrutiny involves teachers determining the defining features of the content and the instructional strategies that best address these features.

There are two design areas in this domain. Design area III addresses proficiency scale instruction, and design area IV addresses general instruction. While these two design areas involve many elements that are used in traditional classrooms, the way teachers employ these elements in a competency-based system has some substantial differences.

Design Area III: Proficiency Scale Instruction

This design area addresses how teachers introduce and initially reinforce the content in the proficiency scales on which they are focusing. It is the starting place for all instructional planning. There are seven elements in this design area.

- IIIa. Chunking content
- IIIb. Processing content
- IIIc. Recording and representing content
- IIId. Using structured practice
- IIIe. Examining similarities and differences
- IIIf. Engaging students in cognitively complex tasks
- IIIg. Generating and defending claims

The following sections detail each one.

IIIa. Chunking Content

The teacher responsibility inherent in this element is to present new content in short, digestible bites. Marzano Academies teachers commonly refer to these digestible bites as *chunks*. Chunking is important simply because students cannot process too much new information all at once. In a competency-based system, chunking content can occur somewhat naturally because the content is already organized as individual learning targets within proficiency scales. Consider the proficiency scale in figure 2.1.

4.0	In addition to score 3.0 performance, the student demonstrates in-depth inferences and applications that go beyond what was taught.
3.5	In addition to score 3.0 performance, partial success at score 4.0 content
3.0	The student will: IMI—Identify the main idea of a text (for example, state that the main idea of Aliki's *A Medieval Feast* is how people in medieval times prepared for a feast).
2.5	No major errors or omissions regarding score 2.0 content, and partial success at score 3.0 content
2.0	IMI—The student will recognize or recall specific vocabulary (for example, *keyword*) and perform basic processes such as: • Annotate repeated words and phrases in a text. • Explain why an author might use repeated words and phrases in a text. • Identify keywords in headings and titles. • Describe what details from different passages of a particular text have in common. • Determine the main topic of a sentence or a short paragraph.
1.5	Partial success at score 2.0 content, and major errors or omissions regarding score 3.0 content
1.0	With help, partial success at score 2.0 content and score 3.0 content
0.5	With help, partial success at score 2.0 content but not at score 3.0 content
0.0	Even with help, no success

Source: © 2016 by Marzano Resources. Adapted with permission.

FIGURE 2.1: Proficiency scale for identifying main ideas, grade 2 ELA.

For instructional purposes, the teacher would likely start with the content at the 2.0 level of the scale. With some modifications, each bullet point might be approached as a single chunk. For example, the teacher would first have students identify repeated words in a passage and then discuss what they might signify in terms of the overall meaning of the passage. After the discussion, the teacher would have students each independently explain why they think the author chose to repeat these specific words and phrases and how this contributes to the overall message of the passage. Again, students would share their ideas. Next, the teacher would have students examine details from different passages, and so on. In effect, teachers can interpret the learning targets (that is, bullet points) in a proficiency scale as chunks of content that they can present to students as distinct, albeit related, segments of knowledge. Of course, lists of learning targets in a proficiency scale will not always fall out into neat, sequential chunks of content. Some more complex learning targets might have to be broken into multiple chunks for processing purposes. However, proficiency scales by and large provide teachers with a good start on chunking content.

When chunking content, teachers should consider both the complexity of the content and their students' background knowledge. The complexity of the content should be a prime determiner of the size of the chunks teachers design. The more complex the content, the smaller the chunks should be. Students' prior knowledge of the content influences the size and quantity of chunks. If students have little prior knowledge of content, chunks should be small in size and large in quantity. If students have substantial prior knowledge, chunks can be large in size and few in number.

Another factor to consider in how chunks are addressed is the extent to which the school's LMS employs playlists. Simply stated, playlists consist of a sequence of information and activities that students use to learn about a measurement topic. Teachers develop playlists and store them within the LMS so that students can experience them at any time. The elements of a playlist should be organized in such a way that students are exposed to chunks of content that progress from simple to complex. Playlists are a core feature of the Empower LMS. Other systems might not use the term *playlist* but have similar features. To illustrate, consider the playlist in figure 2.2, which a teacher has loaded into the Empower system. This playlist involves a series of instructional activities that help students determine the main idea of a passage.

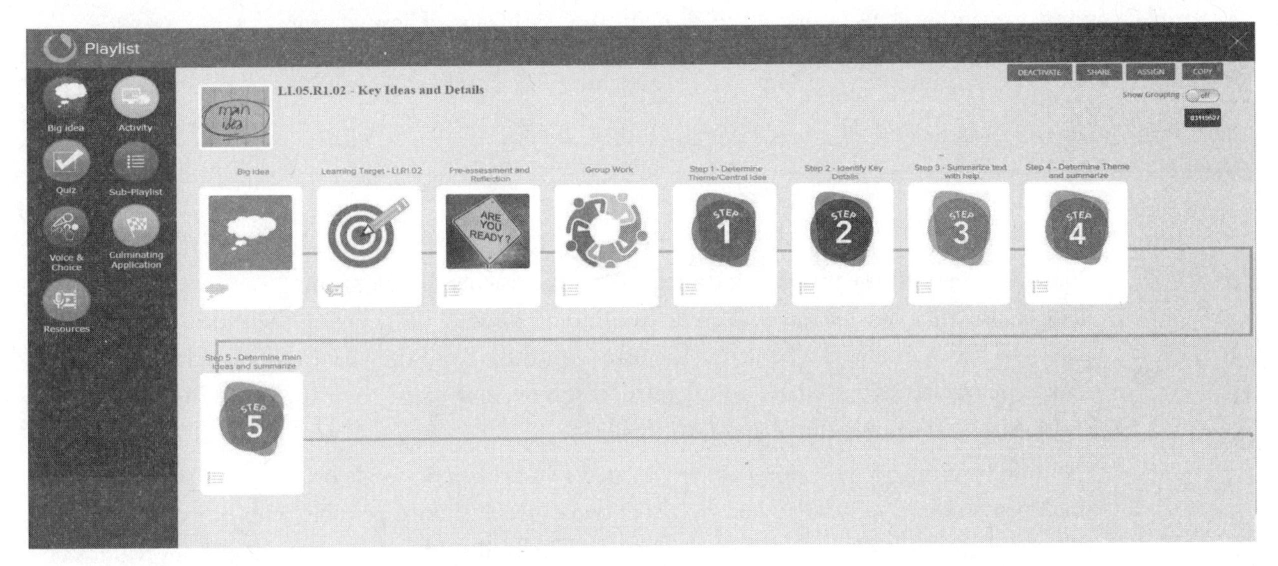

Source: © 2021 by Empower Learning. Used with permission.

FIGURE 2.2: Example of a playlist.

The playlist breaks the process of discerning a main idea into five steps. As depicted in the figure, there is a folder for each of those steps, but these are preceded by four folders that contain necessary background information so that students understand some important features of the concept of main idea. Playlists can also include assessment activities and group activities.

Figure 2.3 (page 44) lists visible evidence for element IIIa.

IIIb. Processing Content

The purpose of this element is to ensure that, as the teacher presents content, students think through each new chunk in ways that help them develop a cohesive understanding of its content. Stated differently, even after presenting an appropriately sized chunk of content to students in a clear manner, teachers must still provide opportunities for students to interact with others about the content, analyze what they have just learned, and determine how it relates to what they already know.

Visible evidence for effective instruction and guidance includes teachers doing the following.
• Presenting new content in larger or smaller chunks based on students' initial understanding of new content • Grouping students to process the chunks of information taught • Presenting new declarative knowledge, ensuring the chunks comprise concepts and details that go logically together • Ensuring the chunks comprise steps in a process that go together when presenting new procedural knowledge
Visible evidence for desired student actions and behaviors includes students doing the following.
• Actively engaging in processing content between chunks • Demonstrating an understanding of the content in each chunk
Visible evidence for students' understanding and awareness includes students doing the following.
• Explaining why the teacher stops at specific points during a presentation of new content • Explaining why chunks help them learn

Source: © *2021 by Robert J. Marzano.*

FIGURE 2.3: Visible evidence for element IIIa.

This is commonly done in some type of cooperative activity. For example, Jot Thoughts (Wincel, 2016) is an easy-to-use processing strategy. After the teacher gives a prompt, each member of a student team writes down ideas that come to mind on a sticky note, saying their ideas aloud as they place their sticky notes on the table. The team continues until they have articulated all their ideas. Next, the teacher asks students to organize, combine, and refine their lists until they can reach a consensus on the group's final and favorite ideas.

Similarly, during a read-aloud activity related to a proficiency scale on character traits, a teacher might ask students to form ad hoc groups of two or three and list possible traits of a character from the text along with supporting textual evidence. Finally, if students were learning about regions of a country, the teacher might split them into different groups to become experts on a particular region. They return later to report their findings and the teacher engages the whole class in a discussion to combine and summarize the information. There are many other similar interaction strategies. These include perspective analysis, reciprocal teaching, concept attainment, think-pair-share, and scripted dyads, as described in *The Handbook for the New Art and Science of Teaching* (Marzano, 2019a).

Virtually all of the most effective processing activities require students to engage in some form of two basic cognitive operations: summarizing and classifying. Simple prompts for summarizing include the following.

- Describe what was most important about what you learned.
- What stands out to you most about what you learned?
- How would you briefly explain what you learned?
- What key ideas stood out in what you learned?
- What is most important to remember from what you learned?
- If you had to briefly tell someone what you learned, what would you say?

Simple prompts for classifying include the following.

- How can these ideas be formed into groups?
- Which ideas are similar to each other?
- What groups of ideas are here, and how are the groups different?
- What are some common characteristics of various ideas?

Figure 2.4 lists visible evidence for element IIIb.

Visible evidence for effective instruction and guidance includes teachers doing the following.

- Having students work in groups to summarize new information, ask clarifying questions, and make predictions
- Employing group processing strategies such as perspective analysis, thinking hats, collaborative processing, jigsaw, reciprocal teaching, concept attainment, think-pair-share, and scripted dyads

Visible evidence for desired student actions and behaviors includes students doing the following.

- Actively interacting with the content and their peers about the content
- Generating summary statements
- Volunteering predictions
- Volunteering questions

Visible evidence for students' understanding and awareness includes students doing the following.

- Explaining what they just learned
- Explaining how processing new information helps to better understand it

Source: © *2021 by Robert J. Marzano.*

FIGURE 2.4: Visible evidence for element IIIb.

IIIc. Recording and Representing Content

The teacher responsibility inherent in this element is to provide students with opportunities to record and represent the new content they are learning. This activity has a number of outcomes that enhance learning. One is that students must mentally recall content to record or represent it. Second, recording and representing are forms of encoding information, which means that students are restating the content in a format that represents their current understanding. In effect, anytime students are describing content as they currently understand it, they are engaging in recording and representing.

The strategies that students can use to record and represent information are many and diverse. For example, during a unit on endangered species, a teacher might direct a group of students to use a process called *generate-sort-connect-elaborate* (Ritchhart, Church, & Morrison, 2011). After a shared reading activity about how scientists are using drones to track right whales and learn more about how they live, students could create a type of graphic organizer called a *running record* that they initially use with the information in the text they have just read (see figure 2.5, page 46). This organizer includes columns to record details about the whales, causes for their endangerment, efforts to help them, and the source of the information. There are also rows for other animals that students learn about during the unit. As they encounter information about new endangered species, they fill in

Animal	Details	Causes of Endangerment	Efforts to Help	Source
Right Whale	Rough patches on head look white. Three different species. Second largest in mass.	Hunting; many killed by large ship propellers	Protected as endangered. Lowered speed limits for ships.	National Geographic

FIGURE 2.5: Running records.

more rows in the running record. For example, later in the unit, students might be asked to summarize an article on shark fin soup and the decimation of the worldwide shark population. They would record this information in another row of the running record. As the unit progresses, more rows are filled in. These activities constitute the generate phase of the generate-sort-connect-elaborate strategy. Next, students sort the animals in their running records into groups that appear alike in their details, causes for endangerment, or efforts to help them. Students then describe how the animals in their various groups are connected and elaborate on these connections in written form.

FIGURE 2.6: Poster highlighting critical information.

To further extend this activity, teams might then choose one of the different species that need help, and create a poster that highlights critical information both visually and linguistically (see figure 2.6). This, too, is a representation of the content. Students author articles on their chosen species to be included in a class book along with original artwork, another form of representing content. The unit continues with a dramatic reading of a play about Dian Fossey and her work with gorillas in Rwanda. The dramatic reading is yet another technique for representing new information. To culminate the unit, students write a proposal on why an animal they have chosen is the most critically endangered and needs the most help from the class. Students vote on which animal they will save, and initiate a coin drive to collect money to donate to the World Wildlife Fund in honor of their animal. While these culminating activities do not involve recording and representing content, they do provide students with closure and final conclusions about what they have learned.

While there are nearly limitless ways for students to record and represent content, the Marzano Academies model asks teachers to use specific types of graphic organizers referred to as *knowledge maps*. To illustrate the use of knowledge maps, imagine that a teacher has students read a story about a demonstration at a political event. The teacher provides students with the simple sequence map (figure 2.7) and the complex sequence map (figure 2.8) and asks students to use the map they think best captures what occurred in the narrative. A student who viewed the story as representing events that occurred one after another would use the simple sequence map. The horizontal line represents time, and the angled vertical lines represent individual events (for example, the crowd started to gather; when a substantial number of people were there, they started chanting and singing; and so on). Another student might choose the complex sequence map, using each horizontal timeline to depict the events from the perspective of a different person—perhaps a participant at the demonstration, a police officer charged with keeping order, and someone viewing the demonstration from their apartment window.

Another option teachers have when using the system of knowledge maps is to present students with multiple types of maps they might use to represent something they have read, heard, or seen. For example, using the account of the demonstration, a teacher might give students the option of using a sequence map or a causation map (depicted in figure 2.9).

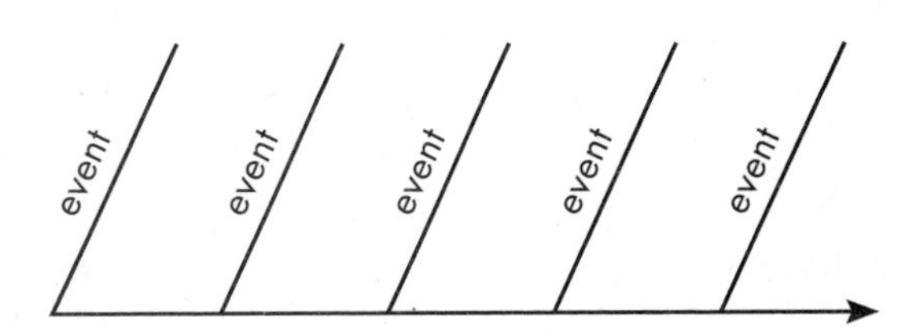

Source: © 2017 by Marzano Resources. Used with permission.

FIGURE 2.7: Simple sequence knowledge map.

Whereas teachers in traditional classrooms tend to use graphic organizers in isolation, knowledge maps are intended to be used in sets. For example, with traditional graphic organizers, teachers might provide students with a specific organizer and ask them to use it to represent information they have read, heard, or seen. In contrast, when using knowledge maps, the teacher will typically present students with two or more types of knowledge maps and ask them to select the type they think best fits the information and to justify their selection. In sum, teachers using the academy model should think of knowledge maps as an integrated system that can help students understand and organize content at all grade levels and in all subject areas. To illustrate the system of knowledge maps used in the academy model, consider figure 2.10 (page 48), which lists fourteen types of knowledge maps. Within most types, the knowledge maps can range from simple to complex. For example, the sequence map has a simple version and a complex version, as does the causation map. The problem-solution map has simple, complex, and advanced versions. This scope and sequence suggests that certain knowledge maps are more appropriate for certain grade-level spans. This is a useful guideline, though we have found that some elementary teachers effectively use more complex knowledge maps with their students, and some secondary teachers find ways to make simpler knowledge maps relevant for older students.

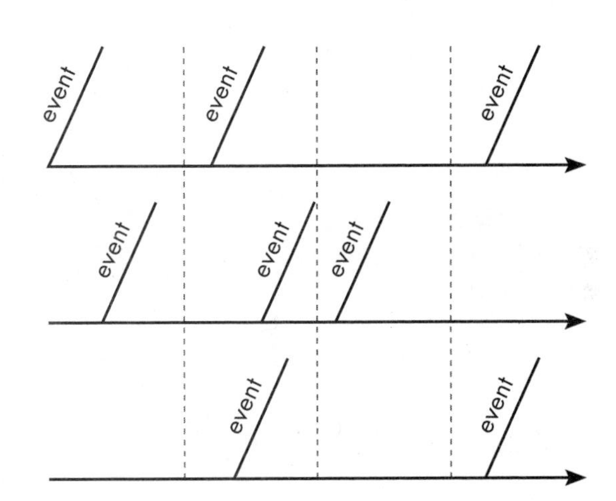

Source: © 2017 by Marzano Resources. Used with permission.

FIGURE 2.8: Complex sequence knowledge map.

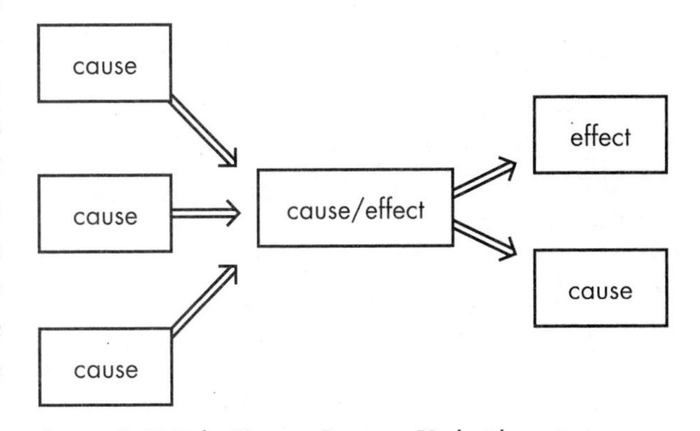

Source: © 2017 by Marzano Resources. Used with permission.

FIGURE 2.9: Simple causation knowledge map.

Figure 2.11 (page 49) lists visible evidence for element IIIc.

Structure	PreK	K–2	3–5	6–8	9–12
1. Basic Relationships	x	x	x	x	x
2. Description	x	x	x	x	x
3. Sequence	simple	x	complex	x	x
4. Causation		simple	complex	x	x
5. Problem-Solution		simple	complex	advanced	x
6. Comparison		x	x	x	x
7. Collection		simple lists	combined lists	intersecting lists	nested lists
8. Classification		simple	complex	x	x
9. Argumentation		simple	complex	x	x
10. Reasoning				inductive	x
				deductive	x
11. Systems		process	x	x	x
		cycle	x	x	x
		flowchart	x	x	x
			system	x	x
12. Episode			x	x	x
13. Metaphor			x	x	x
14. Analogy			x	x	x
TOTALS	3	12	16	18	18

Source: © 2020 by Marzano Academies, Inc. Used with permission.

FIGURE 2.10: Vertical alignment of knowledge maps.

Visible evidence for effective instruction and guidance includes teachers doing the following.
• Engaging students in activities that help them record and represent their thinking in linguistic and nonlinguistic ways • Utilizing strategies such as informal outlines, summaries, pictorial notes, combination notes, graphic organizers, academic notebooks, free-flowing webs, dramatic enactments, mnemonic devices, rhyming peg words, or link strategies • Using a common system of knowledge maps
Visible evidence for desired student actions and behaviors includes students doing the following.
• Producing various types of graphic organizers to represent their thinking • Using the various versions of knowledge maps • Producing summaries that include critical information • Producing mental representations of new information
Visible evidence for students' understanding and awareness includes students doing the following.
• Explaining their mental representations of new information • Explaining their nonlinguistic representations • Remembering the critical content from previous lessons

Source: © *2021 by Robert J. Marzano.*

FIGURE 2.11: Visible evidence for element IIIc.

IIId. Using Structured Practice

The teacher responsibility inherent in this element is to provide students with opportunities for structured practice when they are learning new skills or processes. This is extremely important because without structured practice sessions, students are unlikely to learn a new skill or process to the level of automaticity and fluency.

To implement this element, it is important to understand the distinction between declarative and procedural knowledge. In nontechnical terms, declarative knowledge is informational in nature. When students are learning about things like weather, different types of literature, or types of government, they are learning declarative knowledge. In contrast, procedural knowledge involves skills or processes. Table 2.1 (page 50) provides examples of typical types of procedural knowledge students learn at the elementary level. The distinction between declarative and procedural knowledge is an important one because instruction should be different depending on which type of knowledge a teacher is dealing with. Specifically, teachers should have students *practice* procedural knowledge, but they should help students *deepen* their understanding of declarative knowledge. We consider strategies for deepening declarative knowledge in element IIIe (page 52).

A prerequisite for helping students practice procedural knowledge is that the teacher has already identified the specific steps in the skill or process being taught. This is referred to as *proceduralizing* and is described in depth in the book *Understanding Rigor in the Classroom* (Marzano, 2019b). Although the term *proceduralizing* is not part of everyday vernacular in the general population, it should be an important part of any teacher's classroom practice. It simply means creating a set of

TABLE 2.1: Types of Procedural Knowledge Taught at the Elementary Level

Subject Area	Sample Procedural Knowledge
Mathematics	Dividing fractions
Language arts—reading	Sounding out an unrecognized word while reading
Language arts—writing	Writing a descriptive essay
Foreign language	Using common idioms in informal conversation
Geography	Reading a map
Health	Employing a personal exercise routine
Physical education	Throwing and catching
Arts—music	Playing the scale on violin
Technology—computer science	Troubleshooting a piece of code with errors

Source: Adapted from Marzano et al., 2019.

steps for skills and processes, particularly if those steps are not obvious to students. For example, if a teacher is having a difficult time helping students increase their ability to read poems, he or she can increase their skill by creating an explicit procedure for doing so. These procedures should initially be presented to students in a step-by-step fashion, as exemplified by the following procedure for reading a poem.

1. Look over the poem and find the words you don't understand.
2. Look up those words in the dictionary.
3. Read the poem at least two or three times.
4. Ask yourself who the speaker is in the poem. (Hint: it might not be the poet.)
5. Say the poem in your own words. Do this stanza by stanza.
6. Summarize what the poem means in a few sentences.

This procedure is relatively general, but other step-by-step procedures are for very specific processes. The following process is for sounding out an unrecognized one-syllable word when reading.

1. Identify the vowel sounds in the word.
2. Identify the ending sound and blend it with the vowel sound.
3. Identify the beginning sound in the word and blend it with the vowel sound and the ending sound.

Depending on how much detail a teacher wishes to provide, step-by-step procedures can involve many steps for students to execute in a specific order. To illustrate, consider the following step-by-step procedure, which is also about sounding out one-syllable unrecognized words while reading (Williams, n.d.).

1. Identify the vowel sound.
2. Identify the consonant sound that immediately follows the vowel sound.
3. Blend together the vowel sound with the following consonant sound.
4. If two consonants follow the vowel and can't be easily blended, then do the following.
    a. Isolate the vowel sound and blend it with the first following consonant.
    b. Isolate the sound of the second consonant and blend it with the sound of the vowel and the first consonant.
5. Identify the sound of the consonant letter that comes immediately before the vowel and blend it with the sound of the vowel and the other letters that come after the vowel.
6. If two or three letters come before the vowel, determine if they form a team that make a recognizable sound and blend that sound with the sound of the vowel and the letter or letters that come after the vowel.
7. If two or three consonant letters come before the vowel and don't make a team, start with the consonant nearest the vowel. Identify the sound of the consonant and blend it with the sound of the vowel and the letters or letter that come after the vowel. Then identify the sound of the next adjacent consonant and blend it with the rest of the word that has already been decided. Do the same if there is a third consonant before the vowel.

Creating step-by-step procedures should be one of the first actions a teacher takes when preparing to teach a new skill or process simply because such procedures provide students with a clear picture of what they are expected to do. It is important to note that once students learn a procedure, they typically do not execute it as a series of rigid steps performed in a specific way. Indeed, as students become adept at procedures, they combine steps and commonly develop shorthand versions of the procedure. However, in the beginning, a step-by-step process helps them view the new procedure as a concrete set of actions.

Once students have a working knowledge of the steps provided to them, the teacher should engage them in structured practice sessions. At first, these practice sessions should be spaced closely together (massed) and closely monitored by the teacher. Massed practice sessions provide students with relatively immediate reinforcement of the steps they are learning. If practice sessions are spaced too far apart in the beginning, students will forget the steps involved and have to be reminded of what to do each time they use the procedure. After enough massed practice sessions, students will reach a point where they can execute the procedure without having to remind themselves of the steps. When students begin to develop some ability to execute the steps on their own, the practice sessions become more spread out (distributed). These spaced sessions should continue until students can use the procedure independently without significant error.

Figure 2.12 (page 52) lists visible evidence for element IIId.

Visible evidence for effective instruction and guidance includes teachers doing the following.
• Providing well-structured opportunities for students to practice new skills, strategies, and processes and monitoring students' actions to correct early errors or misunderstandings • Modeling skills, strategies, and processes for students • Creating step-by-step models when teaching procedures • Engaging students in varied practice, fluency practice, worked examples, or practice sessions prior to testing
Visible evidence for desired student actions and behaviors includes students doing the following.
• Actively engaging in practice activities • Asking questions about new procedures • Increasing their competence with the procedure • Increasing their confidence in their ability to execute the procedure • Increasing their fluency in executing the procedure
Visible evidence for students' understanding and awareness includes students doing the following.
• Saying that the practice sessions are making them better • Describing the types of practice that work best for them • Describing how they have changed a procedure to make it more useful to them

Source: © *2021 by Robert J. Marzano.*

FIGURE 2.12: Visible evidence for element IIId.

IIIe. Examining Similarities and Differences

The teacher responsibility inherent in this element is to provide students with opportunities to examine the similarities and differences between the topics they are studying. Again, the distinction between declarative and procedural knowledge is helpful here. As described in the previous section, teachers should provide students with opportunities to practice procedural knowledge but provide them with opportunities to deepen their declarative knowledge. At a very concrete level, this means that activities involving similarities and differences are most appropriate for informational topics such as weather, types of literature, types of government, and the like. Table 2.2 depicts declarative topics across various subject areas that are amenable to analyzing similarities and differences.

Examining similarities and differences can occur in many forms, including comparing, contrasting, classifying, creating analogies, and creating metaphors. In short, teachers can engage students in activities that help them discern similarities and differences and use different strategies in doing so.

Examining similarities and differences works best when students have a fair amount of knowledge regarding the topics they are examining. Consequently, teachers should first provide students with activities that ensure they know about the topics that they will be comparing. During a unit on invasive species, for example, the teacher might first have each student pick a specific type of invasive species to study. Once students have accumulated knowledge of their selections, the teacher would have them design and create a poster to warn the public about the dangers of the species they

TABLE 2.2: Types of Declarative Knowledge Taught at the Elementary Level

Subject Area	Sample Declarative Knowledge
Mathematics	Units of measure
Language arts—reading	Types of literature
Language arts—writing	Types of essay
Foreign language	Customs of people in the target language
Geography	Characteristics of specific locations
Health	Information about caloric intake and health
Physical education	Information about various games or sports
Arts—music	Information about various types of music or art
Technology—computer science	Rules that must be followed within a specific coding language

Source: Adapted from Marzano et al., 2019.

selected and how to mitigate the damage they cause (see figure 2.13). After displaying their posters around the room, students could perform a gallery walk with the intention of identifying and collecting information from each poster about specific categories of characteristics for invasive species (how the species spreads, why it is dangerous, where it comes from, and so on). In effect, during the gallery walk, each would be sorting the various invasive species into categories by comparing the characteristics of the species. After categorizing species, students meet in groups to describe and defend the categories they created. The final activity might be for each group to create a general set of guidelines for how to deal with invasive species.

FIGURE 2.13: Invasive species poster.

As another example of examining similarities and differences relative to factual information, consider a student who has completed a display board about a country she has been researching. Her teacher has tasked the students with finding one country that is similar to the one they researched and one that is different and explaining why. The students view each other's posters, looking for specific similarities or differences that stand out as significant.

Another application of this element is to have students use comparison to improve the quality of their work. Having students compare similarities and differences between their own work and that of others is a powerful way to improve their writing skills. Students might examine other students' writing during a gallery walk or round-table session, with a key focus as to what to look for in their peers' compositions (see figure 2.14). For example, the teacher might direct students to examine how other students begin and end their essays. After students have collected comparative data, they are given a chance to reflect on and record what was similar and different about their peers' writing and their own. Finally, they would then return to their own writing and make revisions based on what they learned.

Note that one of the jobs of a CBE teacher is to create an atmosphere where students feel comfortable giving and receiving peer feedback regarding their strengths and weaknesses. In the beginning, activities that involve such feedback might feel awkward to some students, and teachers may need to provide direct guidance. Once students recognize that everyone has strengths and weaknesses and will therefore receive both positive and constructive feedback, and realize that such feedback is a valuable learning tool, these activities can become highly energizing for students.

It is also important to note that some types of procedural knowledge have declarative components, which can be addressed using similarities and differences. For example, consider the physical education procedure for executing an overhand throw. When a physical education teacher is first introducing this physical procedure to students, he or she would begin by explaining the process to students, describing what they do first, what they do second, and so on. The teacher would also describe some important generalizations about the process such as how tightly to hold the ball, how to shift your weight from back to front, and so on. At this point, the process is information

Photo used with permission.

FIGURE 2.14: Looking for specific characteristics in the writing of peers.

only. Students are not actually executing the overhand throw. Rather, they are learning about it as declarative knowledge. This declarative part of the procedure can be the subject of tasks involving similarities and differences. For example, the physical education teacher might have students compare the process of executing an overhand throw with the process of executing an underhand throw. Similarly, during a mathematics unit on fraction multiplication, teachers might have students examine the similarities and differences between multiplying fractions and adding or subtracting fractions. Students would use declarative knowledge about the procedures of multiplication, addition, and subtraction as the basis for identifying similarities and differences.

Figure 2.15 lists visible evidence for element IIIe.

Visible evidence for effective instruction and guidance includes teachers doing the following.
• Having students identify similarities and differences in two or more elements of content • Having students use graphic organizers (for example, Venn diagrams, T-charts, double bubble diagrams, or comparison matrices) to help students examine similarities and differences • Having students use similes, metaphors, or analogies to help students examine similarities and differences
Visible evidence for desired student actions and behaviors includes students doing the following.
• Actively articulating similarities and differences between the elements being compared • Asking questions about the similarities and differences between the elements being compared • Making summary statements about similarities and differences they have identified
Visible evidence for students' understanding and awareness includes students doing the following.
• Describing what they have learned as a result of identifying similarities and differences • Saying that these activities help deepen their understanding of the content • Suggesting different approaches to identifying similarities and differences

Source: © 2021 by Robert J. Marzano.

FIGURE 2.15: Visible evidence for element IIIe.

IIIf. Engaging Students in Cognitively Complex Tasks

To enact this element, the teacher provides students opportunities to use what they have learned in the context of complex tasks. Complex tasks by their very nature require students to use content in ways they were not directly taught. There are six types of complex tasks in the Marzano Academies model. They are depicted in table 2.3 (page 56). Engaging students in such tasks in a CBE classroom is similar to using complex tasks in a traditional classroom, with one exception—during their execution of complex tasks, students in a competency-based classroom are attempting to demonstrate their knowledge of the content as well as their ability to execute the process inherent in complex tasks. For example, imagine that a teacher engages students in an investigation task regarding what occurred during the Boston Massacre. In a traditional classroom, the emphasis would be on learning the facts about that incident. In a CBE classroom, students would be held accountable for both the facts and the extent to which they accurately executed the process of investigation.

TABLE 2.3: Complex Tasks

Complex Task	Description
Decision making	Decision making is the process of generating and applying criteria to select between alternatives that appear equal.
Problem solving	Problem solving is the process of overcoming obstacles or constraints to achieve a goal.
Invention	Invention is the process of creating a new process or product that meets a specific identified need. In a sense, it might be likened to problem solving in that it addresses a specific need. However, problem solving is limited in duration.
Experimental inquiry	Experimental inquiry is the process of generating a hypothesis about a physical or psychological phenomenon and then testing your hypothesis.
Investigation	Investigation is the process of identifying and then resolving differences of opinion or contradictory information about concepts, historical events, or future possible events.
Systems analysis	Systems analysis is the process of describing and analyzing the parts of a system with particular emphasis on the relationships among the parts.

Source: © 2021 by Robert J. Marzano.

One of the most useful aspects of the complex tasks in table 2.3 is that teachers can use virtually any of them with any subject area. That noted, teachers might look to the preferences and tendencies of their students. For example, students are natural investigators and relish the chance to dig deeper into cloudy or controversial issues. A teacher could propose an investigation task focused on the events surrounding the Boston Massacre—who fired first, and who was to blame? In the Marzano Academies model, instead of simply asking students to investigate this issue, the teacher would provide students with a concrete process for doing so. In effect, teachers should proceduralize all complex tasks they expect students to employ. A straightforward procedure for the complex task of investigation involves the following steps.

1. Clarify the question you have been provided with. What event or idea do you want to explain?
2. Examine the teacher-provided information about your topic. What do people already know?
3. Using the information provided by the teacher, summarize what is already known about your topic. What is the best way to tell about what people already know?
4. Describe something people seem to be confused about or something for which people have different opinions. What confusions do people have about the idea or event?
5. Describe how you would clear up the confusion or the differences in opinion and, if necessary, collect more information to support your resolution. What suggestions do you have for clearing up these confusions? How can you defend your suggestions?

This process is designed for students in grades 3–5 and involves quite a bit of teacher facilitation. For example, in the first step, the teacher provides students with a question or probe. In the case of the Boston Massacre example, the teacher provides the question, What actually happened during the Boston Massacre? In the second step, the teacher would supply students with information about the event such as firsthand accounts, eyewitness testimony from both sides, newspaper articles from the time, and drawings or cartoons that provide insight into the event. Figure 2.16 depicts a playlist for the Boston Massacre that resides within the LMS. Armed with these resources, students would engage in the remaining steps working in small groups or independently. When they are done, students would be asked to report on their conclusions as well as describe how they executed the investigation process.

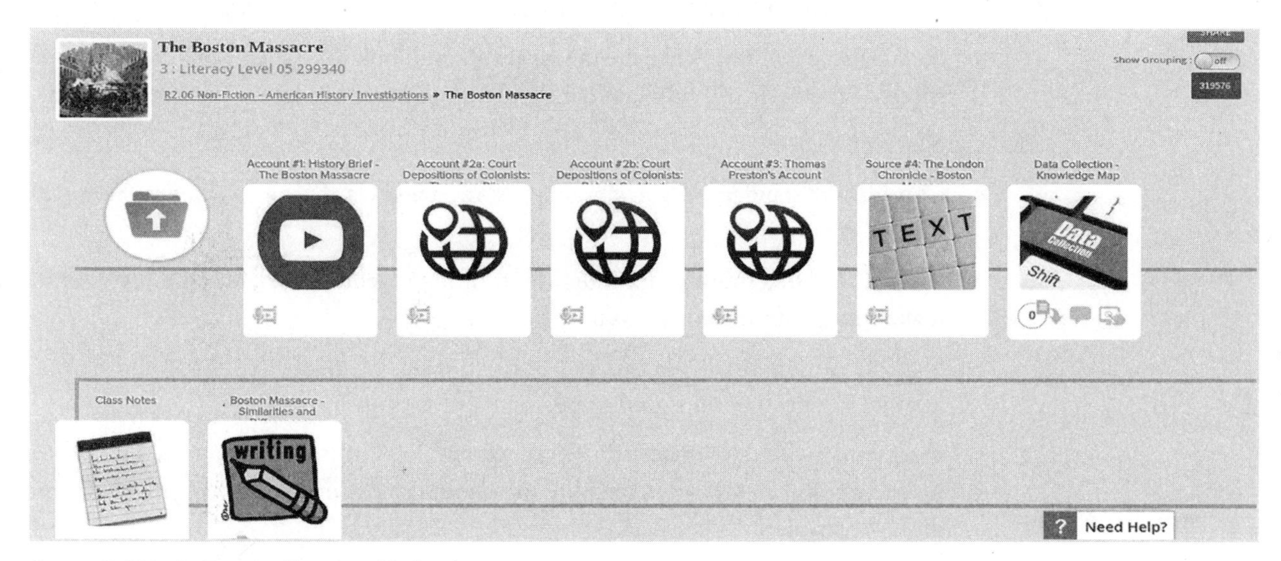

Source: © 2021 by Empower Learning. Used with permission.

FIGURE 2.16: Playlist for the Boston Massacre investigation.

At the primary level, teachers could set up fictional investigations about what "really" happened in classic fairy tales like "Goldilocks and the Three Bears" or "The Three Little Pigs." Intermediate classrooms can easily tie investigations into social studies content (as illustrated by the Boston Massacre example), investigating events of the past. Perhaps a teacher could allow students to investigate their family trees or the homelands of their ancestors, culminating with a multicultural fair where students present their findings along with artifacts or food from their identified countries.

Invention tasks are another natural favorite of elementary students. The teacher might first introduce invention with tasks that can be completed quickly and have high entertainment value. There are multiple STEM resources for classroom engineering projects, some very quick and simple. A primary teacher who assigns a fictional investigation into what really happened to the Three Little Pigs could also have students design and create houses to be "blown over" to see which design the pigs should have utilized. Science teachers can have students use knowledge about how trees and plants spread their seeds to create their own seed carriers and test them for efficiency. A class in need of a break or change of pace could compete to create a structure that holds up the most books, using only five pieces of paper in a time limit of ten minutes (figure 2.17).

FIGURE 2.17: Structure task.

With these interest-piquing experiences under their belts, students could then learn a detailed process for invention like the following for grades 3–5.

Phase 1: Selection

a. Consider the situation I've been asked to make better or the thing I've been asked to invent. What do I want to make, or what do I want to make better?

b. Seek clarity regarding what the invention should look like when I am done and the specific purpose it will fulfill. What standards do I want to set up for my invention?

Phase 2: Drafting

c. Consider the standards my invention must meet and clarify any confusions. How will I know my invention is successful?

d. Make a sketch, a model, or a rough draft of my invention. What is the best way to make a rough draft for my invention?

e. Start developing my invention and think in terms of small steps that build on one another. What steps do I need to take to move forward?

f. Occasionally but systematically step back and look at my invention as a whole to make sure all the parts work together to accomplish my purpose. Does my invention meet the standards I have set?

Phase 3: Revising

g. Try my invention in different situations and note what works well and what doesn't work well. How can I improve on my rough draft?

h. Stop when I feel that my invention has accomplished my initial purpose and has met the standards I have set for it. Is my invention finished?

Again, the teacher would explain, exemplify, and facilitate the eight steps embedded in the three phases of invention. Once students have a working knowledge of the complete process, they could further apply that knowledge by identifying inventions that would improve the day-to-day lives of students in the school or inventions that would improve the lives of people in the community.

Figure 2.18 lists visible evidence for element IIIf.

IIIg. Generating and Defending Claims

Another element of instruction that helps students deepen their content knowledge is providing opportunities to generate and defend claims. At its core, generating claims requires students to construct unique or original conclusions. Defending claims means that students have to provide evidence supporting their conclusions. To support this type of thinking, teachers might first present students with some direct instruction in the nature of claims. For example, a fourth-grade teacher might have students watch a video of people debating a familiar issue, such as a recording of a school board meeting where members and constituents discuss concerns in the district. The teacher would periodically stop the recording and ask students to identify statements for which the debaters should have provided evidence. The teacher might make the point that people make claims frequently in life. Anytime people assert that something is true or untrue, they are making claims. The vast majority of the time, support is not needed for those claims because they occur in

Visible evidence for effective instruction and guidance includes teachers doing the following.
• Engaging students in explicit experimental inquiry tasks • Engaging students in explicit problem-solving tasks • Engaging students in explicit decision-making tasks • Engaging students in explicit investigation tasks • Engaging students in explicit invention tasks • Engaging students in explicit systems-analysis tasks
Visible evidence for desired student actions and behaviors includes students doing the following.
• Actively engaging in their cognitively complex tasks • Asking questions of the various steps of their cognitively complex tasks • Seeking help for various steps of their cognitively complex tasks • Generating and defending conclusions about what they have learned in their cognitively complex tasks
Visible evidence for students' understanding and awareness includes students doing the following.
• Describing the cognitively complex tasks in which they are involved • Describing what they learned from their complex tasks • Explaining and defending the conclusions they have generated

Source: © *2021 by Robert J. Marzano.*

FIGURE 2.18: Visible evidence for element IIIf.

the context of informal discussions. However, in a more formal discussion where the claim might have consequences, one should provide support.

Once students have a working knowledge of the nature of claims, teachers should provide them with a specific process for supporting claims. Primary students might use a simple process like the following set of questions.

1. What is a new idea I have that I want to communicate?
2. What are my reasons for thinking this idea is true?
3. What is the evidence for each of my reasons?
4. What are the situations for which my new idea might not be true?

A more complex version like the following can be presented to students at the upper-elementary level.

1. Identify whether you are stating an opinion that needs to be supported.
2. If so, state your opinion (that is, your claim) as clearly as possible.
3. To support your claim, provide one or more reasons (grounds) why you believe it to be true.
4. For each reason, provide evidence (backing) that indicates your reasons are accurate.
5. If necessary, describe the circumstances (qualifiers) under which you believe your claim would not be valid.

Many activities that involve cognitively complex tasks, as described in element IIIf (page 55), can also create situations for students to generate and defend claims. For example, after investigating the possible theories about the lost colony of Roanoke, students might put together an argument defending which theory they think is the most likely. Students can also be encouraged to generate and defend claims regarding current issues in their school or community. For example, students might attempt to persuade their principal, school board, superintendent, or mayor to make changes within their building, such as offering a wider variety of drink options in the cafeteria. They might put together an action committee to research possible alternatives and write letters containing explicit support for their proposal to the principal and school board to try to enact change. These types of authentic opportunities for students to generate and defend claims are especially powerful.

Technology also provides some unique opportunities for students to generate and defend claims. Online chat rooms, discussion boards, or video-chat platforms like Flipgrid are great places for students to defend their thinking. After a discussion about bullying in schools, the teacher might ask students to read an article about the benefits of assigned seating in the cafeteria. Students would then be prompted to record a video in which they discuss whether they believe assigning seats would help reduce bullying or just cause more problems. Students would then comment on other students' videos to further the discussion.

Figure 2.19 lists visible evidence for element IIIg.

Visible evidence for effective instruction and guidance includes teachers doing the following.

- Introducing the concept of claims and support
- Presenting the formal structure of claims and support
- Providing students opportunities to generate claims, provide grounds, back their claims, and generate qualifiers to their claims
- Having students formally (orally or in writing) present their claims

Visible evidence for desired student actions and behaviors includes students doing the following.

- Generating claims
- Providing grounds for their claims
- Providing backing for their grounds
- Providing qualifiers to their claims

Visible evidence for students' understanding and awareness includes students doing the following.

- Explaining why generating and supporting claims helps them learn more deeply and rigorously
- Describing the claim on which they are currently working and why it is important to them

Source: © 2021 by Robert J. Marzano.

FIGURE 2.19: Visible evidence for element IIIg.

Understanding and Planning for Design Area III

This design area is at the center of instructional planning in a CBE classroom. Its title, proficiency scale instruction, communicates a message: all instruction in a CBE classroom starts with a proficiency scale. As addressed in the discussion of design area I (page 7), proficiency scales make for a highly focused and transparent (1) intended curriculum, (2) taught curriculum, and (3) assessed curriculum. Of these three, design area III focuses on the taught curriculum. Planning units of instruction and lessons within those units begins with an examination of the proficiency scale that is the focal point of the unit. To illustrate, consider the proficiency scale in figure 2.20.

4.0	The student will: • Use mental computation and estimation strategies to assess the reasonableness of an answer at different stages of solving a problem (for example, when given that a boy has 374 more baseball cards than a friend who has 221 baseball cards, and when given that he then buys another 186 cards, use rounding to estimate that the number of baseball cards the boy started with should be close to 600 and the number of cards he ended up with should be close to 800).
3.5	In addition to score 3.0 performance, partial success at score 4.0 content
3.0	The student will: Round a given number to the nearest 10 or 100 (for example, round the numbers 23, 50, 95, 447, 283, 509, and 962 to the nearest 10 and the nearest 100).
2.5	No major errors or omissions regarding score 2.0 content, and partial success at score 3.0 content
2.0	The student will recognize or recall specific vocabulary (for example, *digit, estimate, hundreds, number line, ones, place, place value, round, round down, round up, tens, thousands*) and perform basic processes such as: • Identify multiples of 10 and 100. • Identify relationships between place values. For example, explain that ten 1s are equal to one 10 and that ten 10s are equal to one 100. • Explain that rounding a number to a given place estimates or approximates the value of the number to the nearest multiple of that place. For example, rounding a number to the nearest 10 approximates the value of that number to the nearest multiple of 10. • Explain that rounding a number to a given place will leave a value of 0 in each place that is smaller than (to the right of) the targeted place. For example, rounding a number to the nearest 100 will leave a value of 0 in the tens and ones places. • Use a number line to find the nearest multiple of a specified place for a given number. For example, when given the number 146 represented on a number line, identify 100 as the closest multiple of 100. • Explain that a number will be rounded up to a given place if the digit in the place immediately to the right is greater than or equal to 5, and will be rounded down if the digit is less than or equal to 4. • Identify situations in which rounding might be useful. For example, explain that rounding two addends and quickly calculating their sum can be useful for assessing whether or not the calculated sum of the unrounded addends is accurate.
1.5	Partial success at score 2.0 content, and major errors or omissions regarding score 3.0 content
1.0	With help, partial success at score 2.0 content and score 3.0 content
0.5	With help, partial success at score 2.0 content but not at score 3.0 content
0.0	Even with help, no success

Source: Adapted from Marzano et al., 2019.

FIGURE 2.20: Proficiency scale for the measurement topic of rounding, grade 3 mathematics.

When planning for instruction for this measurement topic, a teacher would determine which of the seven elements in this design area apply to the various learning targets in the proficiency scale.

IIIa. Chunking content

IIIb. Processing content

IIIc. Recording and representing content

IIId. Using structured practice

IIIe. Examining similarities and differences

IIIf. Engaging students in cognitively complex tasks

IIIg. Generating and defending claims

Such deliberations on the part of the teacher might start with the content at the 3.0 level. The content at that level is:

> Explain that rounding a number to a given place will leave a value of 0 in each place that is smaller than (to the right of) the targeted place. For example, rounding a number to the nearest 100 will leave a value of 0 in the tens and ones places.

For this particular learning target, a teacher might decide that she believes it is necessary to provide students with direct instruction about the general rules of rounding such as the fact that rounding a number leaves a value of 0 in each place that is smaller than (to the right of) the targeted place value. To do this, the teacher will employ chunking strategies (element IIIa), whereby she explains this basic rule of rounding and illustrates it using a short series of examples during which she thinks aloud about why she is making specific rounding decisions for each number. She considers each example problem as a small chunk. After each chunk, she will have students interact in small groups to discuss what they have observed her doing (element IIIb). When she has presented all the chunks and students have processed them, the teacher will engage students in some independent structured practice activities (element IIId).

Thus, for this single learning target, the teacher has selected strategies from three instructional elements in design area III (elements IIIa, IIIb, and IIId). Similar deliberations would occur for each of the remaining learning targets in the proficiency scale. In effect, when planning for design area III, teachers ask the following questions for each learning target.

IIIa. **Chunking content:** Should I provide information in small chunks for this learning target?

IIIb. **Processing content:** Should I have students interact in small groups for this learning target?

IIIc. **Recording and representing content:** Should I have students record and represent the information for this target?

IIId. **Using structured practice:** Should I have students practice the content for this target in specific ways?

IIIe. **Examining similarities and differences:** Should I have students examine similarities and differences regarding the information in this target?

IIIf. **Engaging students in cognitively complex tasks:** Should I engage students in complex tasks regarding the information in this target?

IIIg. **Generating and defending claims:** Should I have students generate and defend claims relative to the content in this target?

It is important to emphasize that within the Marzano Academies model, planning for design area III is driven by the nature of the content. The teacher examines the content in a learning target and decides the instructional activities that are most appropriate for its structure and content. The complexity of the content in a specific learning target might dictate that the teacher break it into small digestible chunks, or the equivocal nature of some content might dictate that students should generate and defend claims about it.

Another important part of planning for design area III is for the teacher to determine which content requires virtual resources. Theoretically, virtual instruction and reinforcement can occur for any of the instructional activities described in this design area—chunking can be accomplished in a virtual environment, as can recording and representing, and so on. For example, assume a teacher has parsed information about different types of clouds into three brief presentations that are each about two minutes long. The teacher might record these segments in one presentation, but at the end of each chunk, ask students to stop the video and answer one or more specific questions about what they just saw and heard. The teacher could archive the students' responses so that others could see how their peers reacted to each chunk.

We recommend that teachers continually develop virtual resources for every learning target at the score 2.0, 3.0, and 4.0 levels for every proficiency scale. Of course, this would take a significant amount of time if attempted all at once by an individual teacher. However, when addressed by a team of teachers, the task can be partitioned such that no one is overburdened. To illustrate, assume that the fourth-grade science curriculum involves fifteen measurement topics. Because each proficiency scale has three levels of explicit content (score 2.0, score 3.0, and score 4.0), there are forty-five sets of content for which virtual resources must be developed. If there are three teachers who are responsible for fourth-grade science in the school, they could each be responsible for finding or creating fifteen virtual resources throughout the year. By the end of the first year of this endeavor, the school would have virtual resources for the score 2.0, 3.0, and 4.0 content in each scale. The next year, teachers would continue to add to this resource base.

Teacher-created screencasts are a perfect tool for this purpose. They are easy and inexpensive to make especially when one considers that many schools have licenses for screencast software available to their teachers (in addition to free recording apps). Teachers can sit at their desks or even their kitchen tables and record a screencast regarding the content in a specific proficiency scale in relatively short order. Additionally, if students make video recordings that demonstrate their understanding of the score 2.0, 3.0, and 4.0 content (as described in the discussion of element IIb, using student-centered assessments, page 29), these recordings can be archived so that other students can view them as exemplars of mastery relative to specific learning targets in a proficiency scale.

Design Area IV: General Instruction

When focusing on design area IV, teachers design and execute instructional activities that help students refresh, revise, and integrate their knowledge of specific content. The purpose of these general instruction elements is to engage students in the continual processing of content such that it integrates with and alters what they already know. This design area is referred to as general instruction because all the strategies can apply to any content that has been taught. In design area III, not every strategy makes sense with every piece of content, and the teacher's job is to match the right instructional strategy to the content. In design area IV, every strategy can be applied to any type of content at any time. The teacher's job here is to determine which strategies should be applied to which students based on their needs.

There are seven elements in this design area.

IVa. Reviewing content

IVb. Revising knowledge

IVc. Examining and correcting errors

IVd. Highlighting critical information

IVe. Previewing content

IVf. Stimulating elaborative inferences

IVg. Extending learning through homework

The following sections detail each one.

IVa. Reviewing Content

This element conveys the importance of opportunities for students to review what they have learned previously. Reviewing is standard fare in the Marzano Academies model in that teachers engage students in review activities on a systematic basis.

There are various ways to approach reviewing. Weekly quizzes, for example, can be highly useful review activities. Teachers can create quiz questions designed to review key content that has been previously addressed and then write them on index cards, with the answers on the back. Every week, or at an interval that the teacher finds appropriate, students engage in a "trade quiz" where they mix with their peers around the room, trading flash-card questions with each other. The teacher first hands out an index card to each student and gives them some time to familiarize themselves with the answers. Students then stand and find a partner. One student asks the question and the other student attempts to answer it. If the answer is incorrect, the student who posed the question helps the other partner understand the answer. Then they use the same procedure for the second student's flash card. When both students are done, they trade index cards and look for new partners. As new content is covered or old content revised, the teacher creates more cards and adds them to the quiz card library. This review activity can be done on the way back inside from recess, as students return from the library or specials, or as a break or change-of-pace activity.

Teachers can also make reviewing of content a normal part of their warm-up routines by devoting one day a week to going over previous content. For example, Fridays could become "Review Fridays," where the bell-ringer activities would involve reviewing previously covered content. Students currently learning about word origins and roots might review their previous unit on figurative language, for example.

Over and above such review activities, the Marzano Academies model emphasizes a specific process we refer to as *cumulative review*. The cumulative review process includes three phases.

1. Recording
2. Reviewing
3. Revising

Each phase requires the student to do something different with the content. During the first phase, students record what they remember about the topic that is the focus of the cumulative review process. The teacher reintroduces a topic that the class covered previously or even provides some new information about a previous topic. Students then record what they remember about that content. For example, a teacher might go over some rounding techniques she had previously presented to students. During this first phase, the teacher would ask students to record what they remember about rounding. Students should keep an archive of their cumulative review notes throughout the year. These can take various formats based on students' age. For example, a fifth-grade teacher might ask students to use review journals, or three-ring binders that are tabbed with each measurement topic for the year, which students use to record summaries or serial notes. Kindergarten teachers might provide students with pictographic recording activities to complete during centers. To archive these, teachers might take photos of students' pictographs and keep them in an electronic file, periodically displaying selected ones as a review.

The second phase is the review phase. Here students analyze what they have recorded. The purpose of the review phase is to have students examine or test their understanding of the content they are reviewing. One of the best ways to facilitate this is to provide prompts that require students to go beyond what they initially learned, such as the following.

- Provide more details about what you have recorded.
- Describe and exemplify generalizations and principles you are now aware of.
- Generate and defend inferences.

For example, students who are reviewing rounding might write a generalization they now believe is true about rounding. One student might write that rounding seems to make the most sense when the interval to which you are rounding is not too large relative to the context. The student would provide and explain some examples of this.

Phase three, revising, is the one during which students make substantive changes to their knowledge. Here, they identify previous misconceptions and correct them. They also fill in gaps and make additions. Again, simple prompts like the following aid in this endeavor.

- What are some things you now realize you were wrong about?
- What are some things you now realize you should add to your notes?
- What are some things you still don't understand or know?

The students who are reviewing rounding might be asked to identify some things they now realize they were wrong about. One student might note that she used to think that rounding wasn't supposed to be done with decimals, but now sees that the process for doing so is basically the same as rounding with whole numbers. The products of this type of thinking can be shared in small groups or in a whole-class setting. The cumulative review process requires students analyze what they have previously learned in multiple ways. This helps to sharpen and deepen their understanding.

Figure 2.21 (page 66) lists visible evidence for element IVa.

Visible evidence for effective instruction and guidance includes teachers doing the following.
• Using cumulative review to help students identify and correct misconceptions • Using quick review activities on a spontaneous or planned basis • Having the class summarize previously learned content • Asking review questions
Visible evidence for desired student actions and behaviors includes students doing the following.
• Rethinking what they have previously learned • Asking questions about what they have previously learned • Adding new insights to what they learned previously
Visible evidence for students' understanding and awareness includes students doing the following.
• Describing their previous understanding of content • Describing how their understanding has changed as a result of review activities • Describing what works best for them when they review

Source: © 2021 by Robert J. Marzano.

FIGURE 2.21: Visible evidence for element IVa.

IVb. Revising Knowledge

The teacher responsibility inherent in this element is to provide students opportunities to revise what they have learned. Revising knowledge is a critical part of the learning process. As people gain more experience with specific content, they start to see what they were right about and what they were initially wrong about. The revising process allows students to change the things they were wrong about, and it reinforces the things they were right about. Finally, it allows them to add new information that was not previously part of their knowledge base. As described in the discussion of element IVa, revising is part of the cumulative review process. However, it can also be used in isolation in a wide variety of ways. It is hard to overstate the importance of students' revising their understanding of content, so teachers should use revising strategies liberally and frequently.

Reflection journals are commonly used in CBE classrooms and traditional classrooms. They are a great place to prompt students to revise their thinking and consider how it has changed over time. Whether introducing a new concept or wrapping up a unit of instruction, teachers can use the prompt, "I used to think ______ but now I think ______." This prompt works even when a topic is ostensibly brand new to students, simply because students will have some (albeit limited) background knowledge about some aspects of most topics.

Teachers can use a related approach during whole-class discussions. During such discussions, teachers can prompt students to comment on other students' statements. These added comments are themselves types of revisions. Students making such revisions can be asked to clarify what type of comment they are making. For instance, students who contribute to the discussion first identify whether they are commenting on what someone else has already said, adding new information to what has already been stated, making a revision to what has already been stated, or asking a clarifying question. These four discussion tools should be posted in the room for student reference during discussions until students become familiar with the technique (see figure 2.22).

FIGURE 2.22: Four types of revision comments.

Considering revision in a broader sense, it is important to remember that students in a competency-based classroom are always working toward demonstrating proficiency. Therefore, they are allowed to revise and resubmit assignments and retake assessments to better their scores. Students might make revisions or corrections to their work using a different-colored pencil or pen so that the teacher can easily see the changes in their thinking (the teacher can choose a specific revision color to use across all subject areas if desired). With this in mind, the feedback that teachers provide on assessments and assignments should not give students the correct answer, but lead them toward the revision of their own knowledge.

For example, during a sixth-grade mathematics unit on ratios and unit rates, a student might have a hard time understanding percentages of a quantity as a rate. The student is proficient in the other 3.0 learning goals on the scale, but this one particular goal is giving him a hard time. He has met with his teacher to discuss his overall summative score, and is adamant that he is only currently a 2.5 because he is lacking evidence for the percentages learning goal. His teacher agrees to let him retake the most recent assessment on which he scored a 2.0, as long as he demonstrates he is seeking new information that will help him revise his knowledge, such as instructional videos or more practice items. After receiving some one-on-one instruction from the teacher, completing an extra homework assignment or two, and watching the teacher's instructional video on YouTube, the student retakes his test using a different-colored pen so his teacher can see his changes in thinking. This process can continue as many times as necessary until the student has demonstrated proficiency.

Figure 2.23 (page 68) lists visible evidence for element IVb.

IVc. Examining and Correcting Errors

The teacher responsibility inherent in this element is to help students identify and correct errors in their own reasoning or that of others. Correcting errors is closely related to revising knowledge. Once you realize you have made an error, you seek to correct that error. There are two basic domains of errors on which teachers can focus: errors related to the content in proficiency scales and general errors in reasoning.

The most obvious type of error on which a teacher might focus is errors in students' understanding of content from proficiency scales. Correcting content errors can be done in the context of a cumulative review (as described in the discussion of element IVa, page 64). It can also be inserted into portions of any class period. Figure 2.24 (page 68) depicts a student's answers to some mathematics questions, three of which are incorrect. (Importantly, the student's name has been removed.)

Visible evidence for effective instruction and guidance includes teachers doing the following.
• Reminding students to look for and correct mistakes • Having students identify and fill gaps in their understanding • Providing feedback to students on assignments and letting students revise assignments based on the feedback
Visible evidence for desired student actions and behaviors includes students doing the following.
• Making corrections in what they have previously learned • Seeking information about content to clear up confusions they might have • Demonstrating satisfaction in the increase in their understanding
Visible evidence for students' understanding and awareness includes students doing the following.
• Explaining previous misconceptions they had about content • Describing how the process of revising knowledge has benefited them as learners

Source: © *2021 by Robert J. Marzano.*

FIGURE 2.23: Visible evidence for element IVb.

As a bell-ringer activity, each student would receive a copy and be asked to correct the mistakes and explain possible reasons the student made these errors. Aside from allowing students to analyze the errors in someone else's thinking, it also allows students to feel more comfortable making mistakes in class—they know they are not the only ones who do it. To this end, teachers should make sure that, over time, errors from every student in the classroom will be used (anonymously) for this activity.

A second domain of errors teachers might deal with involves common reasoning errors. There are four categories of errors in reasoning, as depicted in table 2.4.

1. Write the following in exponential form and as a multiplication sentence using only 10 as a factor (for example, $100 = 10^2 = 10 \times 10$).

   a. 1,000 = 10^3 = $10 \times 10 \times 10$

   b. 10,000 = 10^4 = $10 \times 10 \times 10 \times 10$

2. Write the following in standard form (for example, $4 \times 10^2 = 400$).

   a. $3 \times 10^2 =$ 300

   ~~c.~~ $800 \div 10^3 =$ 8.00

   ~~b.~~ $2.16 \times 10^4 =$ 2,160

   ~~d.~~ $754.2 \div 10^2 =$ 75.4

FIGURE 2.24: Error-correction activity.

TABLE 2.4: Common Errors in Reasoning

Category	Error	Definition
Faulty Logic	Contradiction	Presenting conflicting information to support a claim. For example, if a senator says she is for tax increase, and then a little later says she is against a tax increase, she has committed the fallacy of contradiction.
	Accident	Failing to recognize that your evidence is based on an exception to a rule. For example, concluding that the letter *e* always comes before the letter *i* after observing the spelling of the words *neighbor* and *weigh* is an example of an accident.
	False cause	Confusing a temporal (time) order of events with causality or oversimplifying a very complex causal network. For example, if someone concludes that the decision to place a man on the moon was directly caused by America's failed attempt to send a satellite into orbit, he is confusing temporal order with causality. If a person describes only one or two causes of the Civil War, he is making the error of false cause because the reasons for the Civil War were numerous and complexly related.
	Begging the question (circularity)	Making a claim and then supporting it with similar statements that do not constitute evidence. For example, if you say, "That product is not very useful," and then back up your assertion by saying, "You can't do anything with it," you are backing up one statement with another that means just about the same thing.
	Evading the issue	Sidestepping an issue by changing the topic. For example, when asked about his involvement in arms trade to foreign countries, someone changes the topic of conversation to the necessity of weapons. He is evading the issue.
	Arguing from ignorance	Supporting a claim simply because its opposite cannot be proven. For example, arguing that there is no intelligent life beyond planet Earth because we cannot prove that life exists elsewhere is arguing from ignorance.
	Composition and division	Asserting that something is true about the whole because it is true about one of the parts (composition), or asserting that something is true about a part because it is associated with the whole (division). For example, you are making an error of composition if you assume that all members of a family are intelligent because a single member of the family is. On the other hand, you are making an error of division if you conclude that a specific city in the state of Oregon receives a lot of rain simply because the state as a whole is noted for its rainfall.
Attacks	Poisoning the well	Attacking everything that is offered in opposition to your own position. This type of attack manifests as a person being unwilling to listen to or consider anything contradictory to their opinion.
	Arguing against the person	Making derogatory comments about anyone who is arguing against your position. For example, if a politician rejects another politician's stance on nuclear disarmament by attacking the person's heritage, he is arguing against the person.
	Appealing to force	Threatening to psychologically or physically harm anyone who is arguing against your position. Telling someone that you will not like her anymore unless she takes your side on an issue is an example of appealing to force.

continued ➡

Category	Error	Definition
Weak Reference	Using sources that reflect habitual and confirmatory biases	Referencing sources that contain habitual bias or confirmatory bias. Habitual biases sometimes are unconsciously built into people's thinking. For example, you might have a bias toward rejecting ideas from a specific radio talk show host or accepting ideas from a specific television network. Confirmatory bias involves only accepting information that supports what you believe and rejecting information that is contrary to your position.
	Using sources that lack credibility	Using sources that have no documented record of being knowledgeable about a topic or who are known for providing inaccurate information. Information relevant to a topic or issue might come from sources that lack credibility. For example, only using information from a newspaper that is known to support a specific presidential candidate would be using a source that lacks credibility.
	Appealing to authority	Relying on one's superior status (for example, social clout, corporate position) as evidence that your claim is true. For example, someone is appealing to authority if he says something is true (or false) simply because it is stated by a superior.
	Appealing to the people	Asserting that your claim is true because it is a popular position. For example, supporting the claim that "staying up late does not affect my schoolwork" by stating that everyone in school stays up late is an example of appealing to the people.
	Appealing to emotion	Eliciting emotion in support of your claim as the primary evidence that it is true. For example, when a speaker tries to convince people to vote for a particular political candidate by relating a story about the death of a candidate's family in a tragic accident, he is appealing to emotion.
Misinformation	Confusing the facts	Distorting or modifying facts to support your claim. For example, inaccurately describing a particular sequence of events as evidence for your claim would be an example of confusing the facts.
	Misapplying a concept or generalization	Using inaccurate information about a concept or generalization to support your claim. For example, if someone claims that protesters at a rally at city hall should be arrested because they are committing treason, they are misapplying the concept of treason.

Source: Adapted from Marzano & Pickering, 1997.

Teachers should first discuss and exemplify these types of errors with students and then have them apply their knowledge in class. Argumentation units are great places for students to examine errors in reasoning. When reading persuasive articles, students have to figure out not only the grounds and backing that support an author's claim, but also whether or not the grounds and backing contain any of the errors in reasoning. Peer revision and editing persuasive writing in class are also excellent venues to examine errors in reasoning, although students and teachers need to be tactful when pointing out the errors in a classmate's thinking.

Students can apply the common errors in reasoning to real-life content as well. Specifically, students are constantly consuming media of all types. Websites like YouTube and Vimeo are filled with videos that claim all kinds of outlandish things that may have no basis in fact. Classroom teachers can set aside some time during the week to have a "Truth Squad" investigation, where students examine a video, conspiracy theory, or news story for errors. Snopes (www.snopes.com) is a great resource to find recent stories that are misleading, and teachers can easily find relevant stories to bring to class. Videos claiming that mermaids are real, the end of the world is coming, or one of their favorite singers or actors has done something outlandish can be high-interest items for elementary students. Along with recent conspiracy theories and videos, Snopes also debunks a myriad of political stories, which can be fertile sources for identifying errors in reasoning, especially around elections. During the major election years, students can analyze candidates' claims and advertisements, form their own fact-checking teams, and give candidates grades based on their honesty and accurate reasoning.

Figure 2.25 lists visible evidence for element IVc.

Visible evidence for effective instruction and guidance includes teachers doing the following.

- Engaging students in identifying errors in their own reasoning or the overall logic of information presented to them
- Having students identify and rectify specific types of errors in reasoning such as faulty logic, errors of attack, errors of weak reference, errors of misinformation, and errors in logic
- Asking students to examine support for claims, identify statistical limitations, or judge reasoning and evidence in an author's work

Visible evidence for desired student actions and behaviors includes students doing the following.

- Actively identifying and analyzing their own errors
- Actively identifying and analyzing others' errors in materials and resources they encounter

Visible evidence for students' understanding and awareness includes students doing the following.

- Describing and exemplifying the different types of errors one might make
- Explaining how the activities have increased their understanding of the content

Source: © 2021 by Robert J. Marzano.

FIGURE 2.25: Visible evidence for element IVc.

IVd. Highlighting Critical Information

To properly address this element, the teacher provides students with cues regarding content that is particularly important for them to attend to. During virtually every class period, students are bombarded with information coming from the teacher, the textbook, websites, their peers, and so on. Some students might experience all of this information without any way to determine which content is the most important. For these students, the information they receive might seem like a cacophony that results in very little overall understanding. To mitigate such an outcome, teachers can continually point out the critical content within a lesson and across a unit of instruction.

In a school using the Marzano Academies model, proficiency scales should be the primary resource for a teacher trying to determine what to highlight for students. During lessons, teachers can make explicit reference to the content of a specific scale. To facilitate this, teachers might format proficiency scales in ways that help students make connections to specific aspects of lessons. To illustrate, consider figure 2.26 (page 72). Note that the right-hand column of this scale lists lessons and activities students have experienced, which relate directly to specific learning targets in the scale.

Measurement Topic: LI.04.R1.02—Theme (Fiction)		
Target Description: Determine a theme of a story, drama, or poem from details in the text. Summarize the text.		
Proficiency Scale		**Lesson or Example**
Score 4.0	Take it further: the learner can identify multiple texts with similar themes, explaining the similarities and differences between how they are presented by the author.	
Score 3.5	In addition to score 3.0 performance, partial success at score 4.0 content	
Score 3.0	The learner will . . . • Determine a theme of a story, drama, or poem from details in the text. • Summarize the text.	• Choice story theme • Tell me about it . . . • Super Summary
Score 2.5	The learner has no major errors or omissions regarding score 2.0 content, and partial success at 3.0	
Score 2.0	The learner will recognize or recall specific vocabulary (for example, *central idea, detail, summarize, support, text, theme*) and perform basic processes such as: • Summarize a grade-appropriate text using a teacher-provided graphic organizer. • Determine a theme or central idea of a grade-appropriate text. • Identify details that support the theme or central idea of a grade-appropriate text.	• Finding Nemo Theme • Despereaux Theme • Summarize it! • Summary template
Score 1.5	Partial success at score 2.0 content, and major errors or omissions regarding score 3.0 content	
Score 1.0	With help, a partial understanding of some of the simpler details and process and some of the more complex ideas and processes	

Source: © *2021 by Westminster Public Schools. Used with permission.*

FIGURE 2.26: Proficiency scale with links to lessons and activities.

This simple technique helps teachers highlight what is important in a current lesson and it helps students focus on the critical content.

There are also less structured approaches and serendipitous ways to highlight critical information. In these cases, a teacher's personality and presentation style can be a useful tool. A teacher should never be reticent to use dramatic behavior if so inclined. Such behaviors might include singing, shouting, using funny voices, and so on. All of these are legitimate ways to capture students' attention and emphasize important information.

Charts, graphic organizers, and other visuals can also highlight critical information. Teachers can post these artifacts to a playlist, focus board, or whiteboard to remind students of critical content throughout a lesson or unit. Finally, teachers can create procedures to guide students through the content. For example, a teacher progressing through a lesson on text structure and sequence might create a simple visual explaining the steps students should take for this activity: (1) choose and read an article, (2) identify and record sequence words, (3) identify key events that occur in the story, and (4) create and complete a sequence knowledge map. This procedure would be displayed for the duration of the lesson for student reference.

Figure 2.27 lists visible evidence for element IVd.

Visible evidence for effective instruction and guidance includes teachers doing the following.
• Referencing proficiency scales • Repeating the most important content • Asking questions that focus on the most important content • Using tone of voice, gestures, and body position to emphasize important information
Visible evidence for desired student actions and behaviors includes students doing the following.
• Asking questions about highlighted information • Visibly adjusting their levels of attention when critical information is highlighted • Taking notes on highlighted information
Visible evidence for students' understanding and awareness includes students doing the following.
• Describing the level of importance of specific information • Explaining why specific content is important to know • Describing questions they have about the upcoming content

Source: © *2021 by Robert J. Marzano.*

FIGURE 2.27: Visible evidence for element IVd.

IVe. Previewing Content

Previewing content means that teachers provide students with advance notice about what is most important relative to what they are about to learn. The principle underlying previewing is to activate students' prior knowledge about a topic being addressed in class. This element also deals with helping students build mental models as they experience new content. While the term *mental model* is used in many ways, here we refer to the need for students to create mental images of the content they are about to learn along with some descriptive language to go with their images. There are many previewing strategies and activities available to teachers.

The activity generate-sort-connect-elaborate (Ritchhart et al., 2011) is a great way to reveal and organize prior knowledge, helping students make connections before a lesson or unit has begun. We introduced this strategy in the discussion of element IIIc (recording and representing content, page 45), but it also fits nicely with this element. For example, imagine a teacher beginning a unit on human body systems. She passes out sticky notes to small groups of students and gives a prompt for discussion: What do you know about human body systems? In the generating step, students proceed to write down their thoughts, reading them aloud as they are completed and placing them on a larger piece of chart paper. Once the allotted time has expired, the small groups move to the sorting step and spend time sorting and grouping the sticky notes into categories. For this example, categories might range from specific (circulatory system) to general (body parts, body processes). During the connecting step, the groups share their work, with either one student reporting to the class or all groups moving around the room to view other posters. In the final step, elaboration, students describe what they have learned from the three previous steps. This is most directly related to mental models if students use pictures, pictographs, or graphic organizers to illustrate what they have learned. This type of activity can manifest in many forms, but the main elements are usually the same—allowing students time to access prior knowledge, discuss what they think they know with their peers, and play with those concepts a little bit before diving into new knowledge.

Informational hooks are also a fun and effective way to grab students' attention. For example, a YouTube video related to the topic or a story from the news can spark interest and highlight important content. Videos and links can be posted to the playlist for a lesson so students can renew that spark of interest at a later time.

Perhaps one of the best previewing strategies is to use a flipped approach. Generally speaking, flipping occurs when teachers provide activities that help students understand the content before it has been formally introduced by the teacher. For example, an ELA teacher might create a screencast explaining and exemplifying some characteristics of the genre of comedy a week before starting a unit on that type of genre. Students would view the screencast at a time of their own choosing prior to the beginning of the unit. Technology is a great tool for flipped previewing activities. If the LMS allows the teacher to post videos, screencasts, and the like, students can review these resources to help them develop mental models of a topic before a lesson begins.

Figure 2.28 lists visible evidence for element IVe.

IVf. Stimulating Elaborative Inferences

The teacher responsibility inherent in this element is to provide opportunities for students to make inferences about what they are learning. In the academy model, teachers focus on two different types of inferences: default inferences and reasoned inferences. These types have unique characteristics which we describe in the following subsections. However, for students to employ these types of inferences effectively, teachers should ensure that they have a wide variety of opportunities and venues to do so.

Online discussion spaces and platforms like Backchannel Chat, Kialo, YO! Teach, or Google Hangouts are very effective in stimulating elaboration. Students might be asked to respond to a discussion prompt or question, engage with or respond to a peer's comment, or explain and justify their ideas in ways designed to stimulate specific types of inferences. For example, a teacher progressing through a unit on civil rights might ask students to comment in an online discussion

Visible evidence for effective instruction and guidance includes teachers doing the following.
• Preassessing students as a way to preview upcoming content for students • Asking students questions about upcoming content • Utilizing informational hooks, bell ringers, or anticipation guides to preview upcoming content • Helping students make overt linkages between old and new content • Using flipped classroom activities
Visible evidence for desired student actions and behaviors includes students doing the following.
• Actively engaging in the previewing strategies employed by the teacher • Making connections with previous content they have learned • Asking questions about the upcoming content
Visible evidence for students' understanding and awareness includes students doing the following.
• Explaining the links they are making with their prior knowledge • Making predictions about what they expect

Source: © 2021 by Robert J. Marzano.

FIGURE 2.28: Visible evidence for element IVe.

about peaceful protest tactics with the requirement that they provide an example from a specific civil rights leader. This prompt requires students make inferences involving characteristics of protests that are peaceful.

The use of video-recording programs like Flipgrid can allow teachers to have back-and-forth asynchronous discussions with students. A teacher might ask students to choose a character from the classroom's current shared novel and discuss that character's motivation or feeling within a specific episode or chapter. The teacher can then view videos and ask students to respond to specific, targeted questions. He or she can also highlight and share specific videos with the class.

While these general activities accomplish the basic goal of stimulating student inferences, teachers can increase the positive impact of elaboration on student learning if they use planned inferential questions as a primary instructional tool. When planning for elaborative questions, it is useful for teachers to consider two basic types of inferences: default inferences and reasoned inferences. These types of inferences are described in detail in the book *Understanding Rigor in the Classroom* (Marzano, 2019b). We consider them briefly here.

Default Inferences

Default inferences occur when a student automatically assumes that certain characteristics are associated with a particular topic. For example, when students watch a video about a particular type of insect, they might immediately assume that the insect has the following characteristics.

- It will have a shell-like covering on the outside of the body.
- It will have antennae on the top of its head.
- It will crawl or fly.

These are default inferences because students have learned these characteristics of insects either from formal instruction in the classroom or from informal exposure to the content outside of the classroom. Once learned, students will assume that these characteristics apply to any new type of insect they are learning about.

As another example, if you meet someone who is a firefighter, you might assume she is in good physical shape, faces dangerous situations, is brave, and so on. It's important to note that at some point students will make the connection to stereotypes—the association of negative characteristics with categories of people. This is an opportunity to have a discussion regarding the basic nature of human bias, racism, and the like. Obviously, such discussions should be age appropriate and conducted in a manner that is sensitive to students' cultural backgrounds.

These examples illustrate that making default inferences involves knowing something about the category to which a topic belongs. Once people associate a topic with a category, they access their stored knowledge about the characteristics associated with that category and assume they apply to the topic. A teacher can help students access this stored information as they learn new declarative knowledge by using direct questions to identify what students think they already know. These focused and well-structured questions allow the teacher to analyze students' assumptions for accuracy. To aid in the creation of such questions, we recommend that teachers use the prompts in table 2.5.

TABLE 2.5: Common Types of Default Inferences and Questions

Topic	Default Questions
Specific person or type of person (Abraham Lincoln, U.S. president)	What *time period* is associated with this person? What *places* are associated with this person? What *events* are associated with this person? What *accomplishments* are associated with this person?
Specific organization or type of organization (New York Yankees, professional baseball team)	What *beliefs* are associated with this organization or group? What *locations* are associated with this organization or group? What *time period* is associated with this organization or group? What *events* are associated with this organization or group?
Specific intellectual or artistic product or type of intellectual or artistic product (*Mona Lisa*, famous painting)	What *person* is associated with this product? What *time period* is associated with this product? What *event* is associated with this product? What *causes or consequences* are associated with this product? What *places* are associated with this product? What *values* are associated with this product?
Specific naturally occurring object or type of naturally occurring object (linden tree, tree)	What *events* are associated with this object? What *people* are associated with this object? What *time period* is associated with this object? What *location* is associated with this object?
Specific naturally occurring place or type of naturally occurring place (Arctic Ocean, ocean)	What *events* are associated with this place? What *people* are associated with this place?

	What *time period* is associated with this place? What *location* is associated with this place?
Specific animal or type of animal (Secretariat, famous racehorse)	What *events* are associated with this animal or type of animal? What *people* are associated with this animal? What *time period* is associated with this animal? What *locations* are associated with this animal? What *system* is this animal a part of? What *color, number, quantity*, or *dimension* is associated with this object or animal?
Specific manmade object or type of manmade object (Rolls-Royce, expensive passenger automobile)	What *locations* are associated with this object? How is this object *used*? What *larger entity* is this object part of? What is the *process* for making this object? What does this object *look like*? What *value* is associated with this object? What *dangers* are associated with this object?
Specific manmade place or type of manmade place (Coliseum, sports arena)	What *events* are associated with this place? What *people* are associated with this place? What *location* is associated with this place? What *actions* are performed at this place? What *larger entity* is this place part of? How is this place *acquired* or *sold*? What *value* is associated with this place? What *dangers* are associated with this place?
Naturally occurring phenomenon or event or type of naturally occurring phenomenon or event (Mount St. Helens eruption, volcanic eruption)	What *places* are associated with this phenomenon? What *time period* is associated with this phenomenon? What *causes* or *consequences* are associated with this phenomenon? What *happened* or *happens* during this phenomenon?
Specific manmade phenomenon or event or type of manmade phenomenon or event (Macy's Thanksgiving Day Parade, parade)	What *people* are associated with this event? What *time period* or *date* is associated with this event? What *places* are associated with this event? What *causes* or *consequences* are associated with this event? What *happened* during this event? What *equipment* was used during this event? What *problems* were caused or solved by this event?
Specific manmade abstraction or type of manmade abstraction (a function, love)	What are the *features* of this abstraction that distinguish it from other abstractions? What are the necessary *conditions* for this abstraction? What does this abstraction help *explain* or *organize*? What are some *types* of this abstraction? In what *situations* is this abstraction useful or important? Into what *category* does this abstraction fall?

Source: Adapted from Marzano et al., 2019; Marzano & Simms, 2014.

Table 2.5 lists common topics for which a teacher might design default elaboration questions. For each topic, a set of prompts are provided. For example, assume the teacher is introducing the topic of the eruption of Mount St. Helens in 1980. The teacher knows that students have some knowledge of this eruption. However, the teacher does not know the extent of this knowledge or its accuracy. Consulting the categories of default inferences, the teacher decides that the eruption of Mount St. Helens is a type of naturally occurring phenomenon and uses the generic questions associated with this topic.

- What places are associated with this phenomenon?
- What time period is associated with this phenomenon?
- What causes or consequences are associated with this phenomenon?
- What happened during this phenomenon?

The teacher translates these general questions into more specific questions like the following.

- Which specific towns and cities were most affected by the Mount St. Helens eruption?
- When were the first major signs that Mount St. Helens would erupt and what were the signs?
- What was the immediate impact of the eruption in Washington State and across the country?
- What happened during the first twenty-four hours of the eruption?

Using these questions, the teacher can determine what students think they know about the topic and then use that information to help deepen their understanding of the topic. The following steps describe the process a teacher might go through when they use table 2.5 to stimulate default inferences.

1. The teacher identifies how students will receive information about the target topic (for example, listen to a presentation, read about it, watch a video, look up information on the internet, and so on).
2. The teacher structures specific questions for students to answer that will cue them to make default inferences.
3. Prior to presenting the information about the topic, the teacher asks students to answer the questions and explain why they think their answers are accurate.
4. The teacher presents the information and asks students to reexamine their original answers in light of the new information they have received.
5. The teacher asks students to summarize what they have learned and how their thinking has changed.

To illustrate these steps, assume a teacher is involved in a unit on the importance of monuments within a culture. The teacher has students watch a video recording about the Statue of Liberty. However, before watching the video, the teacher asks students to respond to the following questions.

- Where is the Statue of Liberty?
- What does it look like?
- How did the United States get the Statue of Liberty?
- What does the Statue of Liberty symbolize?

As students answer these questions, the teacher periodically asks them how they know their answers are accurate. Students then watch the video and then discuss and reconsider their answers.

Reasoned Inferences

The second type of elaboration involves reasoned inferences. With this type of inference, people use *if-then thinking*: if this is true, then something else should be true. This type of elaboration works best if teachers clearly identify the steps of a process they are teaching students. To do so, the teacher uses the following sequence of activities with students.

1. The teacher focuses students' attention on a step-by-step process to which they have already been introduced.
2. The teacher selects one or more steps in the step-by-step process and asks students to describe what is easy for them and what is hard for them about the step or steps.
3. The teacher asks students to describe how the step or steps could be made easier for them.
4. The teacher has students try out their ideas.
5. The teacher has students summarize what they have learned and discuss how their thinking has changed.

To illustrate, assume that a teacher has provided students with a step-by-step process for sounding out an unrecognized one-syllable word. That process focuses first on the vowel, which is then blended with the ending sounds, and finally blended with the beginning sounds. As a whole class, guided by the teacher, students talk about which part of the process they find most difficult or confusing. The teacher leads the class in a discussion of how they might make the process clearer. The teacher should assist students in structuring their inferences as if-then statements: If I change this step in the following way, then I should expect the following result. The students then try out the new process and discuss how the changes make the process easier.

Figure 2.29 (page 80) lists visible evidence for element IVf.

IVg. Extending Learning Through Homework

The purpose of this element is to use homework activities to further develop students' depth of knowledge and fluency relative to content they are learning. An LMS that allows students to access instruction and activities from home is particularly beneficial to this end. By utilizing playlists and other online tools, teachers can give their students access to in-class assignments while they are at home.

Extending learning through homework has several benefits, the first of which is that students can complete a reading or activity in preparation for the next day's lesson. This flipped assignment can help introduce the students to a new article, story, or concept that the class will be studying. To illustrate, at the beginning of a unit on space exploration, the teacher might ask students to read the article "Disaster in Space" (Tarshis, 2017), which chronicles the Apollo 13 mission. The next day, the teacher begins the lesson by showing a clip from the movie *Apollo 13* (Howard, 1995) starring Tom Hanks, and proceeds with a processing activity where the students discuss the article in groups. Prior to the discussion, the teacher might have students engage in a second reading of the article if the teacher feels that enough students did not do the reading the night before, or if there is evidence that overall comprehension is low. This type of flipped-classroom activity can also be assigned as a shared read with parents, providing some support at home and increasing reading engagement. The teacher can give paper copies of the article to students without internet access, or those preferring to read a hard copy.

Visible evidence for effective instruction and guidance includes teachers doing the following.
• Asking students planned inferential questions • Engaging students in elaborative interrogation • Using question sequences (that is, detail questions, then category questions, then elaboration questions, then evidence questions) • Asking students to expand on their answers
Visible evidence for desired student actions and behaviors includes students doing the following.
• Volunteering answers to inferential questions • Providing explanations for their answers • Asking questions that are inferential in nature
Visible evidence for students' understanding and awareness includes students doing the following.
• Describing the teacher's questions as challenging but helpful • Explaining what an inferential question requires them to do

Source: © *2021 by Robert J. Marzano.*

FIGURE 2.29: Visible evidence for element IVf.

When online classroom platforms are available, homework can also involve students progressing through a playlist or unit at their own pace. Students who are motivated by a particular topic can complete additional assignments, view instructional videos, play skill-reinforcing games, and connect with their peers for online discussions. Students seeking to catch up from a previous learning deficit can complete supporting assignments given by an interventionist, finish missing assignments from a previous unit, or watch tutorial videos to correct any misconceptions in their learning.

Teacher-created videos are wonderful sources of content for homework activities. For example, a teacher might create a mathematics video explaining and demonstrating specific skills (see figure 2.30). He asks students to watch the video and comment on it as a homework assignment. The following day, students come to class having already viewed the video. The teacher would take the first few minutes of class to fill in any gaps or address any misconceptions, and then proceed with an activity designed to further develop their knowledge.

Figure 2.31 lists visible evidence for element IVg.

Understanding and Planning for Design Area IV

Whereas design area III (proficiency scale instruction) focuses on the nature of content, design area IV (general instruction) focuses on students' immediate needs. Specifically, within the purview of design area III, a teacher might decide to chunk content (element IIIa) because that *content* is highly complex and requires parsing to make it more understandable. In contrast, when making decisions about the use of elements in design area IV, the teacher focuses on the current needs of *students* and determines whether the instructional strategies in a particular element are necessary to help the whole class, a small set of students, or even an individual student progress in their knowledge of specific learning targets. For example, the teacher might determine that the majority of students

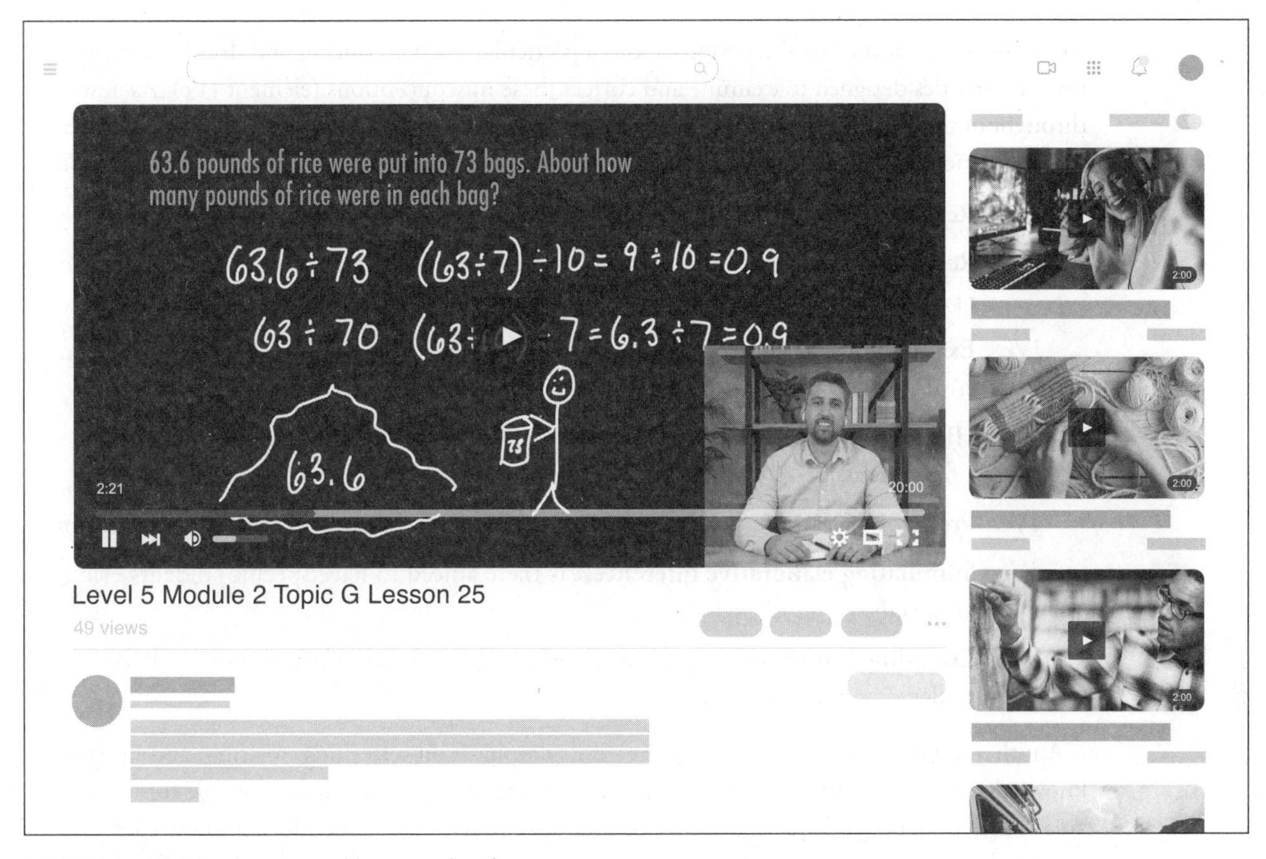

FIGURE 2.30: Teacher-created homework video.

Visible evidence for effective instruction and guidance includes teachers doing the following.
• Assigning homework to preview upcoming concepts or ideas they will study in class • Assigning homework to deepen students' knowledge • Assigning homework that helps students develop fluency in a process or skill
Visible evidence for desired student actions and behaviors includes students doing the following.
• Demonstrating understanding of the purpose of homework • Being prepared for new learning after being assigned homework • Deepening their understanding of the content as a result of the homework • Increasing their speed, accuracy, or fluency as a result of the homework
Visible evidence for students' understanding and awareness includes students doing the following.
• Explaining the purpose of specific homework assignments • Explaining how the homework has helped them

Source: © *2021 by Robert J. Marzano.*

FIGURE 2.31: Visible evidence for element IVg.

still possess significant misconceptions about a particular science concept and decide to engage the class in activities designed to examine and correct these misconceptions (element IVc). As described throughout this section, there are seven elements in this design area. When considering how to use the instructional strategies within these seven elements, teachers can ask the following questions.

IVa. **Reviewing content:** Is there a need to review specific content for specific students?

IVb. **Revising knowledge:** Is there a need to have specific students revise their understanding of specific content?

IVc. **Examining and correcting errors:** Is there a need to have specific students examine errors in their thinking or that of others?

IVd. **Highlighting critical information:** Is there a need to highlight specific content for specific students?

IVe. **Previewing content:** Is there a need to preview specific content with specific students?

IVf. **Stimulating elaborative inferences:** Is there a need to have specific students elaborate on specific content?

IVg. **Extending learning through homework:** Is there a need to assign homework for specific students on specific content?

Another notable aspect of this design area is its emphasis on refreshing, revising, and integrating knowledge once students have an initial understanding of it. The working principle for this design area is that students must recall knowledge they have previously learned if that knowledge is to be further developed. This is a major change in perspective for some classroom teachers.

The cognitive process of recall has been much maligned in K–12 education, most probably because of the popularization of what is referred to as *Bloom's taxonomy* (Bloom, 1956) and its revision (Anderson & Krathwohl, 2001). Both of these works implied that recall was a lower-order process. Specifically, in the 1956 publication, the lowest order of cognition was *recall*; in the 2001 publication, the lowest order of cognition was referred to as *remembering*. This led the K–12 education community to treat recall activities as inferior to activities that require students to use content in various ways. Certainly, applying content to which students have already been exposed is important to the learning experience, but recall is the tool by which students can continually refine their knowledge.

In the neuroscience literature, the act of recall or remembering is generally thought of as one of the most powerful tools in learning. As described in the book *Uncommon Sense Teaching* (Oakley, Rogowsky, & Sejnowski, 2021), when students are engaged in recall, they do not simply download information from permanent memory into working memory in a verbatim fashion. Instead, the very act of recall requires students to reassemble information into a unified whole in working memory. The more they do this, the stronger these new constructions will be. It is through this type of recall that students can fine-tune their understanding by engaging in activities like revising, looking for errors, making elaborations, and so on. In effect, each time students recall information, it provides them with an opportunity to reshape and improve their understanding of the content recalled. Conversely, if students do not recall and reprocess content, it will fade relatively quickly. Design area IV provides teachers with strategies to engage students in recall and remembering activities that operationalize the recommendations of the neuroscience literature.

Summary

This chapter deals with the domain of content in the Marzano Academies instructional model. It includes two design areas, both of which focus on teaching the information defined in proficiency scales. Design area III, proficiency scale instruction, includes seven elements that teachers use with specific learning targets from specific proficiency scales. Decisions as to which strategies to use from this design area are dictated by the nature of the content in the proficiency scales. Design area IV, general instruction, includes seven elements that teachers use to help students review, refresh, and revise their knowledge. Decisions about which strategies to use are dictated by the needs of the students. Visible evidence for teachers and students related to each element aids teachers in determining how effective their actions are relative to the intended outcomes of each element.

CHAPTER 3

Context

As its name implies, the domain of context deals with the overall environment of the classroom—the context that will either support or inhibit learning. While the instructional strategies in this domain certainly are related to academic content, their main purpose is to support the learner. Such support involves ensuring that students have ample opportunities to interact with their peers in ways that deepen their learning. Support must also include activities that keep students engaged in a variety of ways and on a variety of levels. Finally, such support must address students' basic physiological and psychological needs. This domain involves three design areas: design area V, grouping and regrouping; design area VI, engagement; and design area VII, comfort and safety. The strategies in these three design areas work together and must be addressed consciously and concretely.

Design Area V: Grouping and Regrouping

In a CBE classroom, grouping and regrouping play a central role in how teachers set up instruction. Of course, teachers in a traditional classroom group and regroup students. For example, they might form ad hoc groups to talk about new content they just presented or they might have students work together on a class project. The CBE classroom has some mitigating factors that add complexity. Specifically, in a CBE classroom students might be working on different topics within their groups. This requires teachers to think in terms of not only the most beneficial grouping of students but also the most beneficial organization of content.

There are three elements in this design area.

Va. Supporting group interactions

Vb. Supporting group transitions

Vc. Providing group support

The following sections detail each one.

Va. Supporting Group Interactions

The teacher responsibility inherent in this element is to group students in ways that enhance their learning through the formal and informal interactions that occur in the group. One of the first things teachers must do in a CBE classroom relative to organizing students is to determine the various reasons for students to be in a group. Not surprisingly, the starting point in this endeavor is proficiency scales. Obviously, students working on the same proficiency scale can be in a group. At an even more granular level, students working on the same learning targets from a specific proficiency scale can form a temporary group. For example, students working on the score 2.0 learning targets in a specific proficiency scale could constitute a group, students working on the 3.0 targets could constitute a group, and so on. Students remain in these groups until they have mastered the target content.

Another reason to group students is to work on a particular task. This commonly occurs when a teacher wants students to engage in an activity that helps them practice a skill, deepen their knowledge of information, or engage in a knowledge application task. For example, a teacher might wish to organize students into small groups to practice a procedure they recently learned for sounding out unrecognized words while reading. These groups might last for only one or two class periods. Similarly, a teacher might organize students into groups to deepen their understanding of a topic using a classifying activity. For example, to deepen students' knowledge of clouds, the teacher might organize students into groups as they classify the types of clouds they have studied. Finally, a teacher might organize students into groups that form on Monday and disband on Friday. Social studies students in these weeklong groups might have the common knowledge application task of analyzing the 2020 decision to close schools because of the global pandemic. Each group would research the alternatives that were considered and the reasons supporting the final decision that was made. Friday might be the day during which groups report on their findings.

Teachers should always keep in mind that grouping in a competency-based classroom should be flexible. Indeed, some groups might be established on a one-time basis and disband when the need has been met. Students might begin a literacy lesson in a shared meeting space where the teacher shows an introductory video. The teacher might assign students a seat on the floor to facilitate buddy discussions and help with behavior management. After the video, students might mix throughout the classroom and form pairs or groups for a quick processing discussion. From there, students might go to their assigned groups for an activity designed to deepen knowledge. Afterward, they would break out into a fishbowl discussion, inside-outside circle, or three-stay-one-stray activity to share information and receive feedback. The whole lesson would end with students meeting with a friend to reflect on the key content. Finally, students might create a video explaining what they had learned as a resource for their peers.

Teachers should use multiple strategies to ensure that students within groups interact in ways that enhance their learning. Some of those strategies include activities like elbow partners, table groups, close partners, across-the-room partners, inside-outside circles, and the like. For every strategy students are expected to use, the teacher should provide direct instruction as to how to execute the strategy. In all cases the teacher should model the interaction strategy, provide opportunities for students to practice the strategy, and create a poster showing the steps of the strategy if needed.

Figure 3.1 lists visible evidence for element Va.

Vb. Supporting Group Transitions

The teacher responsibility inherent in this element is to ensure that students will move in and out of groups in a manner that supports their individual needs. Within a CBE classroom, how long a group stays together depends on the purpose of the group. As described in the discussion of element Va, there are some groups that stay together for only a few class periods or even a single class period. For these groups, transitions are not a concern. However, for longer-term groups, teachers should seek to ensure that students experience a smooth transition from one grouping to the next.

Home groups are where students address issues that are typically not academic in nature such as checking in with group members as to their well-being, identifying support that group members

Visible evidence for effective instruction and guidance includes teachers doing the following.

- Using protocols for student interaction
- Establishing a clear purpose and goals for groups
- Grouping students for active processing of new knowledge
- Grouping students to practice or deepen their knowledge
- Grouping students for the application of knowledge
- Using multiple grouping strategies to form student groups (for example, elbow partners, table groups, close partners, across-the-room partners, inside-outside circles, and so on)

Visible evidence for desired student actions and behaviors includes students doing the following.

- Moving into groups quickly and with purpose
- Treating each other with respect during group activities
- Interacting in a manner that deepens their understanding
- Working efficiently in groups

Visible evidence for students' understanding and awareness includes students doing the following.

- Describing their group interaction as useful
- Describing what is expected of them in terms of interacting in groups
- Explaining what they like about group work

Source: © *2021 by Robert J. Marzano.*

FIGURE 3.1: Visible evidence for element Va.

might need, ensuring group members are aware of the expectations for the day, identifying and celebrating significant events in the lives of group members, and so on. Home groups should last roughly six weeks. This gives students a chance to get to know each other and develop effective group skills, but prevents the groups from becoming stagnant. When home groups disband, teachers should plan activities that allow students to have closure relative to their home groups. Such activities might involve students communicating about what they learned from their peers, things that happened they particularly enjoyed, and compliments they want to relay to specific individuals.

Groups formed around the content in a specific proficiency scale require special considerations. Students should not stay in these groups beyond the time they benefit from group support nor leave before they are finished benefiting from the group support. To determine where students are in this continuum, teachers should have frequent conversations with students about this issue. These conversations can be as simple as teachers asking students what they are learning from the group and whether they believe they still need to be in the group. In effect, this type of transition occurs when students have reached proficiency on a particular measurement topic.

The most important type of group transition is when a student moves up a level for a given subject area. For example, assume a new student in school has been placed into a grade 3 mathematics group based on an initial assessment given to him on his first day of school. After several weeks of working in grade 3 mathematics, his teacher comes to the conclusion that he has been misplaced and should move up to grade 4 mathematics. His teacher bases this decision on evidence from assessments the student has taken and ongoing discussions she has had with the student. She contacts the administration committee and requests a meeting to discuss the placement. At the meeting, administrators, the grade 4 mathematics teacher, the instructional coach, the school psychologist, and members of the intervention staff consider the student's case. The team agrees with the grade 3 teacher that the student should move up to a grade 4 mathematics class where he would be better served. His parents are immediately contacted and notified, and he begins work in the level 4 class as soon as possible. This same process can occur for existing students within a class who have shown, for one reason or another, that they would benefit from moving up or down a level. Midyear transitions are quite common in a CBE school, especially after students have internalized the requirements for such transitions.

Figure 3.2 lists visible evidence for element Vb.

Visible evidence for effective instruction and guidance includes teachers doing the following.
• Monitoring specific groups to determine if they should continue or be changed • Monitoring specific students to determine if they should stay in a group or move to another • Identifying what specific students need to smoothly transition to a new group or level
Visible evidence for desired student actions and behaviors includes students doing the following.
• Making transitions to new groups or levels and understanding what is expected of them • Being aware of why they are moving to a new group or level
Visible evidence for students' understanding and awareness includes students doing the following.
• Explaining what will be expected of them in their new group or level • Explaining why they are moving to a new group or level

Source: © 2021 by Robert J. Marzano.

FIGURE 3.2: Visible evidence for element Vb.

Vc. Providing Group Support

Groups sometimes have rather fragile infrastructures in that they are dependent on the quality of student interactions with the content and each other. Therefore, the teacher must provide necessary support to specific groups and individuals within those groups. An academy teacher constantly scans the interactions of each active group, determining what types of support are necessary.

First and foremost, strong standard operating procedures (SOPs) should be in place so that students know exactly what they are supposed to be doing in their groups. We address the nature and function of SOPs in depth in a number of subsequent elements. Briefly, though, *SOPs* are written procedures that provide students with explicit direction as to how they should execute specific tasks. SOPs are especially important when groups are constructed as centers where students engage in specific learning activities regarding specific proficiency scale content. Teachers often utilize group or center time to conference with students or conduct small reading groups. When engaged in conferencing, teachers can understandably only provide limited support to groups. Therefore, students need to be able to walk themselves through the center activities and support each other when needed. SOPs for centers should include detailed directions for such activities.

Playlists are great venues for providing group support. In fact, if every playlist a teacher creates includes support resources, students will become adept at seeking out solutions to their own problems. Support within playlists might include online resources or videos. Teachers might also foresee a specific problem that may arise, and create an instructional video or document addressing the problem. For example, a teacher might note that students commonly have difficulty understanding the directions for a specific group activity regarding score 2.0 content. The teacher could make a video explaining the directions more clearly and in more detail, and have every student watch the recording before they start their work in the group. The teacher might also include a Google Form where students can submit questions or needs regarding the group work. This provides an excellent way for students to ask their questions without interrupting the teacher. The teacher then responds to these questions when time is available, perhaps during a preparation period.

Student strength posters are also excellent tools for providing group support. A poster listing all students in the class and their strengths supports students in seeking help from each other if the teacher is occupied (see figure 3.3). Students looking for help with spelling can use the poster to find an expert speller; students needing help with technology can find a tech guru. Students who are proficient with a topic or have already completed a task and are willing to help others might also wear expert badges, lanyards, or hats.

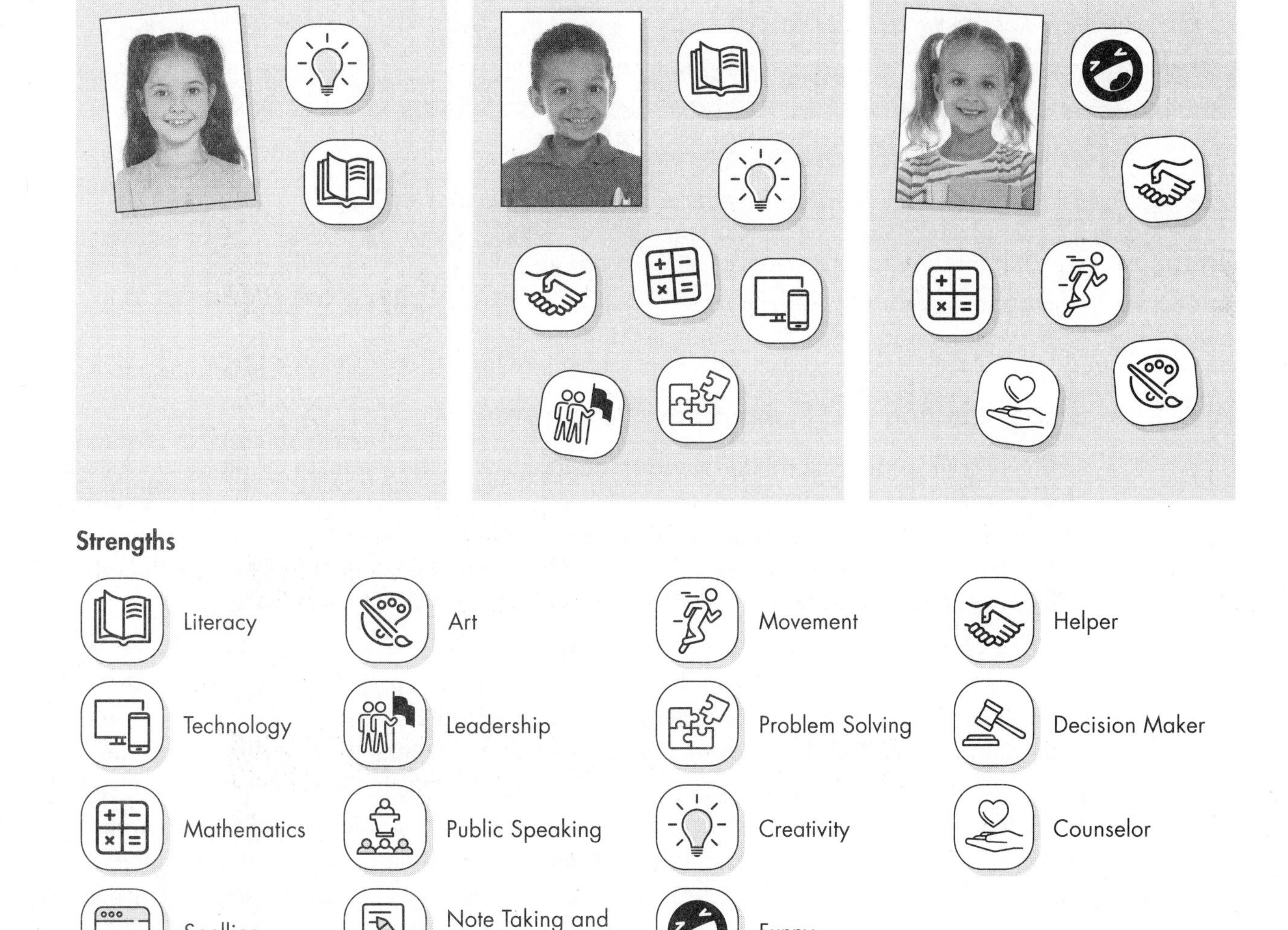

FIGURE 3.3: Student strength posters.

Finally, teachers should always be cognizant of the possibility that students need whole-class instruction relative to specific topics. For example, the teacher might notice that students in multiple groups seem to have the same challenges or misunderstandings with the same topics. The teacher would verify the existence of such common problems using informal assessments like fist to five or other hand signals, whiteboards, exit tickets, a Google Form or online poll, clickers, or Plickers. The information gained from these types of assessments would direct the teacher's next steps relative to specific topics, perhaps indicating that whole-class instruction is necessary.

Figure 3.4 lists visible evidence for element Vc.

Visible evidence for effective instruction and guidance includes teachers doing the following.

- Designing and implementing centers that focus on specific content from proficiency scales
- Identifying specific needs within specific centers
- Determining which topics within a center could benefit from direct instruction or brief whole-class instruction

Visible evidence for desired student actions and behaviors includes students doing the following.

- Being aware of the purpose of the center activities
- Experiencing success in the center activities

Visible evidence for students' understanding and awareness includes students doing the following.

- Describing how groups and centers have met their specific needs
- Describing the purposes of specific center activities relative to specific proficiency scales
- Describing what they understand and don't understand about specific center activities

Source: © 2021 by Robert J. Marzano.

FIGURE 3.4: Visible evidence for element Vc.

Understanding and Planning for Design Area V

Grouping and regrouping are critical parts of an effective CBE classroom. In the preceding discussion, we considered different ways a teacher might organize students into groups, negotiate student transitions, and provide general and specific support to groups. While these are commonly done in CBE and traditional classrooms, a CBE teacher also plans for grouping and regrouping from the perspective of the entire year.

A CBE classroom will likely look very different at the end of the year than it looked at the beginning of the year. At the beginning of the year, CBE teachers will plan the whole year in terms of units of instruction, with each unit addressing one or more proficiency scales. To illustrate, assume that a fifth-grade social studies teacher has twenty-five measurement topics to address in fifteen units of instruction across the year. At the beginning of the year, all students will participate fully in each unit at the same time. Over time, however, some students will start to fall behind in terms of their mastery of the content—that is, taking longer than the allotted time to master the measurement topics for that unit. Likewise, some students might master certain proficiency scales faster than planned and move ahead to topics that the teacher has not yet addressed.

To address this growing heterogeneity in students' status relative to the measurement topics slated for the year, a CBE teacher must establish groups for those students who are falling behind in demonstrating proficiency. For these groups, the teacher would provide students opportunities to work independently or in small groups to improve their status on proficiency scales from units already completed. Similarly, the teacher would establish groups that provide opportunities for students to move at a faster pace than the units are presented. In both cases, it is necessary for the teacher to create virtual resources for the learning targets in each proficiency scale. We described this in the discussion of preparing and planning for design area III, proficiency scale instruction (page 60). If the teacher has created such resources, they provide a wide variety of options for students to work at their own pace individually or in groups.

Design Area VI: Engagement

Engagement is a robust construct in the academy model. When teachers are focusing on design area VI, they are helping students pay attention and feel energized and intrigued. There are eight elements in this design area.

VIa. Noticing and reacting when students are not engaged

VIb. Increasing response rates

VIc. Using physical movement

VId. Maintaining a lively pace

VIe. Demonstrating intensity and enthusiasm

VIf. Presenting unusual information

VIg. Using friendly controversy

VIh. Using academic games

The following sections detail each one.

VIa. Noticing and Reacting When Students Are Not Engaged

The teacher responsibility inherent in this element is to continually monitor students' levels of attention and react when their attention is waning. Attention is the gatekeeper for engagement. If students are not paying attention to what is occurring in class, there is little chance they will engage in the academic activities posed by the teacher. Consequently, one of the classroom teacher's first jobs is to be aware of students' levels of attention. There are several direct approaches for doing this. One simple technique is to visually scan the classroom periodically, looking for signs of engagement and signs of lack of engagement. For example, evidence of student engagement includes the following.

- Students working on the activities that have been assigned to them
- Students making eye contact with the teacher
- Students making notes on the handouts provided to them
- Students writing in their academic journals

Evidence of lack of engagement includes the following.

- Students not making eye contact with the teacher
- Students working on tasks other than those assigned by the teacher
- Students talking with other students about topics that are clearly not related to the content
- Students doing things that distract others

Another strategy for monitoring students' attention levels is to periodically ask them to signal their level of engagement. For this strategy to work, the teacher must assure students that there will be no punitive consequences for them if they indicate that they are not engaged at a given moment. To signal their level of attention when prompted by the teacher, students can use fist to five (with a fist meaning not attending and five fingers indicating complete attention) or other hand signals. Another straightforward approach is for each student to have three colored cards: green for engaged, yellow for partially engaged, and red for disengaged. When prompted by the teacher, students display the card that represents their current level of engagement.

Beyond these direct strategies, developing relationships with students is quite possibly the most effective way to understand when and why particular students are not fully engaged. A close personal bond with students can provide the teacher with an insight into verbal and nonverbal cues a student might be giving off when their engagement drops. Teachers might notice a certain look on a student's face or body language that signals that something is not quite right. A conversation at the onset of a lesson might reveal that a student is having a difficult time at home, or was up late the previous night because a sibling was sick. The teacher would then respond accordingly and make adjustments or accommodations throughout the day.

Once a teacher notices that students are not engaged, there are many different ways to respond. First, the teacher should quickly reflect on why engagement has fallen off. The teacher might find that directions are not clear enough or that the provided resources are too difficult. With such information, a teacher might make a simple adjustment. Sometimes it is the case that one group in particular is off task, talking, or displaying confusion. A quick visit to that group to assess their needs, provide a pep talk, or even move one or all students can take care of the issue.

If the teacher has noticed that the whole class is losing interest, perhaps it is time for a team-building activity or quick game. If the teacher has a set of games that the class plays and enjoys on a regular basis, there is little time wasted on initial setup and introduction of rules and procedures.

A teacher may also decide to abandon a lesson or activity if it is not engaging students. If an activity has major design flaws, time is too short, or everything just seems to be going wrong, a teacher should never be afraid to stop a lesson with complete transparency. He or she might say, "Class, I'm going to go ahead and stop us right now. For some reason, this lesson didn't work, and I'm thinking it's because the article I gave you is too difficult. I'd like to see if I can find something better, and we can try this activity later on. Does anybody have any feedback for me?" Modeling honest and self-reflective behavior is highly beneficial as it shows students how to self-analyze performance and comprehension, as well as provides an authentic opportunity for students to see problem solving in action. Students will appreciate that their teacher is constantly working to meet their educational needs and that their feedback is meaningful.

Finally, it is important to remember that it is legitimate for the teacher to expect students to refocus themselves. Of course, the success of such an approach is age dependent, but upper-elementary students should be overtly working on their self-awareness and agency. Students re-engaging when they realize that they are currently off task is a practical and concrete way to improve both. To this end, teachers should provide students with SOPs designed to help students re-engage. Such SOPs should include diverse options like going for a brief walk, getting a drink, following a mental process, doing some jumping jacks, or briefly visiting with a different teacher or other mentor in the building.

Figure 3.5 lists visible evidence for element VIa.

Visible evidence for effective instruction and guidance includes teachers doing the following.

- Monitoring individual student engagement
- Monitoring overall class engagement
- Asking students to signal their level of engagement
- Boosting the overall energy level of the class when energy levels drop

Visible evidence for desired student actions and behaviors includes students doing the following.

- Being aware of the fact that the teacher is taking note of their engagement levels
- Trying to increase their engagement levels when the teacher cues them

Visible evidence for students' understanding and awareness includes students doing the following.

- Describing their teacher as one who expects high engagement levels
- Explaining the specific things the teacher does that helps them keep engaged

Source: © 2021 by Robert J. Marzano.

FIGURE 3.5: Visible evidence for element VIa.

VIb. Increasing Response Rates

Having students answer questions is one of the quintessential ways to capture their attention. With this element, the teacher provides students with processes for answering questions in such a way that multiple students answer each question. The reason for this is somewhat counterintuitive. When a teacher asks a question, one would think that it automatically stimulates all students to pay attention because they are all thinking about the answer. But this is not necessarily the case. In fact, the way the teacher asks a question can dampen students' need or desire to pay attention to the question. For example, if a teacher only calls on those students who raise their hands, then some students will simply never raise their hand and consequently will never have to think about the questions. Likewise, once a teacher calls on a particular student, every other student in class realizes that they no longer have to consider the answer.

The term *response rates* refers to the number of students who respond to a question the teacher poses. This is the nexus of the utility of questioning as a tool for capturing students' attention. If only one or two students respond to a question posed by the teacher, then the question has a low response rate. If all students respond to a question posed by the teacher, then the question has a high response rate. In effect, the more students that respond to teacher questions, the more the strategy of asking questions becomes a tool to enhance attention. There are a number of strategies available to teachers to increase student response rates.

Random name generators are a good way to increase response rates to questions. The types of random name generators range from the classic popsicle sticks in a jar to newer class management technology like ClassDojo (www.classdojo.com) or Classcraft (www.classcraft.com). Every student should expect to be called on at least once throughout the day, and it is important for students to understand why the teacher has this expectation. Random name generators may increase anxiety, especially for shy students, so it is also important that students have a means to get help when they are called on and do not know the answer. Strategies like phone a friend or answer eliminator can help ease the worry, although students should not get too many passes. If the teacher uses a random name generator regularly for all types of reasons, then students get used to having to respond on a regular basis.

In addition to random name generators, random group selectors and random sequencers can come in very handy. For example, at the beginning of a group activity for which the teacher wants groups to share their results, a random group sequencer can decide which group will present first, second, third, and so on. Random group generators can also select one student within each group to present, or assign other types of jobs.

Technology also provides a plethora of ways for students to respond. Student clickers, cell phones, online polls, and Plicker cards are great ways to increase student response rates. However, such technology tools should not be the only way for students to respond, especially since they can sometimes take longer than other reliable methods like individual whiteboards, hand signals, and individual or choral vocal responses.

Figure 3.6 lists visible evidence for element VIb.

Visible evidence for effective instruction and guidance includes teachers doing the following.

- Engaging all students in answering questions by utilizing strategies like choral response, paired response, response cards, whiteboards, technology-based response platforms, or hand signals
- Pulling random names of students to answer questions
- Utilizing wait time after asking a question and after a student responds

Visible evidence for desired student actions and behaviors includes students doing the following.

- Responding to questions as an entire class or in groups
- Paying attention to other students' answers
- Being aware that the teacher expects all students to respond

Visible evidence for students' understanding and awareness includes students doing the following.

- Describing the teacher as one who expects all students to respond
- Describing specific strategies the teacher uses to elicit answers from all students

Source: © 2021 by Robert J. Marzano.

FIGURE 3.6: Visible evidence for element VIb.

VIc. Using Physical Movement

Physical movement is an essential technique for enhancing students' energy levels. It is safe to say that, at the elementary level, many if not most lessons should incorporate some type of physical movement, even if it's just for a brief period of time. Such quick movement activities include the following.

- **Mix-pair-share:** Students stand, find partners, and discuss a question or share their answers. When the teacher signals, students find another partner with whom they share, again, while standing.
- **Gallery walk:** The teacher posts student work around the room or in the hallway and then provides extended time for students to walk around and observe each other's work, taking notes as they do so.
- **Four-corners voting:** The teacher asks a question and posts four options in the corners of the room. Students walk to the corner that represents their opinion or what they believe is the correct answer.
- **Three stay one stray:** The teacher organizes students into groups of four to work on a specific task. When signaled by the teacher, one group member visits another group to see how they are approaching the task and then returns back to inform his or her group. This is done multiple times throughout the task with students rotating who strays each time.

A teacher might start a lesson off by having students mingle with their peers while listening to music, perhaps using a specific song to indicate a recurring task or action. Students are interacting about academic content, but the music provides a pleasing and energizing backdrop to their discussions. Movement strategies can also be strung together to produce a series of connected movement activities. For example, the teacher might begin by asking a previewing question and prompting students to stand up and find a partner, answer the question, and then share with the whole class. All of this occurs while students remain standing. Students then begin their group work on a specific topic, with the teacher stopping the class at regular intervals to implement brief movement activities or brain breaks. When their work is complete, groups post the products of their collaborative work and students conduct a gallery walk or other movement-based review activity.

An important aspect of this element is that students should be encouraged to self-assess when they might need to stand, stretch, or take their own individual break. The class could even develop an SOP called "My brain is fried" or "I'm feeling tired" with steps ranging from "stand up and get a drink" to "take a short walk." The SOP would provide students suggestions on how they can recognize when to execute the SOP (for example, when they find they are having a hard time thinking about the content). It would also guide students on how to take a break without disrupting others. For example, relative to taking a short walk, it might instruct students to do so in the hallway right outside the room, walk quietly for no more than two minutes, and then re-engage in classwork.

Finally, teachers should consider the arrangement of their classroom to facilitate easy movement. There should be open spaces for students to occupy and gather in, as well as clear pathways for students to move. Students can work in different places around the room, lie on the floor, or sit up against the wall. Strategies for setting up the classroom are described in element VIIa, organizing the physical layout of the classroom (page 105).

Figure 3.7 (page 96) lists visible evidence for element VIc.

Visible evidence for effective instruction and guidance includes teachers doing the following.
• Using physical movement or having students stand up and stretch when energy levels are low • Using physical movement as a response-rate strategy (for example, vote with your feet, corners activity, stand and be counted) • Using physical movement to help students create representations of content (for example, body representations or drama-related activities)
Visible evidence for desired student actions and behaviors includes students doing the following.
• Actively engaging in physical-movement activities • Demonstrating increased levels of energy
Visible evidence for students' understanding and awareness includes students doing the following.
• Describing the physical-movement activities they like the best • Explaining why physical-movement activities keep their interest and help them learn

Source: © *2021 by Robert J. Marzano.*

FIGURE 3.7: Visible evidence for element VIc.

VId. Maintaining a Lively Pace

The teacher responsibility inherent in this element is to ensure that the pace of instruction in the classroom is generally lively, does not drag, and adapts to optimize students' learning at any point in time. An effective pace indirectly and sometimes directly improves the energy levels of students.

To establish a lively pace for the day, teachers should be thoughtful in their planning, purposeful in their routines, adaptive in their instruction, and aware of the "temperature" of their classrooms. Effective planning includes preparing for flexibility: having the next lesson segment ready just in case one takes less time than expected or pushing a lesson to a later date to accommodate a class that needs more time. Students will always give indications, whether verbal or nonverbal, of how much time they need, and it is up to the teacher to be constantly aware of student progress. For example, if a majority of students have stopped working on a task, it is probably the case that they do not need more time. If they are working intently on the task at a rapid pace, it is probably an indication that they need more time. Teachers can also ask students directly how much more or less time they need. A teacher might ask the class to show how many more minutes they need to complete a task by holding up their fingers. For longer tasks, the teacher might establish that each finger is worth two minutes, or three minutes, or more.

Effective routines and transitions are instrumental in keeping the pace of a lesson lively. Of course, establishing routines and protocols for transitions happens in advance. Particularly in the beginning of the school year, classes should articulate such procedures and practice them to the point where students can execute them with little conscious thought. It is almost always useful to state routines and protocols in the form of SOPs. Classroom job assignments can also come in handy, with particular students assigned to collect supplies or turn in work, while others clean up and set up for the next lesson or activity. Either way, routines and transition procedures ensure that every moment of the day is used efficiently.

In addition to planning to maintain a lively pace, teachers should continually ask themselves if things are going too slowly. One indication is if students display a lack of energy and an absence of enthusiasm, or appear distracted or lethargic. In this case, then the teacher might simply pick up the pace or employ some type of activity intended to recapture students' attention. For example, a teacher could reorganize students into ad hoc groups and play a game focused on the academic content that is being addressed. Using academic games is addressed in element VIh (page 101).

Figure 3.8 lists visible evidence for element VId.

Visible evidence for effective instruction and guidance includes teachers doing the following.
• Varying the pace by speeding up or slowing down to meet students' engagement needs • Ensuring all instructional segments occur in a brisk but unhurried fashion • Utilizing motivational hooks to spark students' attention
Visible evidence for desired student actions and behaviors includes students doing the following.
• Quickly adapting to changes in classroom activities and reengaging in the content • Appearing energized by the teacher's pace
Visible evidence for students' understanding and awareness includes students doing the following.
• Reporting that the pace of the class is neither too fast nor too slow • Saying that they like the pace the teacher keeps

Source: © 2021 by Robert J. Marzano.

FIGURE 3.8: Visible evidence for element VId.

VIe. Demonstrating Intensity and Enthusiasm

This element concerns teachers' tendency to display authentic intensity and enthusiasm about the content they are addressing. The teacher's display of enthusiasm and occasional intensity about content can be contagious. Of course, displays of such sentiments must be genuine, or students will recognize their inauthenticity. This is typically no problem for classroom teachers since they enter the teaching profession because of their enthusiasm for helping students learn. Whereas enthusiasm can and should be exhibited continually, intensity is situational. Both are communicated in part by volume, tone of voice, verbal emphasis on specific words or phrases, pauses, and rate of speech.

Foundational to communicating intensity and enthusiasm are the personal connections teachers make with the content. A mathematics teacher might communicate enthusiasm by telling stories about when and why she first became interested in mathematics even though her friends didn't think it was the "cool" thing to do. A science teacher might describe some articles he is currently reading to learn more about Mars and what humans are discovering about it from current explorations of the planet. A literacy teacher might share her recent experience reading a short story by her favorite author. Intensity is demonstrated by the teachers' attention to detail relative to the content. Teachers should share new awareness they gain about the content or fine distinctions they have recently made between similar-seeming pieces of content.

Teachers should consider intensity and enthusiasm when planning units or lessons. They should seek to create units regarding content about which they are sincerely enthusiastic. A teacher looking to design a unit around animals might choose a particular region or animal that they have a personal connection to. For example, a teacher might design a unit around the Serengeti ecosystem in Africa because he has traveled there and can provide many personal stories, pictures, and artifacts. Or, a teacher might design a unit around the reintroduction of wolves to the Yellowstone ecosystem because she has taken classes at the Yellowstone Institute about wolf behavior and can provide insights from this experience. Students will feel an automatic attachment to the content because their own teacher, someone they love, care for, and admire, has experienced these things firsthand.

Figure 3.9 lists visible evidence for element VIe.

Visible evidence for effective instruction and guidance includes teachers doing the following.
• Making direct statements about the importance of content • Making explicit connections between content and the world outside school • Telling personal stories about the content to make it more accessible to students • Using humor to trigger interest in content • Using volume, tone of voice, verbal emphasis on specific words or phrases, pauses, and rate of speech to communicate intensity and enthusiasm
Visible evidence for desired student actions and behaviors includes students doing the following.
• Increasing their attention levels in response to the teacher's intensity and enthusiasm • Increasing their energy levels in response to the teacher's intensity and enthusiasm
Visible evidence for students' understanding and awareness includes students doing the following.
• Saying the teacher likes the content and likes teaching • Saying they like the teacher's enthusiasm

Source: © *2021 by Robert J. Marzano.*

FIGURE 3.9: Visible evidence for element VIe.

VIf. Presenting Unusual Information

Providing students with information that stimulates their interest and intrigue relative to the content is another key element of engagement. Unusual information is intrinsically interesting even if it is only tangentially related to the content of a lesson or unit. Additionally, students are naturally curious and drawn to information that is unusual or out of the ordinary.

This strategy can stimulate students' interest about the content of a lesson or unit they are about to experience. The aforementioned teacher beginning a unit on the Serengeti ecosystem might begin by introducing the students to the man-eating lions of the Tsavo region. Or, a teacher beginning a unit on space exploration might begin by sharing an article about how Elon Musk launched his Tesla Roadster into space.

Another option is for a teacher to plan a "check this out" segment each day, where the class learns about a new, interesting, or unusual piece of information or story. He or she could post these items to a focus board and encourage students to add stories or facts they find. If the teacher has a newsletter, website, or class newspaper, he or she can incorporate a "weird news" or "believe it or not" section.

Students should always be encouraged to highlight facts and information they find to be interesting or unusual. Students who are working through an endangered species unit could design a "fast facts" poster highlighting the most interesting or unusual facts about their chosen species. These posters can be created using an online tool like Lucidpress, printed in color, laminated, and posted in the hallway for everyone to see. Perhaps students are learning about World War II; they might be encouraged to film a historical news segment that highlights a lesser-known story or personal journey from the time.

Unusual information can also be generated by making students aware of different perspectives on issues they are studying. For example, after teaching a unit on the reintroduction of wolves to the Yellowstone ecosystem, a teacher could challenge the students' thinking by introducing them to the perspective of a rancher from Montana who opposed the reintroduction. Personal testimony or video might prompt the students to see the other side of things and gather new unusual information about the topic.

Another option is to develop lessons and units around the results of student interest inventories, student interviews, or parent questionnaires given at the beginning of the year. This is not to say that every lesson a teacher gives needs to center on the latest video game, but teachers can tailor units around broader interest categories. For example, a teacher receiving feedback that her students love pets could design units around interesting species of animals and include information about how people sometimes keep exotic animals as pets. Students can be invited to seek out examples of this and research the possible negative consequences to a species because of this practice.

Similarly, teachers can assess students' level of interest regarding topics for upcoming units by asking questions like, "Which topic would you be most interested in studying: inventors, Nazi Germany and World War II, or rainforests?" Figure 3.10 depicts the results of such an interest survey.

Figure 3.11 (page 100) lists visible evidence for element VIf.

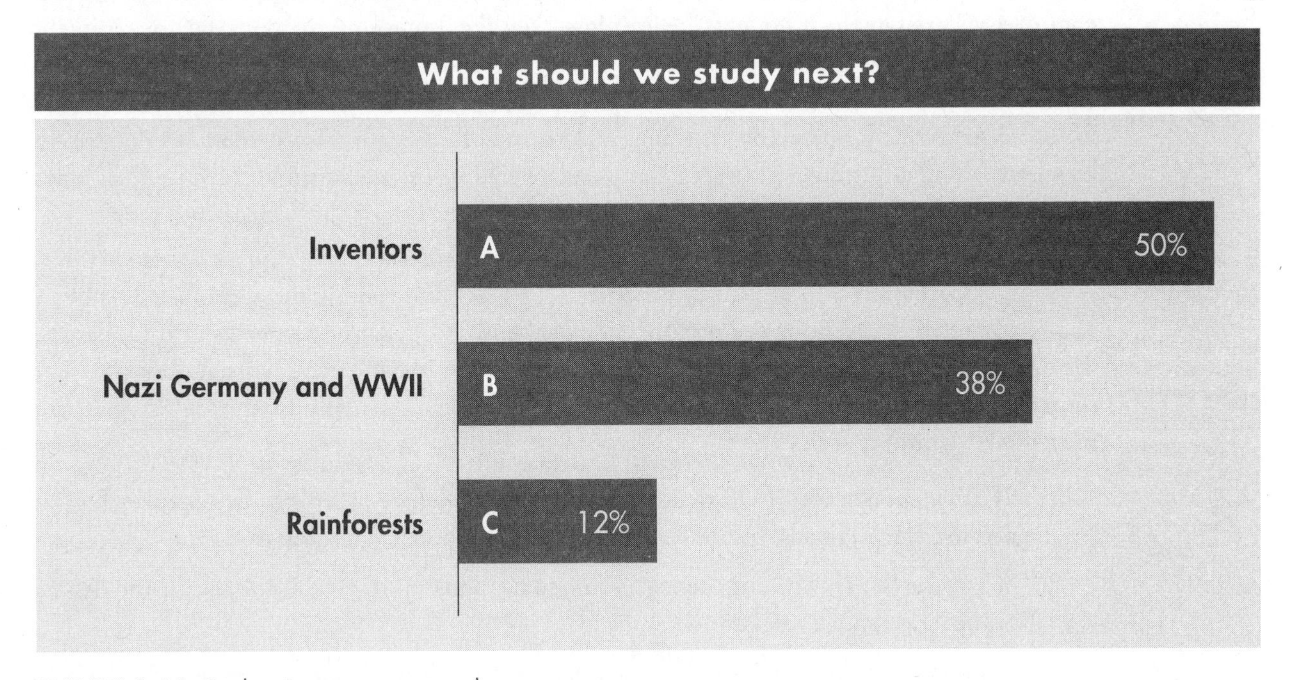

FIGURE 3.10: Student interest survey results.

Visible evidence for effective instruction and guidance includes teachers doing the following.
• Presenting unusual or intriguing information to capture students' attention • Having students explore, find, and share unusual information • Inviting guest speakers to share unusual or intriguing information with the class
Visible evidence for desired student actions and behaviors includes students doing the following.
• Increasing their engagement levels in response to the presentation of unusual information • Asking questions about the unusual information • Sharing unusual information with the class
Visible evidence for students' understanding and awareness includes students doing the following.
• Explaining how the unusual information makes the content more interesting • Describing the types of unusual information they like the most

Source: © *2021 by Robert J. Marzano.*

FIGURE 3.11: Visible evidence for element VIf.

VIg. Using Friendly Controversy

This element involves providing students with opportunities to debate the merits of different perspectives on teacher-selected and student-selected topics. As its name implies, friendly controversy involves students in activities that require them to defend different points of view on an issue and do so in a way that does not include personal attacks. Any activity that involves options or alternatives can become a friendly controversy task. Similarly, any class vote provides an opportunity for friendly controversy. For example, if students are learning about the Serengeti ecosystem, the teacher might ask, "If you were designing a flag for the Serengeti ecosystem, which animal would you put on it?" Students could propose ideas and even campaign for a specific animal. However, students would have to defend their proposals by providing reasons and evidence for why their animal deserves to be selected. Similarly, students learning about endangered species could try to convince their peers that the animal they are studying should be chosen to benefit from a class coin drive.

At a more formal level, students can take part in structured debates. This requires two small teams of students (perhaps two to five students per team): a team representing the affirmative side of an issue and a team representing the negative side of the issue. A chairperson is selected to manage the debate. This can be the teacher or a student in the class. The other students in class represent the gallery who will judge the efficacy of the arguments. The class might use the following debate procedure (Manitoba, n.d.).

1. The first speaker for the affirmative side begins the debate. Then, the first speaker for the negative side responds. In this way, the speakers for both sides speak in turn.
2. When the last speaker for the negative side has spoken, the second round of the debate begins, this time in reverse order.
3. At the end of the second round, one speaker for the affirmative and one speaker for the negative make the final summary comments.

4. The order of speakers must not change from round to round.
5. During the debate, each speaker has a maximum time of ninety seconds. The chairperson checks the time carefully. He or she gives a sign when the speaker has ten seconds to go. When ninety seconds have elapsed, the speaker may finish his or her sentence but then must stop.
6. Interrupting a speaker is forbidden.
7. The audience must not participate in the debate.
8. After the debate, the audience has five minutes to share their impressions and opinions.
9. To end the debate, the audience votes. In the vote, yes and no votes are counted. The majority wins the vote.

The teacher would present this process to students and engage them in guided practice of following the protocol. However, once students have internalized the process, they or the teacher can call for its use regarding any topic that arises.

Figure 3.12 lists visible evidence for element VIg.

Visible evidence for effective instruction and guidance includes teachers doing the following.

- Engaging students in friendly controversy by having them explain and defend their positions on topics about which they disagree
- Having students vote on particular issues and discuss their positions
- Setting up seminars, legal models, town-hall meetings, or debates for students to participate in friendly controversy
- Asking students to take a perspective opposite of their own and defend that position

Visible evidence for desired student actions and behaviors includes students doing the following.

- Readily engaging in the friendly controversy activities
- Presenting well-thought-out arguments for their perspectives

Visible evidence for students' understanding and awareness includes students doing the following.

- Describing friendly controversy activities as stimulating, fun, and interesting
- Explaining how the friendly controversy activities help them better understand the content

Source: © 2021 by Robert J. Marzano.

FIGURE 3.12: Visible evidence for element VIg.

VIh. Using Academic Games

The teacher responsibility inherent in this element is to use games to help students review and forge relationships among academic concepts. Games have always been a highly engaging way to learn. When games focus on academic content to which students have already been exposed, they serve as a powerful form of review as well as energizers for students. Multiple academic games are described in the book *Teaching Basic, Advanced, and Academic Vocabulary* (Marzano, 2020).

Charades is an effective game for vocabulary review. The teacher writes vocabulary words from the current unit or proficiency scale on index cards and students or groups draw cards and silently act out the words. Group charades can help take the pressure off individual students. Games like Pictionary that require students to create nonlinguistic representations are also useful for vocabulary review, and can be organized very quickly and spontaneously. They can also highlight central ideas within a story: students can draw an event, character, setting, and so on.

The game "Which One Doesn't Belong?" (see www.wodb.ca) is great for mathematics warm-ups. Students look at a group of four objects (shapes, numbers, or graphs) and identify patterns and similarities to identify the odd one out. Figure 3.13 shows several examples. The central task in this type of activity is recognizing patterns of characteristics. This skill is an explicit and implicit part of many mathematics standards. Perhaps the most interesting part of this activity is that different figures in a set of four can be described as the outlier depending on which characteristics are used. Consider set 2: If you focus on the color, then the arrow at the bottom right is the outlier since it is the only one with the same border and fill colors. However, if you focus on the shapes, then the circle is the outlier since the other three figures have multiple edges.

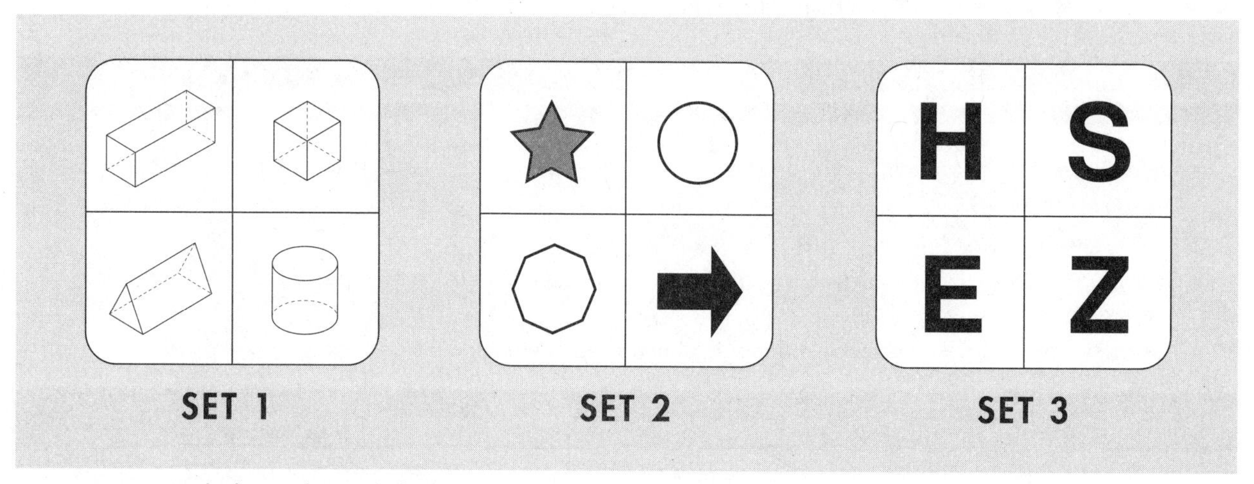

FIGURE 3.13: Which one doesn't belong?

Finally, teachers can include relevant games when designing playlists around specific content. For example, a science unit on ecosystem interactions could include a link to the game "Feed the Dingo," where students strive to create a balanced desert ecosystem. Websites like Legends of Learning (www.legendsoflearning.com) create playlists of games based around mathematics and science curriculum. Interactive online games on websites like Kahoot! (www.kahoot.com) and Quizizz (www.quizizz.com) allow teachers to choose from prepopulated quizzes or create their own. Students can compete against each other and view the results on a real-time leaderboard. Quizlet (www.quizlet.com) allows teachers to input vocabulary words, definitions, pictures, and so on, and create flash cards and other games. Classroom management platforms like Classcraft often have incorporated games. Teachers can input questions and answers, and teams or individuals have a "boss battle" where they fight monsters using knowledge. Correct answers earn points within the platform. Finally, a game day, with students playing classic board games just for fun, is a simple way to break up the typical routine. Playing these types of games can be a reward, or simply a way to promote an atmosphere of collaboration and fun and to allow students to unwind.

Figure 3.14 lists visible evidence for element VIh.

Visible evidence for effective instruction and guidance includes teachers doing the following.
• Using academic games of inconsequential competition to review content from the current unit of study (for example, What Is the Question?, Name That Category, Talk a Mile a Minute, Classroom Feud, and Which One Doesn't Belong?) • Using academic games of inconsequential competition to review content from previous units of study (for example, What Is the Question?, Name That Category, Talk a Mile a Minute, Classroom Feud, and Which One Doesn't Belong?) • Turning questions into impromptu games
Visible evidence for desired student actions and behaviors includes students doing the following.
• Engaging in academic games enthusiastically • Deepening their understanding of content while playing the academic games
Visible evidence for students' understanding and awareness includes students doing the following.
• Describing the content the games were focused on • Explaining how games have enhanced their understanding of the content

Source: © *2021 by Robert J. Marzano.*

FIGURE 3.14: Visible evidence for element VIh.

Understanding and Planning for Design Area VI

Understanding and planning for design area VI begin with an examination of the dynamics of engagement. To do so, it is necessary to consider the various types of memory and how they relate to student engagement. Figure 3.15 depicts three types of memory and how they interact with the outside world. For a detailed discussion of the interaction of these types of memory, readers should consult *Managing the Inner World of Teaching* (Marzano & Marzano, 2015).

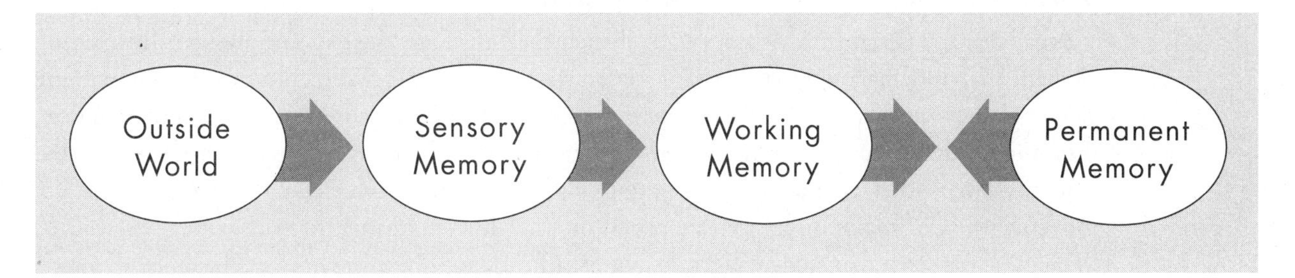

Source: Marzano & Pickering, 2011, p. 7.

FIGURE 3.15: Types of memory and how they interact.

Figure 3.15 depicts the process by which human beings receive and filter incoming information in their working memories and how permanent memory is involved in this process. The outside world constitutes everything that is happening in one's immediate environment. However, a person is not aware of everything that is occurring. Rather, sensory memory encodes specific stimuli from the outside world—images, sounds, smells, tastes, and so on. One might say sensory memory is the conduit to the outside world. Sensory memory stores information for a short period of time only. As John Anderson (1995) noted, "The environment typically offers much more information at one time than we can attend to and encode. Therefore much of what enters our sensory system results in no permanent record" (p. 160).

Working memory's job is to process and make sense out of all the information received by sensory memory from the outside world. It translates the images and other sensations into recognizable persons, places, things, and events. When we say students in a class are engaged, we mean they are paying attention to and making sense out of what is occurring in the classroom, whether it be what the teacher is saying or doing, what their classmates are saying or doing in the context of group work, or what they are reading and watching. However, permanent memory also feeds information into working memory. Permanent memory contains everything a person knows (academic or otherwise) and representations of everything that person has done or thought of doing. Sometimes in a classroom, a student's permanent memory is feeding information to working memory that helps the student learn the content being addressed in class at that moment. For example, if the teacher is presenting a lesson on fractions and permanent memory is feeding the student prior knowledge about fractions, then permanent memory is aiding in the learning process. However, if permanent memory is feeding the student's working memory images of what the student plans to do as soon as school lets out, then permanent memory is detracting from the learning process.

As far as engagement in a classroom setting is concerned, one can think of it as a battle for working memory. In effect, whatever is in a student's working memory at any point in time is what that student is paying attention to. The battle for students' attention can be summarized in the following question: Will students' working memories be filled with what is occurring in the outside world—such as content being presented by the teacher or the activity the teacher has assigned—or will students' working memories be filled with information from permanent memory such as the television program they saw the night before or the conversation they had with friends right before class? At a very basic level, all the elements described as part of design area VI are designed to ensure that students are filling their working memories with the information from the outside world as directed by the teacher. The teacher's job is to determine at any moment in time what type of activity will most probably capture students' interest powerfully enough to override possible distractions from the inner world in students' permanent memories.

Recall that this design area includes eight elements. Of these, teachers should always be employing element VIa, noticing and reacting when students are not engaged. Teachers will use the remaining elements when specific situations arise. For example, when teachers sense a general lack of attention, they might employ strategies from element VIb, increasing response rates. When teachers sense that students' levels of energy are low, they might employ strategies from element VIc (using physical movement), VId (maintaining a lively pace), or VIe (demonstrating intensity and enthusiasm). When teachers sense that students have lost interest in what is occurring in class, they might employ strategies from element VIf (presenting unusual information), VIg (using friendly controversy), or VIh (using academic games). Finally, when planning to use these elements as tools to enhance engagement, teachers should keep in mind that the strategies in elements VIf (presenting unusual information), VIg (using friendly controversy), and VIh (playing academic games) can take a significant amount of time and resources to execute well. Consequently, they require overt planning on the part of teachers. For example, teachers should plan for the specific pieces of unusual information they will present and what they will do to help students react to that content. Although friendly controversy can be executed in an ad hoc manner, the more complex versions such as structured debates must be well thought out and organized. Similarly, a teacher can design academic games on the spot, but those games are typically more effective when detailed and well defined in advance.

Design Area VII: Comfort, Safety, and Order

Design area VII addresses the basic needs of students. These deal with comfort, safety, and order. We refer to these considerations as basic needs because human beings look to see them taken care of before they can fully attend to anything else. If students are not physiologically comfortable in the classroom, they likely will not be able to pay attention to the academic content. If students do not believe they are physically and psychologically safe, they will likely not be able to pay attention to academic content. If students perceive the environment to be disorderly, they will likely not be able to pay attention to academic content. There are six elements in this design area.

VIIa. Organizing the physical layout of the classroom

VIIb. Demonstrating withitness

VIIc. Acknowledging adherence to rules and procedures

VIId. Acknowledging lack of adherence to rules and procedures

VIIe. Establishing and adapting rules and procedures

VIIf. Displaying objectivity and control

The following sections detail each one.

VIIa. Organizing the Physical Layout of the Classroom

The purpose of this element is to provide students with a physically and psychologically comfortable environment. The organization and decoration of a classroom send a message to students. A well-organized classroom communicates planning, preparation, and respect. A poorly organized classroom communicates the opposite.

Students spend many hours within the four walls of a classroom, and teachers should put themselves in their students' shoes and ask themselves what type of environment they would prefer. Generally, a range of seating options is best, as one size definitely does not fit all. High-top tables and regular tables with the legs removed provide varying surface heights, allowing students to stand up to work or sit on the floor. Padded chairs, rocking chairs, and exercise balls provide a comfortable place to sit for an extended period of time while still allowing movement. Areas of the room should be available for students to spread out and work, perhaps lying down or leaning up against a cupboard or wall. Figure 3.16 depicts a classroom with flexible seating options.

FIGURE 3.16: Furniture options.

Having a place for students to come together as a group is critical for both instruction and classroom culture. Most primary classrooms prominently feature a meeting space, often with colorful carpets designating seating patterns. Similarly, intermediate classrooms can have meeting places for student gatherings. In this space, the class can hold meetings facilitated by an appointed classroom leader, take votes on classroom choices, give presentations, view videos, and even gather for extracurricular opportunities like watching a baseball game. The meeting space is like the family room of the classroom.

In addition to furniture placement, the teacher must consider the location of materials and classroom resources. Materials should be stored in ways that students can access them easily and independently. Locating materials where the teacher is not the gatekeeper to the supplies also creates a classroom job for students—materials manager. This manager's job is to ensure that materials are put away correctly, available to students, and not in need of repair or replacement. However, teachers are wise to stash away many of the supplies they get at the beginning of the year and ration them throughout the year to prevent shortages.

Classroom libraries should be an easily accessible and prominently displayed part of the setting. Students should be in charge of the organization and management of the classroom library. Accordingly, class librarian is another job that students can take on. The class librarian can display his or her favorite book, post book reviews written by classmates, and add students' self-published works to the library.

Classroom decorations should be aesthetically pleasing. Houseplants give a soothing touch, and provide students with a responsibility and a job to do. Lamps and other lighting options can be easier on the eyes than overhead fluorescents. As the year progresses, student artwork, work examples, and ideas should be displayed around the room. Teachers can take pictures of the students working—or better yet, give students the camera and assign the role of photographer. Their pictures should be displayed prominently, much as someone would display family photos at their home.

Figure 3.17 lists visible evidence for element VIIa.

Visible evidence for effective instruction and guidance includes teachers doing the following.
• Placing student seats strategically to allow easy grouping and movement within the classroom • Designing classroom décor in a way that makes the classroom feel friendly • Ensuring students have easy access to learning materials • Creating areas for whole-group instruction, group work, and learning centers • Involving students in the design process for the classroom
Visible evidence for desired student actions and behaviors includes students doing the following.
• Moving easily about the classroom • Making use of materials and learning centers • Accessing and using examples of their work the teacher has displayed • Accessing and using the information on bulletin boards
Visible evidence for students' understanding and awareness includes students doing the following.
• Describing the physical environment of the classroom as pleasant and conducive to learning • Explaining what they like about the physical layout of the classroom

Source: © *2021 by Robert J. Marzano.*

FIGURE 3.17: Visible evidence for element VIIa.

VIIb. Demonstrating Withitness

Demonstrating withitness refers to the teacher staying vigilant to everything that occurs in the classroom and taking appropriate actions if any disruptions arise. Even though it is not used outside of education, the term *withitness* has been common in discussions of classroom management since it was first popularized by Jacob Kounin in his 1970 book *Discipline and Group Management in Classrooms*. There he noted that one of the characteristics of effective classroom managers is that they are extremely aware of what is going on and what might go on at all times—hence the term *withitness*.

At a very basic level, withitness manifests as teachers being on the move, whether they are speaking to the whole class or monitoring group and independent work. They use proximity to students as a behavior management tool. Teachers can even sit down at a table with a specific group of students, but still speak to the entire class whenever warranted. Visually scanning the room to monitor student behavior and making eye contact with students are also elements of withitness. Students should be expected to make eye contact with the teacher whenever the teacher asks for their attention.

If teachers observe behavior that needs correcting, they can use nonverbal redirection strategies to manage students without interrupting instruction. These strategies are not specific to a competency-based system; they are common tools of the teaching trade. Standing behind or near a student or group that is talking during instruction, for instance, is a good way to redirect students' attention. Looking in the student's direction, giving a knowing glance, nodding, shaking your head "no," and tapping the desk or shoulder of a student are all ways to let an off-task or disruptive student know that you are aware of their behavior and would like them to stop.

It is important, however, that teachers do not call out students in front of the rest of the class, but make an effort to quietly and discreetly let them know they are expected to do better. With certain students, the teacher can establish a predetermined signal. For example, say a squirmy student has set a goal to stay seated and focused during instruction. The teacher and student might agree that if the student needs to stand up, stretch, or walk around in the back of the room while the teacher is giving instruction, the student will show a specific hand signal for approval. With another student, the teacher might tug on his own ear, or pat his head briefly, to signal that the student needs to follow a set of predetermined steps for redirection. Teachers might also prompt students to employ a hand signal when they are being distracted by other students—the classic peace sign is a good example of a nonverbal peer-to-peer redirection that can be employed as part of an instructional SOP.

In a competency-based system, withitness is not only about knowing how students are behaving, or whether or not they are on task. It is also about knowing each student's current standing relative to the proficiency scales. Teachers need to be able to approach a student or a group of students and know which learning targets they are working on and their progress on those targets. This allows the teacher to deliver precise, on-the-spot instruction, guidance, or support. Awareness of all students' current academic focus can be difficult to manage, which is why an online LMS that readily displays such information is extremely beneficial. Teachers can quickly view real-time reports pertaining to students' status on proficiency scales. If an online platform is not available, teachers might create progression matrices for current proficiency scales and post them in the classroom. Students would identify their current position with a magnet, number, or other nonidentifying marker that the teacher can reference at a glance.

Figure 3.18 (page 108) lists visible evidence for element VIIb.

Visible evidence for effective instruction and guidance includes teachers doing the following.
• Attending to potential problems before they occur • Proactively taking preemptive action to avoid disruptions in the classroom • Occupying all quadrants of the classroom and making regular eye contact with each student • Using a series of graduated actions to address behavior issues
Visible evidence for desired student actions and behaviors includes students doing the following.
• Being aware of the fact that the teacher is noticing their behavior • Extinguishing potentially disruptive behaviors quickly and efficiently
Visible evidence for students' understanding and awareness includes students doing the following.
• Describing the teacher as aware of what is going on in the classroom • Explaining what they appreciate about the teacher's level of awareness

Source: © 2021 by Robert J. Marzano.

FIGURE 3.18: Visible evidence for element VIIb.

VIIc. Acknowledging Adherence to Rules and Procedures

It is every teacher's responsibility to fairly and equitably recognize students for their adherence to rules and procedures. This responsibility is common to teachers at all grade levels, yet it is particularly important at the elementary level and absolutely critical with primary students. To positively reinforce behavior, teachers should let students know that they notice and appreciate adherence to rules and procedures.

There are quite a few online classroom management platforms that facilitate this process, typically using some type of point system. ClassDojo (oriented toward primary students) and Classcraft (for older students) are two that have become popular with both students and teachers. ClassDojo does an excellent job of promoting a growth mindset, and Classcraft emphasizes student engagement. Both allow teachers to assign points to students and groups for specific predetermined behaviors.

Teachers can expand the utility of these platforms by using them to create a token economy. Students can use the points that they earn throughout the day, month, and year to purchase prizes or privileges. Teachers can set up a store that is open once a week (run by students, of course). Particularly effective prizes are those that give students an opportunity to do something special, or apply their reward at a chosen time. For example, a buddy coupon might allow a student who purchases it the option to sit with a buddy, which the student can redeem whenever he or she chooses.

Perhaps the most effective method for acknowledging positive behaviors in class is to give students the chance to recognize each other. During a class meeting, classmates can give kudos to their peers for jobs well done. For example, one student might raise her hand and say, "I'd like to give a kudos to Jesús for helping me hang up my backpack earlier this morning." Classes might keep a record of acts of kindness by writing each on a slip of paper and creating a chain to represent the chain reaction of kindness.

Additionally, students might receive acknowledgment for adhering to the classroom's code of conduct. Competency-based classrooms should also emphasize and reward cognitive, metacognitive, and life skills (which we discuss in depth in design area X, page 137). One way to highlight skill attainment or positive behavior is to have students nominate their peers to receive an icon or badge. This can be linked to the classroom's code of collaboration or current cognitive or metacognitive skill focus. The teacher and the class leadership team select nominees and give out badges during a class meeting. Students might display their badges on icon cards or data notebook covers. Figure 3.19 depicts sample badges.

It is important to note that positive student behavior should not always be linked to a tangible reward. At the end of a lesson, unit, or day, teachers can stop to acknowledge a student or particular group for doing a great job by giving brief shout-outs. No points or rewards need to be given, just a verbal pat on the back, or perhaps a quick email or phone call home to notify parents of a job well done. Technology has made parent communication quite easy with programs like ClassTag (https://home.classtag.com), Bloomz (www.bloomz.com), or Remind (www.remind.com). Teachers make it a habit to spend the first five minutes of their planning time sending home a nice message regarding a student who has done a good job that day.

Finally, schools or classrooms can set up programs where teachers choose one student from their class to be student of the week. The principal reads those students' names over the intercom or visits the classroom to announce the names, and those students receive a predetermined reward like extra recess, gym time with the principal, or a visit from a therapy dog.

Figure 3.20 (page 110) lists visible evidence for element VIIc.

Badges (earned)

Integrity
Effort (Hard Work)
Helpfulness
Positivity
Empathy
Kindness
Friendship

FIGURE 3.19: Badges.

VIId. Acknowledging Lack of Adherence to Rules and Procedures

Just as it is important to acknowledge students' adherence to rules and procedures, it is equally important to acknowledge lack of adherence to rules and procedures. Teachers should do so in a way that makes students aware of what the rule or procedure is and stimulates a desire to adhere to that rule or procedure.

Ultimately, all redirection should come from a place of love and trust. While students might not like what the teacher is saying, it is important for them to understand that the teacher is looking after their best interests. Teachers can only create this through bonding and building trust. When acknowledging lack of adherence to rules and procedures, teachers should, for the most part, attempt to have private conversations with students. Power struggles in front of the whole class will be a detriment to a culture of trust and positivity. Whether conversations happen at the teacher's desk, in a quiet corner of the classroom, in the hallway, or outside on the playground, students begin to understand that these conversations are not negative, and start to view them as coaching sessions with someone who cares about them.

Visible evidence for effective instruction and guidance includes teachers doing the following.
• Using verbal affirmations such as "thank you," "good job," "that's great," and so on • Using nonverbal affirmations such as a smile, nod of the head, thumbs up, and so on • Using privileges, activities, or items as positive consequences for following rules and procedures • Using color-coded behavior cards, daily recognition forms, and certificates to recognize adherence to rules and procedures • Communicating positively with students' parents or guardians recognizing the student for adherence to rules and procedures
Visible evidence for desired student actions and behaviors includes students doing the following.
• Being appreciative of the teacher's acknowledgment • Regularly adhering to rules and procedures
Visible evidence for students' understanding and awareness includes students doing the following.
• Describing their teacher as aware of their good behavior • Describing their teacher as appreciative of their good behavior

Source: © *2021 by Robert J. Marzano.*

FIGURE 3.20: Visible evidence for element VIIc.

Consequences that arise from a lack of adherence to rules and procedures should directly link to the behavior itself. For example, a student destroying supplies like markers or crayons should either have to replace such items or not be able to use them for a specified amount of time. A student having a hard time lining up to leave the classroom might be required to help develop a lining-up SOP and present it to the class, or visit the classroom of younger students and assist in teaching them about the appropriate way to line up.

Lack of adherence to rules and procedures for completing work or turning in assignments represents its own unique category of behavior. One principle of a competency-based system is that students who do not complete tasks and assignments are not providing evidence of their current status on proficiency scales. Ultimately, if no evidence is turned in, then students will not progress beyond their current level. This message should be communicated clearly to students from the beginning, and not come as a surprise at the end of the semester. Teachers can send home weekly progress reports or stay in constant communication with parents regarding students' overall progress and completion of tasks.

Figure 3.21 lists visible evidence for element VIId.

VIIe. Establishing and Adapting Rules and Procedures

The teacher responsibility inherent in this element is to engage students in the design and implementation of rules and procedures. Quite obviously, rules and procedures are necessary for a well-functioning school. Less obviously, the most effective rules and procedures are those that are developed jointly by teachers and students, simply because when students have a say in developing

Visible evidence for effective instruction and guidance includes teachers doing the following.
• Using verbal cues to redirect students who are not following a rule or procedure • Using nonverbal cues to redirect students who are not following a rule or procedure • Pausing or stopping teaching in response to recurring disruptive behavior to create an uncomfortable silence to redirect the behavior • Utilizing time-outs, overcorrections, home contingencies, high-intensity situational plans, and overall discipline plans to address a lack of adherence to rules and procedures
Visible evidence for desired student actions and behaviors includes students doing the following.
• Ceasing inappropriate behavior following the teacher's cues • Accepting consequences for their behavior as a natural part of the way class is conducted
Visible evidence for students' understanding and awareness includes students doing the following.
• Describing the teacher as consistent relative to consequences for not following rules and procedures • Describing the teacher as fair relative to consequences for not following rules and procedures

Source: © *2021 by Robert J. Marzano.*

FIGURE 3.21: Visible evidence for element VIId.

rules, they are more likely to adhere to them. Typically, rules are established first, and then procedures to follow those rules.

An important aspect of this element is that establishing rules and procedures is just the beginning—as indicated by the presence of *adapting* in the title. This means that teachers should systematically monitor and change rules and procedures as needed throughout the year, with a maximum amount of student input. Classroom rules and procedures are continually on teachers' minds with regard to efficacy and adjustments, not just at the beginning of the school year. This is the reason we do not list this element first within this design area; to do so might send the incorrect message that rules and procedures are a starting point that teachers can adequately address once and move on.

In order to create student buy-in and set the foundation for self-efficacy and agency, students should have the chance to provide input to the design of classroom rules and procedures and feedback as to how well they are working throughout the year. A teacher might begin by having groups brainstorm possible rules around safety, responsibility, or other general categories. Groups come to a consensus and identify a handful of rules they feel are the most important. Groups present their rules to the class, which then votes to define a reasonable list of accepted classroom rules. Ultimately, however, teachers should feel free to create a list of non-negotiable rules to have for their classrooms. While soliciting student input is a valuable process, teachers need to protect all students' rights to learn and their own freedom to teach. Thus, the teacher should ensure that rules are in place to protect these rights. For example, the teacher might notice that students have not suggested rules regarding respecting others' privacy, such as not asking their peers about their personal lives unless invited. The teacher could add such a rule to the list.

Rules alone are not enough. They should be accompanied by procedures, which define *how* students follow the rules. In the Marzano Academies model, procedures are usually articulated as standard operating procedures (SOPs). At the beginning of the year, teachers might create several SOPs to help students become comfortable with specific processes like what to do during morning arrival or how to pack up at the end of the day. Once students are familiar with SOPs, however, the class should contribute to their development. SOPs can take the form of a procedural list or a flow chart, and common SOPs should be posted in the classroom for easy and frequent reference. For example, many classrooms have an SOP for going to the restroom. A flow chart for this SOP (see figure 3.22) guides students through considerations like "Is the teacher giving instruction?" and "Would leaving now cause a distraction?" The teacher can then direct students to the SOP if they ask, "Can I use the restroom?" Over time, students no longer ask the teacher for permission to use the restroom but are empowered to use the SOP to select an appropriate time to go. The class can establish an SOP for any process the teacher or students deem necessary. Students should provide input and feedback regarding SOPs—if a process is not working, the class should collaborate to adjust or retire it.

Finally, within the Marzano Academies model, each classroom should develop a shared vision at the beginning of the year. It should be the product of group deliberation and set the cornerstone for student agency. The shared vision should be seen as the classroom's goal for the year and should be derived from the school's shared vision.

The affinity process and power voting are useful tools for collaboratively developing a shared vision. Both are explained in depth in *A Handbook for Personalized Competency-Based Education* (Marzano, Norford, Finn, & Finn, 2017). Briefly, though, the affinity process involves students generating multiple ideas and then categorizing them. Once categories are formed, students prioritize and narrow down the options. This list then becomes the focus of power voting. With power voting, students have multiple votes to cast so they can vote according to the intensity of their opinions. One version of power voting is called Spend a Dollar. With this strategy, students have four votes, each worth $0.25. A student might choose to spend her four votes all on one option, or she might choose to spend $0.25 on each of four options.

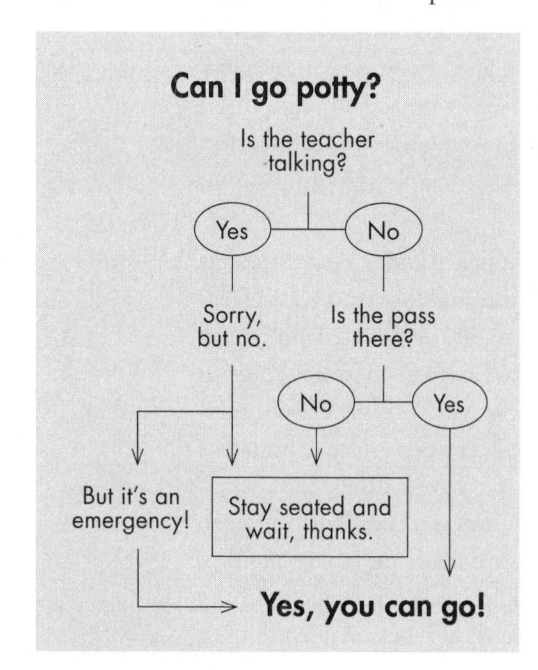

FIGURE 3.22: Primary classroom SOP for using the restroom.

After establishing a classroom shared vision, the class should also articulate a classroom code of collaboration to guide students toward achievement of their shared vision. Again using an affinity process and power voting, students should identify a handful of traits that they feel will benefit their learning and overall moral development. The teacher should provide lessons around the traits and the class can set a goal if there is one trait in particular they want to work on. So that students can monitor and self-assess their progress on these traits, the teacher can create a rubric, as exemplified in figure 3.23. At the end of the day, a teacher might ask students to fill out a self-assessment matrix (figure 3.24), and collect this information to see how the class is doing as a whole. Students who are meeting proficiency according to the rubric can receive a badge, and new traits can be added and others retired if the class feels they have reached overall proficiency.

Figure 3.25 (page 114) lists visible evidence for element VIIe.

Code of Collaboration Rubric	4 I am a role model for others.	3 I can do this myself, without reminders.	2 I have some success with reminders.	1 My teacher is helping me on this goal.
Be helpful to others.	I encourage my classmates to help other people. I discuss with others the importance of being helpful.	I help my teammates when they are struggling. I lend a hand when someone needs it—without being asked. I ask for help from my peers.	I know why it is important to be helpful. Sometimes I have to be reminded to help out when others need me.	I am learning about being helpful. I am trying to be helpful to others.
Be positive.	I am a cheerleader for the class, and always give praise to others for a job well done. I always give a cheer when meeting with partners. I am a school leader for positivity.	I have good things to say about other people. I point out the good parts, rather than focus on the difficult parts. I am a team player.	Sometimes I need reminders to be positive. I sometimes focus on what's difficult, or parts I don't like. I understand the importance of being positive.	I am working with others to try and focus on the things that are good. I can practice being positive with the teacher's help.

FIGURE 3.23: Rubric for code of collaboration traits.

How did I do today? Be truthful. Be thoughtful.	September 17	September 18	September 19	September 20	September 24	September 25	September 26	September 27	September 28
Helpful									
Effort									
Positivity									
Integrity									
What have I mastered?									
Where can I improve?									
What is my goal for the next two weeks?									

FIGURE 3.24: Self-assessment matrix.

Visible evidence for effective instruction and guidance includes teachers doing the following.
• Involving students in the design of rules and procedures • Developing a shared vision and code of conduct • Using a small set (5–8) of classroom rules • Explaining rules and procedures to students • Systematically modifying and reviewing rules and procedures with students • Posting rules and procedures around the classroom • Periodically asking students to self-assess their level of adherence to classroom rules and procedures
Visible evidence for desired student actions and behaviors includes students doing the following.
• Being involved in the processes of designing rules and procedures • Following the rules and procedures • Regulating their own behavior relative to rules and procedures • Engaging in modifying rules and procedures
Visible evidence for students' understanding and awareness includes students doing the following.
• Describing established rules and procedures • Describing how well they do in terms of following classroom rules and procedures • Describing the classroom as an orderly place

Source: © *2021 by Robert J. Marzano.*

FIGURE 3.25: Visible evidence for element VIIe.

VIIf. Displaying Objectivity and Control

By displaying objectivity and control, the teacher behaves in such a way that students perceive him or her as someone who will treat everyone fairly. Whether or not it is always apparent, students look to their teachers for objectivity and personal control. They do not want their teachers to exhibit swings in behavior or mood. While teachers experience pressures from school and home and strong feelings are natural human tendencies, objectivity and control are not feelings. They are behavioral decisions. The message that teachers should convey through their behavior is that what happens in the classroom cannot upset their calm demeanor—even when they might feel anything but calm.

When teachers have a very clear set of rules, expectations, and possible consequences, and they show a high level of consistency when holding students accountable to those rules, students begin to perceive them as someone who is fair and just. SOPs that detail expectations for appropriate behavior are highly useful to this end (see figure 3.26). A defined procedure allows students to clearly understand what processes the teacher will employ. Such SOPs can also have tiers for escalating behavior, with detailed examples of behavior that would cause the teacher to enact each consequence, steps students can take, and steps the teacher will take. This clarity allows teachers to objectively and unemotionally follow the outlined steps.

If a teacher feels as though he or she is reaching the limits of sanity, we recommend joining the class in play. The teacher might join the class for gym, play along with students during recess, or take the class outside for an impromptu break. If the stress is getting too high, teachers can take a break. While a teacher cannot simply leave the classroom at any point in time, some teachers have established relationships with other teachers or school leaders such that they can call on them to take over their classrooms for a short while if needed. Using a less obtrusive approach, teachers can post visual reminders somewhere in their rooms that trigger them to follow specific mental strategies. For example, a teacher might post a picture of a fluffy cloud on the wall. Anytime she begins to feel stressed or perceives that she is beginning to lose control, she can look at the picture of the fluffy cloud and remind herself to take a deep breath and practice a quick mindfulness technique.

While teachers need to be calm and display objectivity and control, it is useful for students to understand that the teacher is constantly working on making this happen. Teachers can share with students some of their personal strategies for monitoring their own feelings and keeping themselves calm. Finally, teachers can take time throughout the day to have students practice mindfulness, self-reflection, or other control strategies. As an aid to developing these skills in students, teachers might also describe times when those very strategies were effective for them.

Figure 3.27 lists visible evidence for element VIIf.

Being Quiet SOP

1. Stop what you're doing

- But what if I'm not finished with what I'm currently working on? Please pause for the moment.

2. Close your computer and limit any distractions

- No drawing, using fidget toys, and so on.

3. Focus

- Listen, face the speaker, establish eye contact, and use active listening.
- What if I have a question or comment? Raise your hand and wait patiently.

4. Be quiet and listen

- No speaking, making sounds, or making noises.
- What if someone talks to me or is noisy around me? Give them the two-finger peace sign and return to active listening.

FIGURE 3.26: SOP for being quiet.

Visible evidence for effective instruction and guidance includes teachers doing the following.
• Monitoring his or her own emotions in the classroom • Maintaining a cool exterior when dealing with conflict in the classroom • Identifying emotional triggers and other sources of stress in the classroom so he or she can recognize them when they occur and utilize coping strategies in order to stay calm • Demonstrating assertiveness in tense situations but doing so while showing respect for students and navigating classroom relationships
Visible evidence for desired student actions and behaviors includes students doing the following.
• Generally appearing calm and relaxed • Quickly settling down when they have been agitated
Visible evidence for students' understanding and awareness includes students doing the following.
• Describing the teacher as someone who is in control of himself or herself and in control of the class • Saying that the teacher does not hold grudges or take things personally

Source: © *2021 by Robert J. Marzano.*

FIGURE 3.27: Visible evidence for element VIIf.

Understanding and Planning for Design Area VII

Design area VII deals with students' perceptions of comfort, safety, and order. These are basic needs for all human beings. The Marzano Academies model for this important aspect of instruction is grounded in the well-known hierarchy of needs and goals developed by Abraham Maslow (1943, 1954). Maslow's hierarchy originally had five levels: (1) physiology, (2) safety, (3) belonging, (4) esteem within a community, and (5) self-actualization. Later versions (Koltko-Rivera, 2006; Maslow, 1969, 1979) included a sixth level referred to as connection to something greater than self. Maslow used the term *needs* to describe the elements of his hierarchy but also alluded to the levels as *goals*.

Robert J. Marzano, Darrell Scott, Tina H. Boogren, and Ming Lee Newcomb (2017) adapted Maslow's hierarchy to meet the purpose and focus of the academy model in the book *Motivating and Inspiring Students*. Briefly, though, the six levels of needs and goals are referred to as a hierarchy because the higher levels are generally not available without fulfilling the lower levels. Students cannot think much about their need for belonging if they believe their physical safety is in jeopardy, for example. Figure 3.28 depicts the organization of all six levels.

The six levels of Maslow's hierarchy are important considerations for classrooms and form the foundations for design areas VII, VIII, IX, and X. Referencing the hierarchy, one might say that students are continually asking themselves the following questions.

- **Level one:** Is this situation physiologically comfortable?
- **Level two:** Does this situation provide me with a sense of physical safety?
- **Level three:** Does this situation provide me with a sense of belonging?
- **Level four:** Does this situation make me feel like I am valued?
- **Level five:** Does this situation allow me to work on things related to my personal interests?
- **Level six:** Does this situation make me feel like I'm a part of something important?

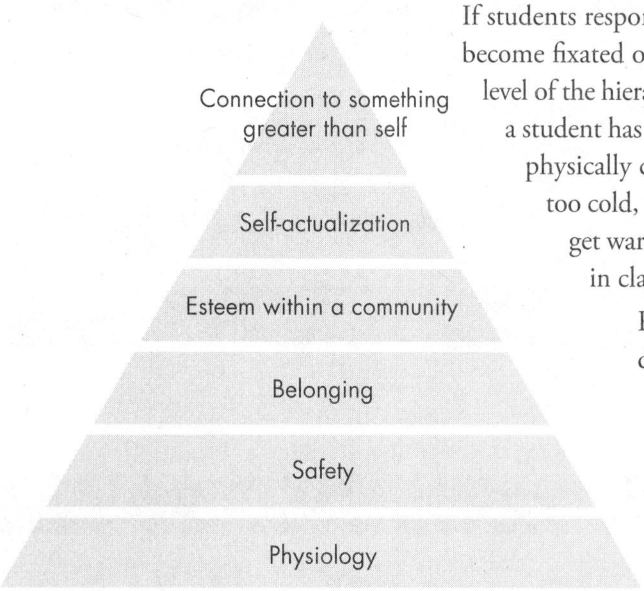

If students respond in the negative to any of these questions, they can become fixated on trying to fulfill the needs or goals at that particular level of the hierarchy, unable to attend to anything else. For example, if a student has a negative answer to the first question (Is this situation physically comfortable?) because the temperature in the room is too cold, the student's focus will likely be on thinking of ways to get warm as opposed to the academic content being addressed in class.

Relative to design area VII, the extent to which students in a classroom feel a sense of comfort, safety, and order is a function of the extent to which the teacher addresses the first two levels of the hierarchy. This design area includes six elements that help the teacher directly address students' needs related to physiological comfort and safety.

Connection to something greater than self
Self-actualization
Esteem within a community
Belonging
Safety
Physiology

Source: Marzano, Scott, et al., 2017, p. 3.

FIGURE 3.28: Maslow's hierarchy of needs and goals.

VIIa. Organizing the physical layout of the classroom

VIIb. Demonstrating withitness

VIIc. Acknowledging adherence to rules and procedures

VIId. Acknowledging lack of adherence to rules and procedures

VIIe. Establishing and adapting rules and procedures

VIIf. Displaying objectivity and control

To a certain extent, teachers should be continually thinking about whether they are adequately addressing each of these elements. In other words, teachers must be prepared for a variety of eventualities relative to this design area. With such preparation and awareness, teachers can make many corrections on the spot, especially for elements such as ensuring adequate acknowledgment of adherence to rules and procedures and lack of adherence to rules and procedures. Some elements like organizing the physical layout of the classroom to meet students' needs for physiological comfort and safety require more time, resources, and preparation to make necessary adjustments. Much of this type of preparation and planning occurs at the beginning of the school year.

Summary

This chapter deals with the domain of context in the Marzano Academies instructional model. It represents the overall environment that teachers create in the classroom. One might think of context as the social-emotional environment in the classroom. It includes three design areas. Design area V addresses grouping and regrouping, which includes three elements and deals with the manner in which the teacher groups students on a short-term and long-term basis to enhance their learning. Design area VI includes eight elements related to engagement, all of which are designed to fill students' working memories with the events and activities that deal directly with what is occurring in the classroom. Design area VII addresses students' basic needs for safety, comfort, and order. Its six elements focus on students' physiological comfort and safety. Visible evidence for teachers and students was described for each element in each design area to aid teachers in determining how effective their actions are relative to the intended outcomes of each element.

CHAPTER 4

Self-Regulation

In the Marzano Academies model, the domain of self-regulation concerns students' ability to monitor and manage their emotions, thoughts, and behaviors in ways that are acceptable to specific situations and produce positive results. Self-regulation is a tacit goal of CBE classrooms in general and Marzano Academies classrooms in particular. The CBE system itself requires students to exhibit self-regulation through activities such as conducting self-assessment, managing the time they take to work through the curriculum, and the like. In the Marzano Academies model, self-regulatory skills and awareness are directly taught through the design areas in this domain.

The design areas and elements in this domain guide teachers to create supportive classroom environments and deliver instruction that fosters students' self-regulation. The domain includes three design areas: design area VIII, belonging and esteem; design area IX, efficacy and agency; and design area X, metacognitive and life skills. Each of these is rooted in various levels of Maslow's hierarchy.

Design Area VIII: Belonging and Esteem

Design area VIII addresses students' perceptions of the extent to which they are welcome as members of the classroom community and whether they are valued members of that community. If students feel excluded or unimportant, it is difficult for them to self-regulate. Stated differently, the skills necessary to self-regulate do not function well if an individual does not perceive he or she is in a community that welcomes and values him or her. Belonging and esteem are basic needs that must be met before one can attend effectively to the self-regulatory skills (Marzano & Marzano, 2015; Marzano & Pickering, 2011; Marzano, Scott, et al., 2017).

There are four elements in this design area.

VIIIa. Using verbal and nonverbal behaviors that indicate affection

VIIIb. Demonstrating value and respect for reluctant learners

VIIIc. Understanding students' backgrounds and interests

VIIId. Providing opportunities for students to talk about themselves

The following sections detail each one.

VIIIa. Using Verbal and Nonverbal Behaviors That Indicate Affection

The teacher responsibility inherent in this element is to provide students with overt messages that he or she cares for them at a personal level. Students want to know that the teacher they have been assigned to has their best interests at heart, and if they are vulnerable and try something new, their vulnerability will be protected and rewarded in the end.

Exhibiting behaviors that show care for students is something that teachers should start the second students enter the building. Teachers should greet students at the entrance to the classroom as often as possible and allow students to choose how they would like to be greeted, perhaps by posting visual depictions for handshake, high five, fist bump, or hug. Teachers should remember that the smiles they give students in the morning might be the first a student has received since he or she left school the previous day. Likewise, teachers should not be afraid to allow students to show them affection. Of course, this must be done appropriately and with caution. It is always wise to let students initiate contact, especially while teachers are getting to know students.

Teachers should engage in regular and natural conversations with students about topics other than schoolwork. Sitting with students at the lunch table, playing with them during recess, joining them at a board game, or conversing with them during a break are all effective ways to develop and strengthen bonds between teachers and students. Academy teachers should take the time to find common interests with their students, and interact with students about those interests throughout the year.

Teachers might also take the time to run student interest clubs that meet during lunch or after school. Puzzle clubs, fantasy football clubs, anime clubs, or clubs centered on anything else students are interested in can be formed. Teachers might also use clubs as rewards for students, like a cartoon lunch group where students who earn the reward eat lunch and watch cartoons with the teacher. If time allows, teachers can try to attend after-school activities that students are involved in such as sporting events, musical events, or art displays. Ultimately, students crave teachers' attention and affection. It is especially powerful when teachers find time to demonstrate affection for students outside of regular class.

Figure 4.1 lists visible evidence for element VIIIa.

Visible evidence for effective instruction and guidance includes teachers doing the following.
• Greeting students at the door of the classroom • Holding informal conferences with students • Attending students' activities outside of school • Utilizing a schedule to seek out and talk with a few students each day • Using physical gestures to signal affection and encouragement for students
Visible evidence for desired student actions and behaviors includes students doing the following.
• Responding positively to the teacher's verbal interactions • Responding positively to the teacher's nonverbal interactions
Visible evidence for students' understanding and awareness includes students doing the following.
• Describing the teacher as someone who cares for them • Describing the classroom as a friendly place

Source: © 2021 by Robert J. Marzano.

FIGURE 4.1: Visible evidence for element VIIIa.

VIIIb. Demonstrating Value and Respect for Reluctant Learners

While teachers must ensure the classroom is a welcoming environment for all students, they should also pay particular attention to reluctant learners and demonstrate that they are valued members of the community. The term *reluctant learner* is a descendant of the term *low-expectancy student.* For a detailed discussion of this term, see the book *The Art and Science of Teaching* (Marzano, 2007). Briefly, though, learners are not reluctant because of any inherent characteristics they might have. Rather, they learn to be reluctant as a result of the way they are treated. Past research (see Marzano, 2003, 2007) on teacher expectations found that educators tend to treat students for whom they have high expectations differently from students for whom they have low expectations. This is not a conscious behavior on the part of teachers, but as human beings, teachers tend to form opinions about students relatively quickly regarding how well or how poorly they will do academically. These initial opinions can be quite inaccurate.

Unfortunately, when teachers form low expectations about particular students, they tend to treat those students differently from those for whom they have high expectations. For example, they ask them fewer questions and the questions they do ask tend to be easier. Students, in turn, begin to interpret such actions as indications that they are not as smart or capable as other students. If this differential treatment continues, students become more and more reluctant to engage in classroom activities over time, particularly complex ones. This creates a vicious cycle. As students become more reluctant, teachers interpret their lack of engagement as a lack of interest or ability and tend to ignore these students even more. Teachers using the Marzano Academies model are constantly working to dismantle this dynamic.

One reliable strategy to use with reluctant learners is to invest a little extra energy and effort into learning about and showing interest in their lives. Often, reluctant learners have experienced trauma of one type or another in their lives and are hesitant to put themselves into a position of vulnerability. Building trust through positive relationships and bonding activities can help break down some of the initial barriers between teachers and reluctant learners. As mentioned in the discussion of element VIIIa, playing games with students, showing interest in their hobbies, involving them in team-building activities, engaging them in casual conversations, or simply asking them what they think about various topics are all ways of showing reluctant learners that you care.

Teachers should use what they learn about reluctant learners' lives and interests when designing their curriculum. A teacher can tally the results from a student interest survey, look for common themes and interests, and create a reference list to use in planning. For example, if a handful of identified reluctant learners show interest in anime, then the teacher can engage these students by incorporating anime into the next lesson. This is not to say that every unit and lesson needs to be tailored to fit the needs of a reluctant learner, but rather that extra consideration should be taken when choosing subject matter. For example, a teacher might choose topics she knows students are interested in when selecting passages to practice fluency in reading or word problems to solve in mathematics. Perhaps a teacher creates a reward for a student who likes sports by allowing that student to spend ten minutes watching highlights from his or her favorite team. Magazines focused on topics of interest, such as *Sports Illustrated Kids, National Geographic Kids, Ladybug Magazine, New Moon Girls,* and *Girls' Life,* can be a great option to have available for independent reading time.

Focusing on specific reluctant learners can have powerful transformative effects. For example, consider a specific third-grade student whose parents contact the teacher at the beginning of the year to voice their concerns about her reluctance and disinterest in school. On an interest survey that students take during the first week of school, she identifies that her favorite show is *Peppa Pig* and she loves all things related to the cartoon. A quick Google search by her teacher reveals an article from Newsela (www.newsela.com) about *Peppa Pig* and the show's popularity and controversy in China. During the first week of school, the teacher decides to use this article to introduce a procedure for close reading, much to the excitement—and disbelief—of this young student who is now viewing her classroom quite a bit differently.

Along with knowing the individual interests of reluctant learners, teachers should ensure that the overall culture of the classroom is one that overtly acknowledges hard work and growth, not just achievement. To begin with, teachers should cultivate a growth mindset with their students by taking the time to identify areas for growth, setting goals around those areas, readjusting when necessary, and celebrating not only student success but also the growth process as a whole. We discuss the growth mindset further in our discussion of design area X (page 137). Additionally, teachers can emphasize and celebrate students' improvement on their proficiency scale tracking matrices, better scores on timed multiplication tests, more words read per minute during fluency practice, and so on. Teachers can take the time to highlight and celebrate some of these daily successes during a daily wrap-up meeting where teachers can give shout-outs and ask for student kudos (see element VIIc, page 108). Shining the spotlight on these small successes can reassure reluctant learners that school and education represent positive and rewarding experiences.

Finally, teachers should examine their own beliefs to ensure that they do not harbor low expectations about specific students. More importantly, teachers should audit their behavior to ensure that they treat all students equitably, particularly as it relates to presenting students with challenging and complex tasks. In brief, this would involve teachers thinking through their class rosters and identifying their beliefs about how capable each student is at complex tasks. Teachers might even rank each student high, medium, or low. With this analysis as a backdrop, teachers would next try to identify the differences in the way they treat high- and medium-expectancy students as opposed to low-expectancy students when assigning complex tasks. The key awareness should be that any differential treatment of low-expectancy students constitutes inequitable behavior, even if the intent is to avoid frustrating or overburdening these students. While it is certainly a good strategy to adapt tasks for some students to ensure they understand the task and have the requisite background knowledge, it is not acceptable to deprive some students the opportunity to engage in complex tasks due to perceptions of their ability. Teachers who do so unwittingly convey to reluctant learners that they are not capable of successfully completing complex tasks.

Self-analysis of inequitable behaviors can be challenging and difficult for teachers because it discloses their biases. It's important to remember that all human beings have biases that they are probably not even aware of. In other words, biases are a natural human tendency. However, people can identify and change their biases. This type of self-analysis can apply to all areas of one's life with positive benefits for self and others. For a detailed discussion of how teachers might use such analysis, readers should consult *Managing the Inner World of Teaching* (Marzano & Marzano, 2015).

Figure 4.2 lists visible evidence for element VIIIb.

VIIIc. Understanding Students' Backgrounds and Interests

One way to communicate to students that they are welcome and valued is to know something about their personal lives and their backgrounds. Thus, teachers should seek out information about individual students in such a way as to demonstrate that they are interested in the lives of those individual students. While the previous section focused on communicating to reluctant learners that

Visible evidence for effective instruction and guidance includes teachers doing the following.
• Identifying differential treatment of reluctant learners • Using nonverbal and verbal indicators of respect with reluctant learners • Identifying and reflecting on expectation levels for all students working to ensure that he or she has high expectations for each student
Visible evidence for desired student actions and behaviors includes students doing the following.
• Treating each other with respect • Reluctant learners engaging in activities with the same frequency as other students
Visible evidence for students' understanding and awareness includes students doing the following.
• Saying the teacher cares for all students • Reluctant learners saying the teacher understands them

Source:

FIGURE 4.2: Visible evidence for element VIIIb.

they are valued and respected, this element is focused on getting to know more about all students in class to communicate that the teacher is interested in them as individuals.

Teachers should systematically set aside classroom time for the purpose of students openly sharing personal details, thoughts, and feelings. The 180 Connections program developed by Rachel's Challenge (Scott & Scott, 2018) provides a structure for both students and teachers to share information about themselves through daily prompts and conversations. Each day, students throughout the school respond to a single prompt, ranging from relatively mundane issues (for example, What is your favorite animal?) to fairly consequential issues (for example, What is something that has made you very sad?). One approach is that students in the class gather in a circle and take turns sharing their specific response while passing a talking stick or other item that indicates whose turn it is to speak. The teacher responds to the daily prompt first and students then follow in turn. Students always have the option of passing if they do not feel comfortable sharing.

During this sharing time, teachers can learn a wealth of information about their students. These conversations often shine a light on significant events in students' lives, allowing teachers to perhaps have more patience and understanding for their aberrant or off-task behavior. In extreme cases, students may reveal instances of abuse or neglect, or share thoughts of self-harm or suicide. Of course, if this ever occurs, it is mandatory for teachers to report significant incidents to the proper authorities in their state or province. Perhaps more commonly, students may reveal information that does not rise to the level of a crisis but still prompts the teacher to involve the school counselor or psychologist.

Another way to find out about students' background and interests is to ask the people who know them best—their parents and guardians. Teachers can survey families at the beginning of the year to get parents' input about their students' interests, perceived academic needs, and effective ways to make them comfortable and motivate them. This not only allows teachers to learn more about their students, but also allows parents' voices to be heard. Figure 4.3 (page 124) depicts a sample questionnaire that parents might fill out to aid the teacher in addressing their children's specific needs.

Parent Questionnaire

Student Name: ____

Parents/Guardians/Family Members:

Name: ______________________________ Relationship: ______________

Best way to reach you: ______________________________________

Name: ______________________________ Relationship: ______________

Best way to reach you: ______________________________________

What is your student's biggest strength? ______________________

____

____

What is your student's greatest area of need? __________________

____

____

How can I best motivate your student? ________________________

____

____

What is your student's favorite thing to do? ___________________

____

____

Is there anything else I should know about your student? _______

____

____

We are looking for volunteers of all shapes and sizes. Flexible schedule. Can work from home. No experience needed. Will train.

Possible work situations include: weekly or bi-weekly classroom help; special events; cut, paste, and staple materials.

- I can come in on Friday mornings to file papers for Friday Folders.
- I can help in the classroom on occasion. Please call when help may be needed.
- I can help outside the classroom on occasion. Please send materials home with my child when the need arises.
- I can send in prizes.

FIGURE 4.3: Questionnaire for parents.

Of course, teachers can also survey students directly by administering interest inventories. Such surveys are quite easy to construct; teachers need only design a small set of short constructed-response questions like the following.

- What is your favorite topic to study?
- What do you like to do for fun?
- What type of animal do you have as a pet or would you like to have as a pet?

These questions are general, but interest inventories can also focus on topics of study in class. For example, before starting a unit on weather, a teacher might pose questions like the following.

- What is the most interesting type of weather you have experienced?
- What types of storms do you like to be in?
- What types of storms do you not like to be in?
- What questions would you like to answer about weather?

Finally, teachers can learn a lot about students when they allow them to make choices throughout the day. Since choice is a cornerstone of a competency-based classroom, teachers have many opportunities to glean information about students' interests. For example, assume the class is working on a learning target that deals with summarizing content one has read. Rather than provide all students with the same reading passage, teachers might allow students to visit a site like Newsela and pick an article from a preselected set of options with a range of subjects. Since the learning goal of summarizing content is not affected by the subject of the article, it behooves the teacher to allow students to select their article based on their personal interests.

Figure 4.4 lists visible evidence for element VIIIc.

Visible evidence for effective instruction and guidance includes teachers doing the following.
• Utilizing student background surveys, opinion questionnaires, or informal class interviews to better understand students • Utilizing informal conferences, parent-teacher conferences, or informal conversations with students to get to know them • Having students set personal learning goals and connecting them to the learning goals within the content of the course
Visible evidence for desired student actions and behaviors includes students doing the following.
• Responding positively to the teacher's queries about them • Volunteering information about themselves • Being interested in the lives of their peers
Visible evidence for students' understanding and awareness includes students doing the following.
• Describing the teacher as someone who knows them or is interested in them • Saying that they feel that their teacher values them • Saying they know something about their peers in the class because of the teacher's efforts

Source: © 2021 by Robert J. Marzano.

FIGURE 4.4: Visible evidence for element VIIIc.

VIIId. Providing Opportunities for Students to Talk About Themselves

This element is similar to element VIIIc in that they both deal with information about students. However, the major distinction between the two is that this element is much more open ended in its intent, which is simply to provide opportunities for students to express themselves. It may even go beyond students talking about themselves and include talking about things they have seen, heard, or read that they find interesting or unusual. To enact this element, the teacher invites students to articulate things that are of interest to them personally. Doing so communicates that they are valued and respected as individuals.

It can be difficult for teachers to give up valuable instructional time to allow students to have personal conversations, but the return on investment is a strong classroom culture. Such activities are quite common at the beginning of the school year, but after this initial get-to-know-you phase of the school year is over, students should still have opportunities to share information about themselves. To this end, a teacher might have students create "passion presentations," where once a week they have time to share a passion of theirs (even if it is new). This could include a show-and-tell element where students bring something they would like to show off or are proud of.

Another way to give students the chance to share information about themselves is called Classmate of the Week or star students (Scott & Scott, 2018). Here, the teacher chooses one student per week to highlight. That student writes a short bio and reads it aloud at the morning meeting on Monday, and provides a picture of him- or herself for the teacher to hang on the board. Throughout the week, other classmates write compliments to the student. The student whose week it is receives special time to share information, stories, artifacts, and pictures. At the end of the week, the class creates a card that everyone signs and gives to the Classmate of the Week before he or she leaves on Friday.

Another way for students to share information about themselves, without having to stand up in front of the class and speak, is through the use of strength icons. We briefly discussed strength icons as part of element Vc, providing group support (page 88). Within the context of that element, students identify their strengths in terms of specific measurement topics so that their peers can call on them for help. Here, students identify more general strengths, which might have little to do with school.

At the beginning of the year, students choose icons that identify their strengths, such as drawing, humor, leadership, working through tough problems, making people feel welcome, spelling, reading, mathematics, technology, and so on. Students display their icons on posters that permanently hang in the classroom. As the year progresses, students can nominate their peers to receive special icons that represent specific traits the class is focusing on, like empathy, teamwork, and so on. The teacher can also create icons for instructional units, like "Wolf Ambassador" or "History Buff," to hand out to students who master the content. Class clubs can also have their own icons for members. These icon posters give students the chance to display traits and share strengths in a nonlinguistic way.

In addition to dedicated time for personal sharing, brief team-building activities can take place intermittently throughout the day. Students can quickly share something about themselves through organized activities like the following.

- **Inside-outside circle:** Half the class forms the inside circle and the other forms the outside circle. Students on the outside face in, and students on the inside face out so that every student is face to face with another student. The teacher provides a question or prompt and gives the students about a minute to think about their answers. Students describe their answers to their partners who in turn share their responses. When partners are done sharing, the teacher instructs the outer circle to rotate one person to their left (or right) to form new partners. The process repeats using the same prompt or a new prompt from the teacher.

- **Classroom mix and share:** Mix and share is a less structured activity where students stand and form groups of two or three and respond to a teacher question or prompt. On the teacher's signal, students move around and form new groups in which they share again.
- **Would you rather:** The teacher prompts students to state their preference between two hypothetical options, such as the ability to fly or the ability to become invisible. Would-you-rather questions are a fun and effective way to discuss both serious and silly things; students can also be prompted to share personal experiences, talk about their weekends, and so on.

Figure 4.5 lists visible evidence for element VIIId.

Visible evidence for effective instruction and guidance includes teachers doing the following.
• Providing systematic ways to highlight the personal interest of every student throughout the year • Engaging in informal discussions with students about their personal lives • Administering interest surveys • Administering student learning profiles • Planning breaks during instructional time so that students can draw links between what they are studying and their lives • Relating content to students' lives by relating content to what they know about students' interests and personal experiences
Visible evidence for desired student actions and behaviors includes students doing the following.
• Demonstrating interest in the lives of their peers • Engaging in activities that help them make connections between their personal interests and the class content • Sharing information about their personal interests
Visible evidence for students' understanding and awareness includes students doing the following.
• Saying that they are interested in the lives of their peers • Saying that the teacher is interested in them personally • Explaining how making connections between content and their personal interests makes class more interesting and enhances their content knowledge • Describing class as being relevant to them personally

Source: © 2021 by Robert J. Marzano.

FIGURE 4.5: Visible evidence for element VIIId.

Understanding and Planning for Design Area VIII

Design area VIII addresses students' senses of belonging and esteem, which are levels three and four of Maslow's hierarchy of needs and goals (see figure 3.28, page 116). As mentioned previously, when teachers are focusing on this design area, they are working to ensure students answer the following questions affirmatively.

- **Level three:** Does this situation provide me with a sense of belonging?
- **Level four:** Does this situation make me feel like I am valued?

Teachers using the academy model have the strategies in four elements at their disposal to produce positive responses to these questions.

VIIIa. Using verbal and nonverbal behaviors that indicate affection

VIIIb. Demonstrating value and respect for reluctant learners

VIIIc. Understanding students' backgrounds and interests

VIIId. Providing opportunities for students to talk about themselves

Of these, element VIIIa might be considered the omnibus element in that it relates to all students and both the belonging and esteem levels of the taxonomy. Element VIIIb focuses on the reluctant learner. (We also focus on the reluctant learner in two of the elements in design area IX, pages 134 and 135.) This focus is important because, by definition, reluctant learners are those for whom many of the general strategies teachers use do not work well. Teachers should maintain a constant awareness of these students with an eye toward making adaptations to meet their specific needs. Elements VIIIc and VIIId focus on students' sense of esteem by acknowledging their unique characteristics. All four of the elements in this design area contain strategies that teachers can use at a moment's notice as they become aware of opportunities to send the message that all students are welcome and valued.

Teachers should also plan to employ these strategies in advance, perhaps focusing on individual students. For example, for element VIIIa, a teacher might plan to demonstrate affection for specific students who have lately seemed withdrawn or troubled. For element VIIIb, the teacher might decide to pay particular attention to a reluctant learner who still appears disenfranchised in class. Similarly, the teacher might identify a student who has just joined the class and plan for ways to find out more about the student's background and interests (element VIIIc) and to encourage the student to talk about herself (element VIIId).

Design Area IX: Efficacy and Agency

Design area IX deals with the related constructs of efficacy and agency. Efficacy deals with beliefs, whereas agency deals with actions. One might say that these two constructs provide the necessary energy behind self-regulation. If an individual in a given situation does not believe she can exert control over that situation and does not take steps to exert that control, she cannot regulate her behavior in that situation. There are four elements in this design area.

IXa. Inspiring students

IXb. Enhancing student agency

IXc. Asking in-depth questions of reluctant learners

IXd. Probing incorrect answers with reluctant learners

The following sections detail each one.

IXa. Inspiring Students

The teacher's responsibility relative to this element is to design and execute activities that inspire students. Inspiring students may be one of the most important things classroom teachers can do.

It is certainly true that teachers inspire students in schools all across the country, and this has always been the case. The difference within the Marzano Academies model is that inspiration is something teachers plan for on a regular basis. While some students come to school with a natural enthusiasm for learning, many students need someone or something to elicit inspiration. Inspiration is a function of beliefs—when students see evidence of their ideals in action, they feel inspired (Marzano, Scott, et al., 2017). To aid in student inspiration, teachers need not aspire to be motivational speakers, psychologists, or life coaches. Merely being in touch with their students' needs, wants, and personalities provides teachers with great insights into things they can do to help them believe that their ideals and aspirations might be possible.

Within the classroom, motivational posters and quotes can provide inspiration for wandering eyes. The teacher might provide daily quotes for students to ponder at the class's morning meeting. Discussion of these quotes or reflection journal entries can prompt students to explore their meaning in more depth. Additionally, students can identify specific quotes that speak to them—quotes that will become a part of their personal code of ethics. Students might memorize these quotes, and talk about what they mean to them personally.

To foster inspiration, teachers can create projects or units designed to enhance students' self-actualization or connection to something greater than self. As described previously (page 116), these are the top two levels of Maslow's hierarchy. When human beings engage in activities that make them feel self-actualized or connected to something greater than themselves, they are inspired. A teacher might have students take part in a series of change-making or community service activities throughout the year. These activities are designed to make a difference in the students' classroom, school, community, and world. The teacher can design an initial activity to get things started—perhaps a school-supply drive or fundraising effort. Students create posters (see figure 4.6 and figure 4.7, page 130), spread the word, collect items from the donation bins, and so on. Such projects should happen quarterly, with students taking on more of the design and implementation elements as the year progresses. Ultimately, students should feel that they and their classmates are making a change in the world.

Source: © 2018 by Westminster Public Schools. Used with permission.

FIGURE 4.6: Canned food drive poster.

Students who are inspired by class service projects might be inclined to start or participate in a philanthropic or service club. The club might meet before or after school or during lunchtime, set goals around who they want to help, and initiate school- or community-wide projects to meet those goals. Perhaps the club holds a Halloween costume drive to give free costumes to local families, or maybe they organize a canned soup drive to benefit a local food pantry. These types of service projects could take place throughout the year and provide the students and school with an experience of giving back.

Teachers can help students experience the power of positive change by setting up situations whereby they can mentor younger students. Students can work with a

Source: © 2018 by Westminster Public Schools. Used with permission.

FIGURE 4.7: Candy drive poster.

class at a lower grade level or an individual younger student and provide role modeling and support in regular mentoring sessions. A common version of this is reading buddies, in which upper-elementary students partner with primary students to help them practice reading fluency. Teachers should discuss what mentoring means, and provide strategies on how to effectively mentor younger students. Regular mentoring time can be scheduled daily or weekly, followed by reflection for the mentor. Mentoring can also work in a buddy-classroom scenario, where two classrooms pair up and work together on projects or other school-culture-building activities.

Another way to provide inspiration is to show students examples of people who make a difference in the world. One resource is CNN 10—CNN's student-oriented news site (www.cnn.com/cnn10)—which includes a regular segment called CNN Heroes. Each CNN Heroes segment identifies a person who is making a difference in his or her community. Students could keep track of all the heroes they learn about over the course of the year, perhaps by using a data collection knowledge map in their reflection journals. Eventually, the teacher might ask students to choose a hero to research in more depth. Students might even write letters of appreciation to those heroes.

Visits from real-life heroes also allow students to see people making a difference in action. Students can nominate heroes from within or outside the school. Perhaps an office staff member presents about her charity work at the local animal shelter, or a student's uncle who is a firefighter can come in to speak with the class. These encounters with exemplary citizens can help light a spark of inspiration within an individual student or an entire classroom.

Finally, thinking about their future careers or life paths can also be inspiring to students. In order to help students set long-term goals and promote self-efficacy, teachers can organize an investigation into jobs and careers where students explore what they believe will be their dream job. Students can do research on careers; organize information into a flyer, pamphlet, poster, or display board; and present it to the class in a mock career fair. Students might even write a letter to and interview someone who has their dream job.

Figure 4.8 lists visible evidence for element IXa.

IXb. Enhancing Student Agency

The teacher responsibility inherent in this element is to engage students in activities that are specifically designed to enhance their sense of agency. Providing students with voice and choice relative to their learning is a powerful tool to this end. From the outset of the school year, teachers should begin building a culture based on student voice and choice. Voice and choice have been tacit aspects of virtually every design area discussed thus far, but within this element, they become the focal point.

Visible evidence for effective instruction and guidance includes teachers doing the following.
• Exposing students to inspirational stories and quotations on a systematic basis • Sharing with students what motivates and inspires them • Having students engage in projects that are relevant to them personally • Engaging students in altruism projects that connect them to something greater than themselves • Having students keep gratitude journals • Having students practice mindfulness
Visible evidence for desired student actions and behaviors includes students doing the following.
• Engaging in activities designed to inspire them • Engaging with community members in meaningful ways • Working on projects that are personally meaningful to them • Engaging in activities that increase their mindfulness
Visible evidence for students' understanding and awareness includes students doing the following.
• Describing the teacher as one who inspires them to do things they might not otherwise do • Describing class altruism projects that are personally fulfilling • Describing the gratitude and mindfulness activities as personally meaningful

Source: © *2021 by Robert J. Marzano.*

FIGURE 4.8: Visible evidence for element IXa.

Teachers can literally give students a voice by inviting them to provide constant and constructive feedback. By creating a pipeline for multiple forms of student input, teachers can gather data and check on students' well-being as well as the effectiveness of their instructional techniques. The following techniques enable teachers to listen to what their students have to say.

- **Daily data collection:** A routine activity where students submit data to the teacher regarding their status or growth on the proficiency scales for specific measurement topics
- **Weekly conferences:** A routine conference between teacher and students to discuss academic topics and bring up any issues and concerns
- **Parking lot:** A piece of chart paper or section of whiteboard where students can leave comments about how the class functions, often divided into sections for positive comments, questions, ideas, and things that need to change
- **Peaks and valleys:** A feedback opportunity, perhaps during daily or weekly wrap-up meetings, where students share their highs and lows from a certain time period or experience

As the year progresses, teachers should give their students more and more opportunities for choice. These efforts combine to provide students with a sense of ownership of their own learning. Providing students with leadership roles and job opportunities within the classroom is a particularly effective way to develop their sense of agency. When students take on roles and responsibilities, the classroom becomes a place where they no longer sit on the sidelines but play an active part in their educational journey. Primary teachers do this regularly with line leaders, door holders, and light switchers, thus helping students feel like valued members of their classroom community. This concept can be extended in higher grade levels by allowing student leaders to monitor class procedures and behavior through the use of predetermined rubrics, goal setting, and progress monitoring. For example, appointed classroom leaders could be responsible for monitoring the line-up procedure every day, providing the class with feedback, and ultimately using a rubric to give the class a score. They also track these scores and lead the class to set goals and earn rewards. This process can be applied to any procedure or segment of the day—morning arrival, carpet time, lining up, recess, hallway, lunch, end of day, and so on. Even more empowering, teachers can grant classroom leaders the autonomy to identify an area of needed growth within the classroom, lead the class in creating a rubric and setting goals and rewards, and monitor throughout the course of a predetermined cycle.

Another strategy is *enrichment time*. This involves dedicated daily time for a self-sustaining system of roles and responsibilities run entirely by students. It both increases student agency and incorporates voice and choice. To illustrate, for roughly thirty minutes every day, students engage in various roles, responsibilities, and tasks according to their weekly assignment. The teacher or class can establish several categories of jobs, which students rotate through. For example, a class might decide to create jobs in the categories of outreach, classroom maintenance, and magazine publishing.

Outreach deploys students throughout the building to participate in making their school a better place. Some students act as mentors to younger students, teach lessons, help with technology, or assist the teacher. Other outreach students go to the office to greet guests and lend a hand or to the library to shelve books and read to students. After spending time in their respective outreach roles, students return to their classroom and reflect on how they have helped make a difference within their school.

Students with classroom maintenance duties help keep the classroom tidy and running smoothly. For example, a student librarian organizes the classroom library, and posts reading recommendations. The health and wellness advisor is in charge of breakfast, lunch count, and snack, as well as giving out kudos to students who eat healthy during lunchtime. He or she might also help his or her peers track their heart rate and other vital signs that relate to their overall health, thus helping all students develop healthy life habits. The class meteorologist heads outside with handheld weather instruments to make observations, and posts the results in the classroom for their peers to see. Other classroom maintenance jobs include announcer and calendar person.

The third enrichment-time category in this example is magazine publishing. Imagine that a teacher decides to promote agency by having students publish a classroom magazine. Students decide to name it *The Falcon Report*, after the school's mascot. Each reporter gets to choose a topic within the guidelines of the magazine's four subsections—The Arts, The Science Page, Current Events, and The Back Page (humor). The reporters essentially execute short research projects of their choosing and report their findings to the community. Copies of the magazine are sent home and disseminated throughout the school. Because many members of the school community will see the magazine, students are writing for an authentic audience. The student reporters hold revising and editing circles and celebrate after the magazine goes to "press."

Finally, enrichment time is overseen by the class's head supervisor. This student holds many roles throughout the day, essentially acting as the classroom leader, and serves as the supervisor and evaluator during enrichment time. He or she uses rubrics and SOPs to determine how well the class performs during enrichment time. He or she also has lists of possibilities for students who are all done with their classwork. The primary purpose of enrichment time is for students to work on the content in their proficiency scales, but if they are up to date on their work, they can engage in other activities. Enrichment time ends with a class meeting led by the head supervisor during which students reflect and give out kudos. The head supervisor and *Falcon Report* editor choose one student as their star student of the day and recognize him or her for a job well done.

SOPs, as described in the discussion of element VIIe (page 110), are another classroom tool for developing student agency. In addition to creating and following SOPs for common classroom routines, the class can develop SOPs for any obstacles the teacher or students are facing in class. For example, a teacher who is having issues with students talking or being distracted during direct instruction can lead the class to develop a focus SOP with the purpose of reminding students of the steps they should take to exercise self-control and focus on the teacher. To develop such an SOP, the teacher would first engage students in a brainstorming session about what they believe are the biggest causes for the talking and distractions. Next, students generate possible solutions and strategies, and the class votes on their top choices. The teacher finalizes the SOP at a later point, adding or taking away elements as appropriate, and presents it to the class the following day. The teacher must also intentionally model and reinforce the new SOP's implementation as well as set daily goals and guide students in reflection until it becomes a regular part of the classroom.

Another set of activities that help students develop a sense of agency are those that foster their understanding of their own thought processes. These include growth mindset thinking and other metacognitive skills (see element Xc, page 143) but can also incorporate thinking that focuses on *future possible selves*. This concept is a subset of the theory of *possible selves thinking* (Markus & Nurius, 1986; see Marzano, Scott, et al., 2017, for a discussion of this theory's application to education). Future possible selves activities begin with students identifying the type of people they want to be—not necessarily what they want to accomplish in life but how they want to behave with other people, how hard they want to work, and so on. The teacher would start by explaining to students that all human beings have mental images of the way they would like to be in life. This typically involves traits like treating other people well, dedicating oneself to something or someone, living an honest life, and so on. However, people frequently don't live up to these images of their potential selves. As an act of individual agency, a person can compare the way he or she actually behaves on a daily basis with how he or she would like to behave. This simple act helps individuals identify specific behaviors they would like to foster in themselves. For example, a particular student might want to be patient with others. However, when he examines his day-to-day behavior, he finds that his actions are more consistently those of someone who is impatient. Teachers should lead such activities by describing the discrepancies they find in their own lives, and how they are working to bring their day-to-day selves more in line with their ideal possible selves. Teachers and students alike can identify behaviors they are going to work on and share how well they are doing with their target behaviors on a weekly basis.

Figure 4.9 (page 134) lists visible evidence for element IXb.

Visible evidence for effective instruction and guidance includes teachers doing the following.
• Involving students in the design and implementation of SOPs • Involving students in activities that provide them with a voice in how the classroom is run, such as affinity diagrams, parking-lot activities, plus-or-delta strategies, exit slips, or class meetings • Involving students in activities that involve choice, such as choice boards, choice menus, must-do and may-do lists, or options for demonstrating proficiency • Explicitly teaching about a growth mindset and cultivating it in students by praising effort rather than intelligence and having students reflect on their level of effort • Engaging students in possible selves activities to imagine what they could develop into later in life
Visible evidence for desired student actions and behaviors includes students doing the following.
• Actively being involved in the design and implementation of SOPs • Expressing their opinions and beliefs about how the classroom should be run • Making choices about the learning activities in which they are involved and the manner in which they demonstrate their knowledge
Visible evidence for students' understanding and awareness includes students doing the following.
• Saying that they are involved in the design of rules and procedures used in class • Saying they are allowed to express their opinions about how the class should be run • Saying they are allowed to make choices about how they learn and how they demonstrate what they have learned

Source: © *2021 by Robert J. Marzano.*

FIGURE 4.9: Visible evidence for element IXb.

IXc. Asking In-Depth Questions of Reluctant Learners

As described in the discussion of element VIIIb (page 121), the term *reluctant learners* refers to students for whom teachers have lower expectations. Educators tend to inadvertently treat these students differently from students for whom they have high expectations, causing a self-reinforcing cycle of academic disengagement. The teacher responsibility inherent in this element is to challenge reluctant learners in the same way they challenge other students.

Asking questions is one of the more concrete ways teachers send messages about their expectations for students. Specifically, teachers often ask reluctant learners fewer and easier questions. Of course, this sends a message to reluctant learners that they are not as capable as others. However, when teachers ask questions of reluctant learners that are as challenging as those posed to other students, it sends a message that reluctant learners are capable of complex thinking.

One way to ensure that you ask complex questions of all students is to keep a chart of which students you have asked questions of and which students you have not. Keep this chart at your desk and check off students' names as you ask them questions. It is important to remember that reluctant learners might struggle when answering complex questions. A key strategy when this occurs is to stay with the student who is struggling and restate or rephrase the question. This often allows the student to find an aspect of the question that he or she knows and thus experience success with the answer.

In all cases, teachers should ensure that no other students make negative comments about incorrect answers.

Finally, when any student demonstrates success or even strong effort with complex questions, the class can engage in quick cheers or other celebrations. Snapping fingers or tapping desks can be a quick way to recognize the effort of fellow students. One fun cheer is the rainstorm, in which students tap their fingers on the tops of their desks, slowly and quietly at first but then with increasing cadence and intensity to simulate a rainstorm. Other cheers include sparkles (snapping fingers), the roller-coaster cheer, the fireworks cheer, the trucker cheer, raise the roof, the wave, and the cheese grater cheer, just to name a few. All of them represent energizing and catchy ways to signify a celebration.

Figure 4.10 lists visible evidence for element IXc.

Visible evidence for effective instruction and guidance includes teachers doing the following.
• Asking complex questions of reluctant learners • Giving reluctant learners equal response opportunities as eager learners • Staying with reluctant learners when they struggle to answer a question by restating the question, utilizing wait time, or giving cues • Avoiding inappropriate reactions to incorrect answers from reluctant learners, including telling students they should have known the answer, ignoring a student's response, making subjective comments, or allowing negative comments from other students
Visible evidence for desired student actions and behaviors includes students doing the following.
• Responding to complex questions, even though they are typically reluctant to do so • Seeking help for complex questions without feeling embarrassed to do so
Visible evidence for students' understanding and awareness includes students doing the following.
• Saying the teacher expects everyone to participate • Saying the teacher asks difficult questions of everyone

Source: © *2021 by Robert J. Marzano.*

FIGURE 4.10: Visible evidence for element IXc.

IXd. Probing Incorrect Answers With Reluctant Learners

This element is directly related to the previous one. In addition to asking them challenging questions, teachers should query reluctant learners when they respond incorrectly to questions just as they would query students for whom they have high expectations. Again, this goes back to the unwitting differential treatment of students for whom teachers have low expectations. In general, teachers tend to challenge the incorrect answers of students for whom they have high expectations, but do not do so for students for whom they have low expectations.

One of the best strategies to reverse this trend is to utilize *elaborative interrogation* with all students, reluctant learners or otherwise. As its name implies, elaborative interrogation involves asking students how they know that their answer is true. This is especially important to ask when their answers are incorrect. Elaborative interrogation steers students to identify and correct their own errors, which is possibly one of the most powerful things students can do to enhance their own learning. It also communicates to students that having errors in their thinking is simply part of the learning process. Teachers should overtly point this out, perhaps by describing times when they, too, misunderstood content and how their understanding was enhanced when they looked for the misconceptions in their own thinking. The basic message should be that, rather than feeling embarrassment when they answer a question incorrectly, students should think of an incorrect answer as an opportunity to delve deeply into a topic.

One important qualifier to keep in mind for this strategy is to be aware when students are becoming frustrated during elaborative interrogation. If this is the case, teachers should temporarily let students off the hook so they can compose themselves and have more time to think without feeling pressured. Students who get stuck when attempting to answer a question can also receive lifeline strategies like answer eliminator, ask the audience (that is, the class), or phone a friend. These are fun ways to support students in answering questions while still holding them accountable for answering the question.

Figure 4.11 lists visible evidence for element IXd.

Visible evidence for effective instruction and guidance includes teachers doing the following.

- Responding appropriately to incorrect answers of reluctant learners by demonstrating gratitude for the student's response and pointing out what is correct and what is incorrect about the response
- Temporarily letting students off the hook if they become frustrated or embarrassed while answering a question
- Using elaborative interrogation techniques to help a student know their answer is defensible

Visible evidence for desired student actions and behaviors includes students doing the following.

- Continuing to answer questions when probed by the teacher even though they are typically reluctant to do so
- Demonstrating that they are not embarrassed when they provide an incorrect answer

Visible evidence for students' understanding and awareness includes students doing the following.

- Saying the teacher won't let them off the hook
- Saying the teacher won't give up on them
- Saying the teacher helps them think deeply about the content
- Saying the teacher helps them answer difficult questions correctly

Source: © 2021 by Robert J. Marzano.

FIGURE 4.11: Visible evidence for element IXd.

Understanding and Planning for Design Area IX

Design area IX addresses students' efficacy and agency. These qualities are directly related to the top two levels of Maslow's hierarchy of needs and goals, self-actualization and connection to something greater than self (see figure 3.28, page 116). By planning for this design area, teachers are trying to ensure that students have affirmative answers to the following questions.

- **Level five:** Does this situation allow me to work on things related to my personal interests?
- **Level six:** Does this situation make me feel like I'm a part of something important?

These questions deal with self-actualization and connection to something greater than self respectively, and the relationship between these two levels of the hierarchy and efficacy and agency is tautological. When individuals are engaged in being self-actualized and connected to something greater than self, they are experiencing efficacy and agency, and when they are experiencing efficacy and agency, they are engaged in self-actualization and being connected to something greater than self.

There are four elements embedded in this design area.

IXa. Inspiring students

IXb. Enhancing student agency

IXc. Asking in-depth questions of reluctant learners

IXd. Probing incorrect answers with reluctant learners

While they all relate to the general construct of efficacy and agency, each element relates to different aspects of these phenomena. For example, a sense of efficacy is a function of one's beliefs. Some beliefs support a sense of efficacy; others extinguish it. Element IXa, inspiring students, deals directly with beliefs. Indeed, inspiration is defined by the beliefs it elicits. As mentioned previously, inspiration occurs when a person recognizes evidence that one or more of his or her ideals could actually be true (Marzano, Scott, et al., 2017). For example, when a fifth-grade student reads about a young girl with a similar background to hers who became an astronaut, the fifth grader will be inspired. The story provides evidence for the ideal that anything is possible for her. This is the essence of inspiration.

The strategies in element IXb, enhancing agency, are designed to engage students in tangible characteristics of agency, such as voice and choice. When teachers use strategies in this element, students experience the very actions that demonstrate agency. For example, when a student adds a comment to a parking lot, the student is most probably operating from a belief that his recommendations regarding what should occur in class will benefit his learning and that of others.

Elements IXc and IXd both deal with providing challenging tasks for all students while focusing on reluctant learners. Such learners, by definition, have given up on their ability to succeed in school—the antithesis of efficacy and agency. Presenting these students with challenging tasks and supporting them in their efforts to overcome these challenges provides reluctant learners with concrete proof that efficacy and agency are attainable in their academic and nonacademic lives.

Careful planning enhances the elements in this design area. Activities to inspire students (element IXa) should occupy a specific time and place within a unit of instruction or as a daily activity. Activities to enhance student agency (element IXb) should also be well thought out such that they maximize students' opportunities to have their voices heard and make choices in the learning process. Planning for elements IXc and IXd commonly focuses on specific reluctant learners and ensuring that the teacher asks them challenging questions, acknowledges their correct answers, and probes their incorrect thinking.

Design Area X: Metacognitive and Life Skills

The three design areas in this domain build on each other to achieve the goal of student self-regulation. Design area VIII (page 119) addresses the foundational perceptions of belonging and esteem students must have before they can self-regulate. Design area IX (page 128) addresses the beliefs and actions of efficacy and agency that students must have to be self-regulated. Finally, design area X focuses on the acquisition and use of specific skills for self-regulation. This design area involves three elements related to developing students' metacognition and skills that will help them be successful in life.

Xa. Reflecting on learning

Xb. Using long-term projects

Xc. Focusing on specific metacognitive and life skills

The following sections detail each one.

Xa. Reflecting on Learning

To enact this element, teachers systematically have students analyze their own behavior as learners. This is highly metacognitive in nature because metacognition, in its most basic form, is simply reflecting on one's own thinking. In turn, metacognition is foundational to the overall process of self-regulation. If students are not aware of their perceptions, interpretations, and actions, self-regulation is difficult—if not impossible.

Reflection journals can provide students with daily opportunities to process their thoughts, track their development, and deepen their understandings. Students might make journal entries about their personal interactions with the topics being addressed in class, recording insights, ideas, connections, and revisions on previous thinking. Consider the following post-learning journal prompts for a primary classroom.

- Today I discovered ________.
- Today I explored ________.
- Today I learned ________.
- I predict that ________.
- I want to know more about ________.

Intermediate students can be prompted to more complex levels of reflection. Consider the following prompts.

- I used to think ________ but now I think ________.
- What information from today should I remember in five years?

Benchmark assessments are great opportunities for students to reflect on their academic development. Teachers and administrators typically use such data to inform grouping and instruction, but students rarely ever see these data. When given the opportunity to analyze their own test scores, students can glean a better understanding of their academic status, identify areas of potential growth, and celebrate areas of success. To enable this analysis, students can keep a running record of their benchmark assessment data, with teachers conducting a reflection session with the class as data become available. Again, students can record their thoughts in reflection journals, identify areas of need, and set goals. Students can also track their growth and progression over the long term by keeping a data picture—an overall snapshot of their learning from a variety of perspectives—in their data notebooks. For example, figure 4.12 shows a data picture that provides scores from three different external assessments: annual state assessments (CMAS/PARCC), a third-party reading exam administered as a benchmark (DIBELS), and other subject-specific benchmark assessments (Scantron Mathematics and Reading). Students can record their scores throughout the year in the rows for beginning of the year (BOY), middle of the year (MOY), and end of the year (EOY).

DATA PICTURE FOR ______________________

School Year: ________ My Grade Level: 3rd 4th 5th

MY PERFORMANCE LEVELS	Literacy	Mathematics	Science	Social Studies

CMAS/PARCC	Scale Score	Performance Level	Growth Percentile	Scale Score Goal	Growth Goal
Mathematics					
English Language Arts					
Science					

Performance Levels for Mathematics and ELA: Did Not Yet Meet Expectations (Level 1): 650–699, Partially Met Expectations (Level 2): 700–724, Approached Expectations (Level 3): 725–749, Met Expectations (Level 4): 750–789, Exceeded Expectations (Level 5): 790–850

DIBELS	Composite Score	Composite Goal	DORF Words Correct Score	DORF Words Correct Goal	DORF Accuracy Score	DORF Accuracy Goal	DORF Retell Score	DORF Retell Goal
BOY								
MOY								
EOY								

Score Levels: Above Benchmark (Blue), At Benchmark (Green), Below Benchmark (Yellow), Well Below Benchmark (Red)

DIBELS	DORF Retell Quality Score	DORF Retell Quality Goal	DAZE Adjusted Score	DAZE Adjusted Score Goal
BOY				
MOY				
EOY				

Score Levels: Above Benchmark (Blue), At Benchmark (Green), Below Benchmark (Yellow), Well Below Benchmark (Red)

Scantron Mathematics	Scantron Annual Growth Target ________ My Annual Growth Goal ________					
BOY Scale Score	MOY Scale Score	Gain (BOY–MOY)	Mid-Year Goal Achieved (Yes or Not Yet)	EOY Scale Score	Gain (BOY–EOY)	Annual Goal Achieved (Yes or Not Yet)

Scantron Reading	Scantron Annual Growth Target ________ My Annual Growth Goal ________					
BOY Scale Score	MOY Scale Score	Gain (BOY–MOY)	Mid-Year Goal Achieved (Yes or Not Yet)	EOY Scale Score	Gain (BOY–EOY)	Annual Goal Achieved (Yes or Not Yet)

Source: © 2021 by Westminster Public Schools. Used with permission.

FIGURE 4.12: Data picture for individual students.

In addition to reflecting on academic content, students can write reflections focused on any metacognitive skill (see element Xc, page 143). We particularly recommend that teachers guide students to reflect on growth mindset thinking. For example, a teacher might prompt students to write a growth-mindset-based entry as a warm-up activity before instruction, or as a post-learning activity. When writing journal entries for the purpose of growth-mindset reflection, it is important that students make regular journal entries so they can see their conceptual development over time. Consider the following journal prompts for growth-mindset reflection.

- One thing I have accomplished that I didn't think I could is . . .
- One of the biggest mistakes I made recently is . . .
- One thing I want to get better at right now is . . .

In addition to growth mindset, students can reflect on the acquisition of any metacognitive skills and chronicle the ups and downs of their progress. Consider the following journal prompts for the metacognitive skill of resisting impulsivity.

- What judgments did I make today that were impulsive?
- What are the things I do that indicate that I'm being impulsive?
- In what situations am I usually impulsive?
- What are some situations where it's OK to be impulsive?

Students can also reflect on their daily progress with metacognitive skills through individual and class data tracking. By providing students with rubrics and tracking matrices, teachers can support the process of student self-evaluation. For example, the class might have a goal to increase their ability to stay focused when answers and solutions are not immediately apparent. The teacher would guide students in creating a rubric that translates this skill into concrete behaviors in the classroom. At the end of the day, the teacher would have students reflect on their current status and daily progress with these behaviors, collecting student evaluations through Plickers, Google Forms, four corners, or other data collection tools. The teacher would then chart progress on a class graph, with goals and celebrations for reaching those goals.

Figure 4.13 lists visible evidence for element Xa.

Xb. Using Long-Term Projects

The teacher responsibility inherent in this element is to provide students with opportunities to engage in extended projects that are of interest to them personally, and over which they have maximum control. In effect, long-term projects allow students to pursue an area of interest while learning valuable metacognitive and life skills. These projects can be done in groups or as individuals, depending on age, interest, ability, and purpose. There are a number of ways personal projects can manifest.

One option for personal projects is akin to Google's practice of genius hour, in which employees can spend 20 percent of their time on projects of their own design. Similarly, students take time away from their traditional studies to pursue an avenue of interest. These projects should not be intentionally linked to proficiency scales, and should not include too many guidelines, limits, or barriers put in place by the teacher. In fact, the primary role of the teacher is to help students acquire and develop project management skills: help students identify an area of interest, define

Visible evidence for effective instruction and guidance includes teachers doing the following.
• Posing reflection questions such as "What could you do differently to improve your work?" or "What could you do differently to improve your learning?" • Having students reflect on specific cognitive and metacognitive skills that were addressed in the lesson
Visible evidence for desired student actions and behaviors includes students doing the following.
• Posing questions about the best ways to accomplish specific tasks • Posing questions about their own strategies for learning • Making comments about their own progress or lack thereof relative to specific skills
Visible evidence for students' understanding and awareness includes students doing the following.
• Describing what they are clear about and what they are confused about • Describing their levels of effort and the relationship of their effort to their learning • Describing what they might do to improve their learning

Source: © *2021 by Robert J. Marzano.*

FIGURE 4.13: Visible evidence for element Xa.

success criteria, set goals and deadlines, communicate needs, acquire resources, reflect on successes and failures, and celebrate the journey in the end.

Primary teachers often begin with a whole-class approach to long-term projects, as the management required of individual projects can be daunting when rolling out long-term projects for the first time. Class projects might be designed as part of a unit of instruction, or happen spontaneously in response to a community need. For example, a class might identify a problem within the school they wish to solve—perhaps students are having a hard time crossing the street after school. The class might decide to petition to get a stop sign, speed bump, or crosswalk added to keep kids safe. As another example, after reading a Scholastic article titled "I Was Homeless" (Lewis, 2014), a class might choose to hold a clothing and canned food drive to benefit a local food pantry. Community projects might also be inspired by a school club. For example, a school might have a Students Give Back club formed around philanthropy. The purpose of the club is to design projects to benefit their school or community. Student council groups or kindness clubs can engage in long-term projects designed to help their peers. Extracurricular organizations can also provide the structure for community projects and long-term learning. For example, Girls on the Run is a nonprofit organization that teaches girls ages 8–13 life skills and leadership through direct instruction and running activities.

In the upper-elementary grade levels, students should be encouraged to work independently on individual projects. Ideally, these projects focus on personal goals. With this version of long-term projects, the teacher prompts students to identify things about which they are passionate and provides activities that help them set long-term goals, make plans, and monitor and adjust along the way. To illustrate, consider a student who is just beginning work on his personal project. His teacher has asked him to think about what he would do if he knew he would not fail, an exercise designed to help the student "think big." The student is passionate about food and is always talking about being a chef when he grows up, so he determines that if he knew he wouldn't fail, he would open a five-star restaurant in Manhattan and become a famous chef. Because the student loves sushi, the teacher helps him discover the chef Masaharu Morimoto. The student learns that Morimoto first wanted to be a baseball player but had to quit because of injury. Based on this information, the student concludes that Morimoto is successful because he was determined and persevered when things got tough. The student decides that being determined and persevering when things get tough are two traits he would like to develop within himself.

Next, the student comes up with the idea of writing his own cookbook based on his favorite meals and family recipes. He identifies his cousin, who is currently attending culinary school, as a mentor and a person who can help him be successful with his project. With the help of his teacher, the student defines specifically what success on this project will look like: he will use the Book Creator app to publish an online cookbook that contains a minimum of twenty recipes for breakfast, lunch, dinner, and dessert. He will collect these recipes from his family and will represent both his favorite meals and dishes from his cultural heritage. Additionally, he will print and spiral bind thirty copies of his book to hand out to his family, friends, and classmates. During the class personal project celebration, he will make one of his favorite dishes to share with everyone.

The student then creates specific deadlines and goals for himself, and works both in class and at home to meet these goals. His teacher checks in with him frequently, offering inspiration and tips on determination and perseverance. At one of their meetings, the teacher offers the student several quotes about determination and perseverance, and the student chooses one by Vince Lombardi as his own personal mantra and displays it on the cover of his data notebook.

As he is working on his cookbook, the student realizes that he needs to extend a deadline he has set for himself, and must adjust the rest of his project. He also realizes that he is going to need to get some help with printing and binding his cookbooks, a task which his close friends happily agree to help with during a handful of lunches and recesses. In the end, the student publishes his cookbook and his friends and family attend the class's personal project celebration, where students present their projects and celebrate their hard work. The student reflects on what he has learned about the culinary world, as well as the traits and skills he has acquired along the way.

Figure 4.14 lists visible evidence for element Xb.

Visible evidence for effective instruction and guidance includes teachers doing the following.
• Engaging students in long-term projects of their own design • Explicitly building the use of metacognitive and life skills into long-term projects
Visible evidence for desired student actions and behaviors includes students doing the following.
• Actively engaging in the design and execution of long-term projects • Working on specific metacognitive skills or life skills as they engage in their long-term projects
Visible evidence for students' understanding and awareness includes students doing the following.
• Saying that they are excited about working on their long-term projects • Describing the specific metacognitive or life skills they are working on within their long-term projects

Source: © *2021 by Robert J. Marzano.*

FIGURE 4.14: Visible evidence for element Xb.

Xc. Focusing on Specific Metacognitive and Life Skills

This element refers to overtly teaching specific metacognitive and life skills. These skills are probably a tacit part of the curriculum in the classrooms of many teachers, simply because teachers want to pass on skills to their students that they can use in their lives inside and outside of school. In the Marzano Academies model, such skills are an explicit part of the curriculum. As the name of this element states, there are two sets of skills: metacognitive skills and life skills. There are ten metacognitive skills, depicted in table 4.1, and four life skills, depicted in table 4.2 (page 144). Many teachers choose to add to the list of life skills and even involve students in the identification of additional skills. For example, teachers might engage students in developing the life skills of being prepared for school, cultivating new friendships, and the like.

TABLE 4.1: Metacognitive Skills

Metacognitive Skill	Description
Staying focused when answers and solutions are not immediately apparent	This skill helps students overcome obstacles and stay focused when challenges arise. It also helps students to recognize how much effort they are putting into accomplishing a specific task.
Pushing the limits of one's knowledge and skills	This skill helps students set goals and engage in tasks that are personally challenging. When using this skill, students will strive to learn more and accomplish more.
Generating and pursuing one's own standards for performance	This skill enables students to envision and articulate criteria for what a successful project will look like.
Seeking incremental steps	This skill helps students take on complex tasks using small incremental steps so they do not become overwhelmed by the task as a whole.
Seeking accuracy	This skill helps students vet sources of information for reliability and verify information by consulting multiple sources known to be reliable.
Seeking clarity	This skill helps students identify points of confusion when they are learning new information. This allows students to independently seek a deeper understanding.
Resisting impulsivity	When faced with a desire to form a quick conclusion, this skill helps students refrain from doing so until they can gather more relevant information prior to taking action.
Seeking cohesion and coherence	When students are creating something with a number of interacting parts, this skill helps them monitor the relationships between what they are currently doing and the overall intent of the project in which they are engaged.
Setting goals and making plans	This skill helps students set short- and long-term goals, create timelines or blueprints, monitor progress, and make necessary adjustments.
Growth mindset thinking	This skill helps students take on challenging tasks with an attitude that helps them succeed, even when confronted by major obstacles.

Source: © 2017 by Marzano Resources. Adapted with permission.

TABLE 4.2: Life Skills

Life Skill	Description
Participation	Participation involves the set of decisions and actions that helps students add to group discussions and engage actively in questioning and answering questions.
Work completion	Work completion involves the set of decisions and actions that helps students manage their workload and complete tasks efficiently and effectively.
Behavior	Behavior involves the set of decisions and actions that helps students follow classroom rules and norms designed to create an efficient and orderly learning environment for all.
Working in groups	Working in groups involves the set of decisions and actions that helps students function as productive and supportive members of groups designed to enhance the learning of the students within those groups.

Source: © 2017 by Marzano Resources. Adapted with permission.

There are many ways to build metacognitive and life skills into day-to-day instruction in conjunction with other elements in the model. For example, the metacognitive skill of seeking accuracy can be employed while a teacher is using strategies from element IVb, revising. When one is revising a composition, for example, ensuring accuracy is an important goal of the revision process. Staying focused when answers and solutions are not apparent can be used when students are engaged in element IIId, structured practice. Structured practice can be difficult and frustrating, particularly when one is first learning a new skill, so students must stay focused even when they feel like giving up.

In addition to coupling metacognitive and life skills with academic activities, Marzano Academies teachers should overtly teach and reinforce these skills with students just as they would with academic knowledge and skills. To begin, teachers should introduce students to the proficiency scales for the metacognitive skills on which they are focusing. Figure 4.15 depicts the scale for the metacognitive skill of growth mindset thinking for grades K–2 and figure 4.16 (page 146) depicts the equivalent scale for grades 3–5.

Scales for metacognitive and life skills follow the same format as the proficiency scales for academic content. The 3.0 level represents proficiency. At the grades K–2 level, the expectation is that, when cued by the teacher, students recognize whether they are currently operating from a growth mindset perspective. At the grades 3–5 level, the expectation at the 3.0 level is that, when cued by the teacher, students can execute a specific process that stimulates growth mindset thinking. As students move up the grade levels in the metacognitive skills, the expectations embedded in the proficiency scales shift from teachers guiding and directing the use of these skills to students creating their own versions of the skills and monitoring their own performance.

The 2.0 level represents the content that teachers should directly present to students so that they can achieve 3.0 status. For example, in the grades 3–5 scale, students must understand more advanced vocabulary, such as *ability*, *developed*, *effort*, *failure*, *innate*, and *intelligence*. They should also be able to recognize common mistakes or pitfalls associated with growth mindset thinking (for example, having a growth mindset in one area but a fixed mindset in others; starting out with a positive attitude but getting discouraged easily).

4.0	The student will: • Provide a rudimentary description of what it looks like when someone develops a growth mindset.
3.5	In addition to score 3.0 performance, partial success at score 4.0 content.
3.0	The student will: GMT1—When asked by the teacher, accurately recognize when he/she is or is not operating from a positive mindset (for example, the teacher asks, "Are you thinking positively about what you can accomplish in this upcoming task?" and the student correctly evaluates him/herself).
2.5	No major errors or omissions regarding score 2.0 content, and partial success at score 3.0 content.
2.0	GMT1—The student will recognize or recall basic vocabulary associated with growth mindset thinking (for example, *fixed mindset, growth mindset, learning from mistakes, trying*) and perform basic processes such as: • Understand that a growth mindset is a positive way to think about what you can accomplish (for example, that you can learn to do almost anything if you are willing to work hard). • Recognize situations in which growth mindset thinking might be useful (for example, when you are learning a new skill, when you have a goal that is not easy for you to accomplish).
1.5	Partial success at score 2.0 content, and major errors or omissions regarding score 3.0 content.
1.0	With help, partial success at score 2.0 content and score 3.0 content.
0.5	With help, partial success at score 2.0 content but not at score 3.0 content.
0.0	Even with help, no success

Source: © 2017 by Marzano Resources. Adapted with permission.

FIGURE 4.15: Growth mindset proficiency scale, grades K–2.

When introducing metacognitive and life skills, teachers can present them such that students feel like they are adding tools to their mental toolboxes. As much as possible, metacognitive and life skills should be taught within a real-world context. Teachers can provide students with example videos, scenarios, or personal anecdotes for analysis and reflection. For example, a teacher might show students a recording of Jesse Owens's performance at the 1936 Olympics in Germany, where he won four gold medals in track and field at a time when African Americans had to overcome many obstacles to be recognized internationally and even within the United States for their athletic accomplishments. Students might investigate Owens's journey to the Olympics and the obstacles he had to overcome from the perspective of the metacognitive skill of setting goals and making plans.

Students can create role-playing scenarios for skills on their own, perhaps even videotaping a series of how-to videos. Additionally, while metacognitive and life skills are easy to incorporate into daily lessons, they are especially effective within long-term units and projects. Teachers should plan units and projects with at least one metacognitive skill in mind, and include lessons about specific metacognitive skills both in isolation and in conjunction with other content. For example, a teacher planning a unit during which students will be asked to investigate various theories of global warming might explicitly build in the metacognitive skill of seeking accuracy. The teacher would include

4.0	The student will: • When cued by the teacher, explain how well he/she operated from a positive mindset.
3.5	In addition to score 3.0 performance, partial success at score 4.0 content.
3.0	The student will: GMT1—When cued by the teacher, execute a simple teacher-provided strategy for growth mindset thinking (for example, [1] notice how you are thinking about your ability to accomplish the upcoming task, [2] try to change any negative thoughts to positive thoughts [for example, change "I can't do this" to "I can accomplish some good things, if I try"; change "This is going to be boring" to "I can make this fun"; change "This is useless" to "I can learn something valuable from this"], [3] promise yourself that you are going to try your best and not let yourself get discouraged).
2.5	No major errors or omissions regarding score 2.0 content, and partial success at score 3.0 content.
2.0	GMT1—The student will recognize or recall advanced vocabulary associated with growth mindset thinking (for example, *ability, developed, effort, failure, innate, intelligence*) and perform basic processes such as: • When asked by the teacher, accurately recognize when he or she is operating from a positive mindset (for example, when asked "Are you thinking positively or negatively about your ability to do this?"). • Recognize common mistakes or pitfalls associated with growth mindset thinking (for example, having a growth mindset in one area but a fixed mindset in others; starting out with a positive attitude but getting discouraged easily).
1.5	Partial success at score 2.0 content, and major errors or omissions regarding score 3.0 content.
1.0	With help, partial success at score 2.0 content and score 3.0 content.
0.5	With help, partial success at score 2.0 content but not at score 3.0 content.
0.0	Even with help, no success

FIGURE 4.16: Growth mindset proficiency scale, grades 3–5.

direct instruction on this skill and have students examine how and how well they employ it as they gather information.

Finally, students and teachers can create checklists to accompany metacognitive and life skills instruction. These checklists can take the form of a personal tracking matrix (see element Ib, page 13) so students can monitor their progress over time to see which metacognitive skills they are addressing on a regular basis.

Ultimately, in the Marzano Academies model, the acquisition of metacognitive and life skills is considered at least as important as academic knowledge skills. Consequently, as students master specific metacognitive and life skills, their hard work should be recognized, whether through the addition of badges to student icon cards; pins, buttons, or stickers; or formal celebrations like all-school assemblies.

Figure 4.17 lists visible evidence for element Xc.

Visible evidence for effective instruction and guidance includes teachers doing the following.
• Providing proficiency scales for specific metacognitive skills • Engaging students in activities that help teach and reinforce specific metacognitive skills • Providing proficiency scales for specific life skills • Engaging students in activities that help teach and reinforce specific life skills
Visible evidence for desired student actions and behaviors includes students doing the following.
• Actively engaging in learning specific metacognitive skills • Actively engaging in learning specific life skills
Visible evidence for students' understanding and awareness includes students doing the following.
• Describing the specific metacognitive skills on which they are working • Describing their level of development relative to specific metacognitive skills • Describing the specific life skills on which they are working • Describing their level of development relative to specific life skills

Source: © *2021 by Robert J. Marzano.*

FIGURE 4.17: Visible evidence for element Xc.

Understanding and Planning for Design Area X

Design area X addresses what might be referred to as the *skill set* for the top two levels of Maslow's hierarchy. People commonly find it difficult to reach and maintain these high-level needs and goals without the skills and experiences included in this design area. Stated differently, effective use of the skills and experiences in design area X can help students develop affirmative responses to the following hierarchy questions.

- **Level five:** Does this situation allow me to work on things related to my personal interests?
- **Level six:** Does this situation make me feel like I'm a part of something important?

The most general skill within this design area is reflecting on learning (element Xa). The activities in this element help students experience a quintessential metacognitive skill—reflecting on one's own thinking. This might be thought of as the gatekeeper to human self-awareness. People who cultivate the habit of reflecting on their own thinking will become aware of their patterns of thinking and how it affects their behavior. Element Xb, using long-term projects, provides students with opportunities to apply selected metacognitive and life skills in the context of a self-regulated project that is inherently motivating to them. Finally, element Xc, focusing on specific metacognitive and life skills, provides students with processes and procedures for specific metacognitive and life skills for which teachers provide explicit instruction and reinforcement throughout the year.

Thoughtful planning enhances the effectiveness of the elements in this design area, especially for element Xb (long-term projects) and element Xc (specific metacognitive and life skills). Whereas opportunities for reflecting on learning (element Xa) can occur quite spontaneously, teachers must plan long-term projects in terms of where they fit into a unit of instruction, how long they will last, the types of resources that will be provided to students, and the extent to which students will do them independently or while working in groups. Finally, determining which metacognitive skills and life skills will be the focus in a given year requires detailed preparation. In a single year, a teacher should address a few metacognitive and life skills that address the unique needs of their students. Making these selections is best done on a schoolwide basis with certain grade levels and subject areas being responsible for certain metacognitive and life skills. This process is described in the book *Leading a Competency-Based Elementary School* (Marzano & Kosena, 2022). If such decisions are not made schoolwide, then individual teachers should make these determinations by considering their students' specific needs relative to the various metacognitive and life skills.

Summary

This chapter deals with the domain of self-regulation. In the Marzano Academies model, this refers to students' ability to monitor and manage themselves in ways that produce controlled, positive results in their lives. The domain includes three design areas. Design area VIII addresses students' perceptions of their belonging and esteem within the school community (levels three and four of Maslow's hierarchy). Design area IX addresses students' efficacy and agency, which are foundational to levels five and six of Maslow's hierarchy. Design area X involves metacognitive and life skills, which are the tools students use when involved in activities related to those top two levels of the hierarchy. Visible evidence for teachers and students was described for each element in each design area to aid teachers in determining how effective their actions are relative to the intended outcomes of each element.

CHAPTER 5

The CBE Mindset

In the previous chapters, we have presented strategies for forty-nine categories of CBE instruction, which we refer to as *elements*. Some of the strategies we presented are quite different from strategies employed in a traditional classroom. So too are some of the attitudes and beliefs—or *mindsets*—held by CBE teachers, particularly those using the Marzano Academies model. The term *mindset* was popularized in education by Carol Dweck's (2006) book *Mindset: The New Psychology of Success*. There, she stresses the importance of making students aware of the distinctions between a fixed mindset and a growth mindset and fostering their belief in the latter. At a more general level, *mindset* means a person's established set of attitudes and beliefs relative to a specific topic or issue. In keeping, we assert that there is a mindset for CBE instruction. Table 5.1 summarizes some of the attitudes and beliefs that are explicitly or implicitly part of the ten design areas of the academy model.

TABLE 5.1: Attitudes and Beliefs for the Design Areas of the Academy Model

Design Area	Attitudes and Beliefs
Design area I: Proficiency scales	• Proficiency scales should constitute the intended curriculum for each subject area. • Proficiency scales should be transparent to teachers, parents, and students.
Design area II: Assessment	• Proficiency scales should constitute the assessed curriculum for each subject area. • A single score on a single test should never be considered the final status for an individual student relative to a specific measurement topic. • To determine summative scores for students, teachers should examine the pattern of scores for each student on each proficiency scale.
Design area III: Proficiency scale instruction	• Proficiency scales should constitute the taught curriculum for each subject area. • Teachers should plan to use specific instructional strategies for the learning targets in each proficiency scale.
Design area IV: General instruction	• Teachers should continually have students refresh and revise their understanding of the content that has been presented to them so that they might continually update and sharpen their knowledge.
Design area V: Grouping and regrouping	• Teachers should group students regarding their short-term needs within a unit of instruction. • Teachers should group students on a long-term basis such that students can move through measurement topics at a pace appropriate to their individual needs.

continued ➡

Design Area	Attitudes and Beliefs
Design area VI: Engagement	• Engagement should be thought of as a multifaceted construct involving attention, energy, interest, and intrigue. • Teachers should use a wide variety of strategies to address the different types of engagement in the classroom.
Design area VII: Comfort, safety, and order	• Teachers should involve students in activities that ensure they have a sense of comfort, safety, and order.
Design area VIII: Belonging and esteem	• Teachers should involve students in activities that ensure they have a sense of belonging and esteem.
Design area IX: Efficacy and agency	• Teachers should involve students in activities that develop their sense of efficacy and agency.
Design area X: Metacognitive and life skills	• Teachers should engage students in activities that develop specific metacognitive and life skills. • Teachers should consider metacognitive and life skills equally as important as the knowledge and skills in traditional subject areas.

Source: © *2021 by Robert J. Marzano.*

In addition to these attitudes and beliefs, there are others we have not yet concretely addressed that are critical to the CBE mindset. Here we deal with three other important aspects of the CBE mindset: (1) CBE skills and processes for students, (2) teaching as facilitating and evaluating, and (3) new metrics for grading and reporting.

CBE Skills and Processes for Students

Certainly, teachers must acquire new knowledge and skills to effectively execute competency-based instruction. Similarly, students must acquire new knowledge and skills to effectively learn in a competency-based classroom. To ignore this requirement is to undermine some of the most important outcomes of a CBE system. Of course, CBE skills and processes for students are explicit in the Marzano Academies model itself—design area IX, student efficacy and agency (page 128), and design area X, metacognitive and life skills (page 137), are two prime examples. In addition to these, CBE teachers should continually look for opportunities to teach and reinforce skills that will help students solve problems and make reasoned decisions.

Additionally, students should learn about the basic nature of the CBE process: They will be expected to devote the requisite time to master the content in the proficiency scales, and the time they take is not constrained in any way. Sometimes they will reach proficiency quickly; sometimes they will not. In all cases, their job is to devote their full attention and energy to learning with the assurance that their teachers and, indeed, the system itself are working to support their success. This awareness on the part of students will not develop naturally. Rather, it requires a change in perspective on teachers' parts. They should continually look for opportunities to teach students about the importance of taking responsibility for their own learning and providing them with opportunities to do so.

Students should also know that, as part of the CBE process, they can demonstrate their competence in a variety of ways, not only through pencil-and-paper tests. In fact, their own perceptions regarding their knowledge of specific content are an important part of the assessment process. Indeed, students are encouraged to advocate for themselves, as is evident in element IIb, student-centered assessments (page 29). The clear implication here is that students have the right and the invitation to take major responsibility for how they are evaluated. Again, to develop this awareness and skill in students, teachers must continually prompt them to self-evaluate and design their own ways of demonstrating their current status on specific measurement topics.

Teaching as Facilitating and Evaluating

The CBE process ultimately changes the role of the teacher. Traditionally, the teacher's role has been limited to presenting new information and skills to students and then taking actions to ensure they become proficient at the same. While this dynamic still occurs in a CBE classroom, the system more strongly emphasizes providing students with the necessary resources to direct their own learning, sometimes with minimal help from the teacher. Stated differently, one of the teacher's primary responsibilities within a CBE system is to be a facilitator of learning, as opposed to solely an instructor of content.

This shift should occur gradually throughout the school year as teachers transfer some responsibilities from themselves to their students. To illustrate, at the beginning of the year, a CBE teacher might take the stance of presenting content and engaging students in activities to help them learn that content. However, over time, the teacher starts to step back from this role as students become more adept at utilizing the resources available within the system. As students become increasingly more facile with the virtual resources in the LMS, the teacher's role changes accordingly, with students potentially becoming self-sufficient relative to learning the content in proficiency scales and demonstrating competence. To make this shift, teachers must design a system that includes the following resources and processes: highly transparent proficiency scales, options for students to submit evidence of their status on specific content within specific proficiency scales, virtual instructional resources in the form of playlists, and so on. As described throughout the previous chapters, the Marzano Academies model includes all these elements.

Evaluating students' status on proficiency scales is another primary role of a CBE teacher. As described in the discussion of design area II (page 25), teachers will use a wide variety of assessments to determine students' status on the learning targets in a specific proficiency scale. They may also enter students' evidence scores into a calculator that determines the most accurate current summative score. However, the teacher is the final judge as to whether or not students have demonstrated proficiency. In concrete terms, this means that once a teacher is convinced a student is proficient regarding the content of a specific scale, that student should be free to move on to another topic. This is qualitatively different from the assessment role of teachers in a traditional classroom. In the traditional classroom, teachers design, administer, and score tests, but the grade is the ultimate determiner of a student's status. For example, if the cut score for a grade of A is 90 percent, a traditional teacher will typically let that score determine a student's status. If a student receives a score of 89 percent on a summative test, that student will receive a B, not because of a reasoned decision-making process that includes all information about the student, but simply because of a pre-established cut-score policy.

The evaluative role of the CBE teacher should be the safeguard against falling into the trap of the "activity curriculum." Such a curriculum exists when students are simply required to complete activities and assignments that are associated with certain numbers of points or a certain percentage score. This is a trap into which traditional teachers and, indeed, even CBE teachers can fall. To counteract this, CBE teachers must hold the validation of students' competence as one of their most important responsibilities.

New Metrics for Grading and Reporting

Beliefs about grading and reporting in a CBE system are among the most divergent from those underpinning a traditional system. In a traditional system, a student's status is typically reported as an omnibus grade at the end of the semester or school year using letter grades or percentage scores. A CBE system uses different metrics.

One popular CBE metric is to report how many of the proficiency scales at a given grade level and subject area the student has mastered. For example, assume that there are twenty proficiency scales for fifth-grade mathematics. If a student has reached proficiency (that is, demonstrated competence at the score 3.0 level) for ten of these scales, the student's status would be represented as the simple ratio 10/20.

Another important metric of student progress in a CBE system is pace. Pace refers to whether a student is moving through the measurement topics for a given year at a rate such that he or she will demonstrate proficiency on all of the scales by the end of the school year. The most straightforward way to report pace is to divide the school year into equal units based on the number of proficiency scales students must complete within a year. Again using fifth-grade mathematics as an example, students must complete the twenty proficiency scales by the end of the school year, which is thirty-six weeks in length. To accomplish this, students should complete a proficiency scale once every 1.8 weeks (that is, $36 \div 20 = 1.8$). Assume that after eighteen weeks of the school year, a particular student has completed ten proficiency scales. That student would be considered on pace, whereas a student who had completed eight proficiency scales would be considered behind pace, and a student who had completed twelve proficiency scales would be considered ahead of pace. These and other approaches to grading in a CBE elementary school are discussed in depth in the book *Leading a Competency-Based Elementary School: The Marzano Academies Model* (Marzano & Kosena, 2022).

While not preferred, traditional grades can also be adapted and used in a CBE system. To illustrate, assume that it is the end of a nine-week grading period and a teacher has addressed seven measurement topics during that period. Each student would have a current summative score on each of these topics. One particular student might have the following set of summative scores: 2.5, 3.5, 3.0, 3.0, 2.5, 2.5, 2.0. These summative scores can be combined using a weighted or unweighted average. The unweighted average for this student's seven summative scores is 2.71 (that is, $19 \div 7 = 2.71$). This can be transformed into an overall grade using a conversion scale like that in table 5.2.

Based on the conversion chart, this student's average score of 2.71 would translate to an overall grade of 84 percent or B. This grade now represents the student's central tendency in terms of the seven measurement topics. One might say that the student's overall tendency for this particular nine-week grading period was to demonstrate solid understanding of the foundational knowledge at the score 2.0 level and high-partial understanding of the score 3.0 content. Once the student is

TABLE 5.2: Converting Proficiency Scale Scores to Percentages and Letter Grades

Scale Score	Percentage	Grade	Scale Score	Percentage	Grade	Scale Score	Percentage	Grade	Scale Score	Percentage	Grade
4.00	100	A	2.30 to 2.34	76	C	1.30 to 1.31	50	F	0.73 to 0.75	25	F
3.90 to 3.99	99	A	2.25 to 2.29	75	C	1.28 to 1.29	49	F	0.70 to 0.72	24	F
3.80 to 3.89	98	A	2.20 to 2.24	74	C	1.26 to 1.27	48	F	0.67 to 0.69	23	F
3.70 to 3.79	97	A	2.15 to 2.19	73	C	1.24 to 1.25	47	F	0.64 to 0.66	22	F
3.60 to 3.69	96	A	2.10 to 2.14	72	C	1.22 to 1.23	46	F	0.61 to 0.63	21	F
3.50 to 3.59	95	A	2.05 to 2.09	71	C	1.20 to 1.21	45	F	0.58 to 0.60	20	F
3.40 to 3.49	94	A	2.00 to 2.04	70	C	1.18 to 1.19	44	F	0.55 to 0.57	19	F
3.30 to 3.39	93	A	1.95 to 1.99	69	D	1.16 to 1.17	43	F	0.52 to 0.54	18	F
3.20 to 3.29	92	A	1.90 to 1.94	68	D	1.14 to 1.15	42	F	0.49 to 0.51	17	F
3.10 to 3.19	91	A	1.85 to 1.89	67	D	1.12 to 1.13	41	F	0.46 to 0.48	16	F
3.00 to 3.09	90	A	1.80 to 1.84	66	D	1.10 to 1.11	40	F	0.43 to 0.45	15	F
2.95 to 2.99	89	B	1.75 to 1.79	65	D	1.08 to 1.09	39	F	0.40 to 0.42	14	F

continued ➡

2.90 to 2.94	88	B	1.70 to 1.74	64	D	1.06 to 1.07	38	F	0.37 to 0.39	13	F
2.85 to 2.89	87	B	1.65 to 1.69	63	D	1.04 to 1.05	37	F	0.34 to 0.36	12	F
2.80 to 2.84	86	B	1.60 to 1.64	62	D	1.02 to 1.03	36	F	0.31 to 0.33	11	F
2.75 to 2.79	85	B	1.55 to 1.59	61	D	1.00 to 1.01	35	F	0.28 to 0.30	10	F
2.70 to 2.74	84	B	1.50 to 1.54	60	D	0.98 to 0.99	34	F	0.25 to 0.27	9	F
2.65 to 2.69	83	B	1.48 to 1.49	59	F	0.96 to 0.97	33	F	0.22 to 0.24	8	F
2.60 to 2.64	82	B	1.46 to 1.47	58	F	0.94 to 0.95	32	F	0.19 to 0.21	7	F
2.55 to 2.59	81	B	1.44 to 1.45	57	F	0.91 to 0.93	31	F	0.16 to 0.18	6	F
2.50 to 2.54	80	B	1.42 to 1.43	56	F	0.88 to 0.90	30	F	0.13 to 0.15	5	F
2.45 to 2.49	79	C	1.40 to 1.41	55	F	0.85 to 0.87	29	F	0.10 to 0.12	4	F
2.40 to 2.44	78	C	1.38 to 1.39	54	F	0.82 to 0.84	28	F	0.07 to 0.09	3	F
2.35 to 2.39	77	C	1.36 to 1.37	53	F	0.79 to 0.81	27	F	0.04 to 0.06	2	F
			1.34 to 1.35	52	F	0.76 to 0.78	26	F	0.01 to 0.03	1	F
			1.32 to 1.33	51	F				0.00	0	F

Source: Marzano, 2018, pp. 100–101.

able to demonstrate mastery on all seven measurement topics, he or she will have earned an overall grade of A at least as indicated by the conversion table.

Finally, an issue that can come up in a CBE classroom that uses traditional omnibus grades is that some students might be working on proficiency scales from different grade levels. For example, a fifth-grade student might be working on one or more sixth-grade topics for a specific subject area. Teachers must have a consistent method of combining scores on topics at multiple grade levels within a given subject area. One method is the weighting scheme depicted in table 5.3. This scheme weights scores based on how much above or below grade level the topic is. Scores on topics below grade level are adjusted to be lower, and scores on topics above grade level are shifted higher.

To illustrate how this system is employed, assume that a fifth-grade student is working on ten measurement topics during a grading period for a specific subject area. Seven of those topics are at the fifth-grade level and three topics are at the sixth-grade level. At the end of the grading period, the student receives a current summative scale for each of the ten measurement topics. These scores are depicted in figure 5.1 (page 156).

TABLE 5.3: Weighting Scheme for Students Working on Topics at Different Grade Levels

Measurement Topics Two Levels Below Grade Level		Measurement Topics One Level Below Grade Level		Measurement Topics One Level Above Grade Level		Measurement Topics Two Levels Above Grade Level	
Earned Score	Weighted Score	Earned Score	Weighted Score	Earned Score	Weighted Score	Earned Score	Weighted Score
4.0	1.0	4.0	2.0	4.0	7.0	4.0	8.0
3.5	0.5	3.5	1.5	3.5	6.5	3.5	7.5
3.0	0.0	3.0	1.0	3.0	6.0	3.0	7.0
2.5	0.0	2.5	0.5	2.5	5.5	2.5	6.5
2.0	0.0	2.0	0.0	2.0	5.0	2.0	6.0
1.5	0.0	1.5	0.0	1.5	4.5	1.5	5.5
1.0	0.0	1.0	0.0	1.0	4.0	1.0	5.0
0.5	0.0	0.5	0.0	0.5	3.5	0.5	4.5
0.0	0.0	0.0	0.0	0.0	3.0	0.0	4.0

Source: © 2021 by Robert J. Marzano.

Measurement Topic	Grade Level	Unweighted Score	Weighted Score
Topic 1	5	3	3
Topic 2	5	3.5	3.5
Topic 3	5	4	4
Topic 4	5	3	3
Topic 5	5	2.5	2.5
Topic 6	5	3	3
Topic 7	5	4	4
Topic 8	6	1.5	4.5
Topic 9	6	1.0	4
Topic 10	6	0.5	3.5
Total		26	35
Average		2.6	3.5

Source: © 2021 by Robert J. Marzano.

FIGURE 5.1: Example weighted scoring scenario.

For the seven fifth-grade topics, the student received relatively high scores: two scores of 4.0, three scores of 3.0, one score of 3.5, and one score of 2.5. However, on the three sixth-grade topics, the student received much lower scores: 1.5, 1.0, and 0.5. This, of course, is because the student has recently started working on these more difficult, higher-level topics. The simple average for these ten scores is 2.6, which translates to a grade of B using the conversion scale in table 5.2. However, the fourth column of figure 5.1 lists the weighted scores: the student's scores for the fifth-grade topics stay the same, but the scores for sixth-grade topics are weighted to account for the fact that they are above the student's chronological grade level. The weighted average using this scheme is 3.5, which translates to a letter grade of A.

Summary

This chapter describes the different perspective teachers must take and the ways of thinking they must cultivate to manifest a competency-based system in their classrooms. We refer to this as the *CBE mindset*. It is not enough for CBE teachers to employ a new instructional model. While they retain their traditional role of teaching students new knowledge and skill, teachers in a CBE classroom must simultaneously enhance students' abilities to manage their own learning and advocate for their current levels of knowledge and skill.

This book has described the nature and function of teaching in a competency-based elementary classroom using the Marzano Academies model. It has laid out a comprehensive instructional model with its forty-nine elements in great detail. Additionally, it has described the rationale for and underlying dynamics of the strategies in the model. Perhaps most importantly, the book has attempted to communicate the attitudes and behaviors that are at the core of competency-based teaching.

As we stated in the introduction, while this book is certainly intended for teachers in schools that are Marzano Academies or are in the process of becoming so, it is also intended for teachers in other schools who wish to use some of the components of the academy model within their current system. In other words, individual schools and individual teachers should feel free to adopt and adapt any of the concepts and processes we have presented as tools to enhance student learning. Ultimately, though, we believe competency-based education represents the inevitable and bright future of education throughout the United States and the world. We sincerely hope that this book helps all school systems and all teachers manifest that future.

REFERENCES AND RESOURCES

Anderson, J. R. (1995). *Learning and memory: An integrated approach*. New York: Wiley.

Anderson, L. W., & Krathwohl, D. R. (Eds.). (2001). *A taxonomy for learning, teaching, and assessing: A revision of Bloom's taxonomy of educational objectives*. New York: Longman.

Bandura, A. (1977). Self-efficacy: Toward a unifying theory of behavioral change. *Psychological Review, 84*(2), 191–215.

Bandura, A. (1993). Perceived self-efficacy in cognitive development and functioning. *Educational Psychologist, 28*(2), 117–148.

Bandura, A. (1997). *Self-efficacy: The exercise of control*. New York: W. H. Freeman.

Bloom, B. S. (Ed.). (1956). *Taxonomy of educational objectives: The classification of educational goals. Handbook I—Cognitive domain*. New York: David McKay.

Dodson, C. W. (2019). *The critical concepts in social studies*. Accessed at https://www.marzanoresources.com/critical-concepts-social-studies.html on March 1, 2021.

Donohoo, J., Hattie, J., & Eells, R. (2018). The power of collective efficacy. *Educational Leadership, 75*(6), 40–44.

DuFour, R., & Marzano, R. J. (2011). *Leaders of learning: How district, school, and classroom leaders improve student achievement*. Bloomington, IN: Solution Tree Press.

Dweck, C. S. (2006). *Mindset: The new psychology of success*. New York: Ballantine Books.

Hattie, J. A. C. (2009). *Visible learning: A synthesis of over 800 meta-analyses relating to achievement*. New York: Routledge.

Hattie, J. A. C. (2012). *Visible learning for teachers: Maximizing impact on learning*. New York: Routledge.

Hoegh, J. K. (2020). *A handbook for developing and using proficiency scales in the classroom*. Bloomington, IN: Marzano Resources.

Howard, R. (Director). (1995). *Apollo 13* [Film]. United States: Imagine Entertainment.

Koltko-Rivera, M. E. (2006). Rediscovering the later version of Maslow's hierarchy of needs: Self-transcendence and opportunities for theory, research, and unification. *Review of General Psychology, 10*(4), 302–317.

Kounin, J. S. (1970). *Discipline and group management in classrooms*. New York: Holt, Rinehart and Winston.

Lewis, K. (2014, January). I was homeless. *Scholastic Storyworks*, 14–17.

Manitoba. (n.d.). *Conducting a debate*. Accessed at https://www.edu.gov.mb.ca/k12/cur/socstud/frame_found_sr2/tns/tn-13.pdf on October 8, 2021.

Markus, H., & Nurius, P. (1986). Possible selves. *American Psychologist, 41*(9), 954–969.

Marzano, R. J. (2000). *Transforming classroom grading*. Alexandria, VA: Association for Supervision and Curriculum Development.

Marzano, R. J. (with Marzano, J. S., & Pickering, D. J.). (2003a). *Classroom management that works: Research-based strategies for every teacher*. Alexandria, VA: Association for Supervision and Curriculum Development.

Marzano, R. J. (2003b). *What works in schools: Translating research into action*. Alexandria, VA: Association for Supervision and Curriculum Development.

Marzano, R. J. (2004). *Building background knowledge for academic achievement: Research on what works in schools*. Alexandria, VA: Association for Supervision and Curriculum Development.

Marzano, R. J. (2006). *Classroom assessment and grading that work*. Alexandria, VA: Association for Supervision and Curriculum Development.

Marzano, R. J. (2007). *The art and science of teaching: A comprehensive framework for effective instruction*. Alexandria, VA: Association for Supervision and Curriculum Development.

Marzano, R. J. (2010). *Formative assessment and standards-based grading*. Bloomington, IN: Marzano Resources.

Marzano, R. J. (2017). *The new art and science of teaching*. Bloomington, IN: Solution Tree Press.

Marzano, R. J. (2018). *Making classroom assessments reliable and valid*. Bloomington, IN: Solution Tree Press.

Marzano, R. J. (2019a). *The handbook for the New Art and Science of Teaching*. Bloomington, IN: Solution Tree Press.

Marzano, R. J. (2019b). *Understanding rigor in the classroom*. West Palm Beach, FL: Learning Sciences International.

Marzano, R. J. (2020). *Teaching basic, advanced, and academic vocabulary: A comprehensive framework for elementary instruction*. Bloomington, IN: Marzano Resources.

Marzano, R. J., Brandt, R. S., Hughes, C. S., Jones, B. F., Presseisen, B. Z., Rankin, S. C., et al. (1988). *Dimensions of thinking: A framework for curriculum and instruction*. Alexandria, VA: Association for Supervision and Curriculum Development.

Marzano, R. J., Dodson, C. W., Simms, J. A., & Wipf, J. P. (2022). *Ethical test preparation in the classroom*. Bloomington, IN: Marzano Resources.

Marzano, R. J., Heflebower, T., Hoegh, J. K., Warrick, P. B., & Grift, G. (2016). *Collaborative teams that transform schools: The next step in PLCs*. Bloomington, IN: Marzano Resources.

Marzano, R. J., & Kendall, J. S. (1996). *A comprehensive guide to designing standards-based districts, schools, and classrooms*. Alexandria, VA: Association for Supervision and Curriculum Development.

Marzano, R. J., & Kosena, B. J. (2022). *Leading a competency-based elementary school: The Marzano Academies model*. Bloomington, IN: Marzano Resources.

Marzano, R. J., & Marzano, J. S. (1988). *A cluster approach to elementary vocabulary instruction*. Newark, DE: International Reading Association.

Marzano, R. J., & Marzano, J. S. (2015). *Managing the inner world of teaching: Emotions, interpretations, and actions.* Bloomington, IN: Marzano Resources.

Marzano, R. J., Norford, J. S., Finn, M., Finn, D., III, Mestaz, R., & Selleck, R. (2017). *A handbook for personalized competency-based education.* Bloomington, IN: Marzano Resources.

Marzano, R. J., Norford, J. S., & Ruyle, M. (2019). *The new art and science of classroom assessment.* Bloomington, IN: Marzano Resources.

Marzano, R. J., & Pickering, D. J. (1997). *Dimensions of learning: Teacher's manual* (2nd ed.). Alexandria, VA: Association for Supervision and Curriculum Development.

Marzano, R. J., & Pickering, D. J. (2011). *The highly engaged classroom.* Bloomington, IN: Marzano Resources.

Marzano, R. J., Pickering, D. J., & Pollock, J. E. (2001). *Classroom instruction that works: Research-based strategies for increasing student achievement.* Alexandria, VA: Association for Supervision and Curriculum Development.

Marzano, R. J., Rains, C. L., & Warrick, P. B. (2021). *Improving teacher development and evaluation: A guide for leaders, coaches, and teachers.* Bloomington, IN: Marzano Resources.

Marzano, R. J., Scott, D., Boogren, T. H., & Newcomb, M. L. (2017). *Motivating and inspiring students: Strategies to awaken the learner.* Bloomington, IN: Marzano Resources.

Marzano, R. J., & Simms, J. A. (2014). *Questioning sequences in the classroom.* Bloomington, IN: Marzano Resources.

Marzano, R. J., Warrick, P. B., Rains, C. L., & DuFour, R. (2018). *Leading a high reliability school.* Bloomington, IN: Solution Tree Press.

Marzano, R. J., Warrick, P. B., & Simms, J. A. (2014). *A handbook for high reliability schools: The next step in school reform.* Bloomington, IN: Marzano Resources.

Marzano, R. J., Yanoski, D. C., Hoegh, J. K., & Simms, J. A. (2013). *Using Common Core standards to enhance classroom instruction and assessment.* Bloomington, IN: Marzano Resources.

Marzano, R. J., Yanoski, D. C., & Paynter, D. E. (2015). *Proficiency scales for the new science standards: A framework for science instruction and assessment.* Bloomington, IN: Marzano Resources.

Marzano Resources. (n.d.). *The Marzano compendium of instructional strategies.* Centennial, CO: Author.

Maslow, A. H. (1943). A theory of human motivation. *Psychological Review, 50*(4), 370–396.

Maslow, A. H. (1954). *Motivation and personality.* New York: Harper & Row.

Maslow, A. H. (1969). The farther reaches of human nature. *Journal of Transpersonal Psychology, 1*(1), 1–9.

Maslow, A. H. (1970). *Motivation and personality* (2nd ed.). New York: Harper & Row.

Maslow, A. H. (1979). *The journals of A. H. Maslow* (R. J. Lowry, Ed.). Monterey, CA: Brooks/Cole.

Mid-Continent Research for Education and Learning. (2014). *Content knowledge: Online edition—Browse the online edition standards and benchmarks.* Accessed at www2.mcrel.org/compendium/browse.asp on August 6, 2021.

Oakley, B., Rogowsky, B., & Sejnowski, T. J. (2021). *Uncommon sense teaching: Practical insights in brain science to help students learn.* New York: TarcherPerigee.

Ritchhart, R., Church, M., & Morrison, K. (2011). *Making thinking visible: How to promote engagement, understanding, and independence for all learners.* San Francisco: Jossey-Bass.

Scott, M., & Scott, D. (2018). *180 connections: Classroom strategies.* Denver, CO: Rachel's Challenge.

Seligman, M. E. P. (2006). *Learned optimism: How to change your mind and your life.* New York: Vintage Books.

Simms, J. A. (2016). *The critical concepts (Final version: English language arts, mathematics, and science).* Accessed at www.marzanoresources.com/the-critical-concepts.html on October 5, 2017.

Tarshis, L. (2017, February). Disaster in space. *Scholastic Storyworks,* 4–10.

Thrash, T. M., Elliot, A. J., Maruskin, L. A., & Cassidy, S. E. (2010). Inspiration and the promotion of well-being: Tests of causality and mediation. *Journal of Personality and Social Psychology, 98*(3), 488–506.

Williams, J. E. (n.d.). *How to sound out words.* Accessed at https://weallcanread.com/how-to-sound-out-words/ on October 7, 2021.

Wincel, M. (2016). *Cooperative learning for primary: Book 2.* San Clemente, CA: Kagan Cooperative Learning.

INDEX

D

E

F

G

H

I

J

K

L

M

N

O

P

Q

R

S

T

U

V

W

A Handbook for High Reliability Schools™

Robert J. Marzano, Philip B. Warrick, and Julia A. Simms

Usher in the new era of school reform. The authors help you transform your schools into organizations that take proactive steps to prevent failure and ensure student success. Using a research-based five-level hierarchy along with leading and lagging indicators, you'll learn to assess, monitor, and confirm the effectiveness of your schools. Each chapter includes what actions should be taken at each level.

BKL020

Leading a High Reliability School™

Robert J. Marzano, Philip B. Warrick, Cameron L. Rains, and Richard DuFour

How do educators build High Reliability Schools (HRS) that consistently produce excellent results? The key is to establish interdependent systems that focus on continuous school improvement. A critical commitment to leading a high reliability school is the implementation of the PLC at Work® process. This user-friendly resource provides guidance on establishing and maintaining a high reliability school.

BKF795

A Handbook for Personalized Competency-Based Education

Robert J. Marzano, Jennifer S. Norford, Michelle Finn, and Douglas Finn III

Ensure all students master content by designing and implementing a personalized competency-based education (PCBE) system. This handbook explores approaches, strategies, and techniques that schools and districts should consider as they begin their transition to a PCBE system. The authors share examples of how to use proficiency scales, standard operating procedures, behavior rubrics, personal tracking matrices, and other tools to aid in instruction and assessment.

BKL037

Scheduling for Personalized Competency-Based Education

Douglas Finn III and Michelle Finn

A challenge at the heart of personalized competency-based education (PCBE) is grouping and scheduling students according to their learning needs rather than their age. With this guidebook, you'll take a deep dive into the why and how of these foundational PCBE components. Gain clear guidance for gathering standards-based data and then using the results to create schedules that promote student proficiency.

BKL049

Motivating and Inspiring Students

Robert J. Marzano, Darrell Scott, Tina H. Boogren, and Ming Lee Newcomb

Bringing motivation and inspiration to the classroom is not easy. With this practical resource, you'll discover a results-driven framework—based on a six-level hierarchy of student needs and goals—that you can use to provide engaging instruction to students. The authors share comprehensive understandings of the nature of motivation and inspiration and detail specific strategies to connect with your students.

BKL025

Visit MarzanoResources.com or call 888.849.0851 to order.